Barbara Drosten

Self-Efficacy Shapes Modernization

Demokratie und Entwicklung

herausgegeben von

Rainer Tetzlaff und Cord Jakobeit

Institut für Politische Wissenschaft

Universität Hamburg

Band 72

LIT

Barbara Drosten

Self-Efficacy Shapes Modernization

Evidence from Smallholder Farmers in Ghana

LIT

Cover image: Lea Drosten

Bibliographic information published by the Deutsche Nationalbibliothek
The Deutsche Nationalbibliothek lists this publication in the Deutsche Nationalbibliografie; detailed bibliographic data are available on the Internet at http://dnb.d-nb.de.

ISBN 978-3-643-91041-7 (pb)
ISBN 978-3-643-96041-2 (PDF)
Zugl.: Hamburg, Univ., Diss., 2016

A catalogue record for this book is available from the British Library.

Klosbachstr. 107
CH-8032 Zürich
Tel. +41 (0) 44-251 75 05
E-Mail: zuerich@lit-verlag.ch http://www.lit-verlag.ch
Distribution:
In the UK: Global Book Marketing, e-mail: mo@centralbooks.com
In North America: Independent Publishers Group, e-mail: orders@ipgbook.com
In Germany: LIT Verlag Fresnostr. 2, D-48159 Münster
Tel. +49 (0) 2 51-620 32 22, Fax +49 (0) 2 51-922 60 99, e-mail: vertrieb@lit-verlag.de
e-books are available at www.litwebshop.de

For Lea, Ruben and David

Self-Efficacy Shapes Modernization

Evidence from Smallholder Farmers in Ghana

Abstract:

Self-efficacy is the belief in one´s abilities and as such, the critical link between environment, culture, institutions, and modernization. It is the primum movens of intentional change by enabling modernization as reacting to stimuli with adaptive learning and develops continuously everywhere in response to environmental and circumstantial demands and rewards for action. Responsiveness and supportiveness of an environment decide about its levels, grades of robustness and generality.

Self-efficacy is not genetic, but learned and culturally transmitted, and therefore susceptible to intentional support. Individuals and communities with high self-efficacy believe to be able to learn and change their behaviour to favourably influence the outcome of their actions and their environment through effort. Past success thus begets future success as high self-efficacy fosters opportunity recognition, higher risk taking, more cooperation, and higher and longer investment. In contrast, people experiencing an environment that does not reward more efforts with f.ex. more profit, thereby not fostering learning and behavior change, are likely to keep their low self-efficacy beliefs. In a self-fulfilling prophecy, low self-efficacy subsequently tends to resist or avoid change for fear of failure, avoid risk, not recognize opportunity as easily, and seek ways to circumvent and exploit the system.

Developed and less developed countries alike need continuous modernization to adapt to challenges that could pose threads to their structural stability and social cohesion. A lack of self-efficacy in leaders, elites, and general population stifles economic and political progress: fears of losing privilege and a favourable status quo without the necessary self-efficacy to be able to keep or regain it, lead to lying, manipulating and harming institutional functioning, and preventing the learning and developing high SE of potentially competing others.

In a study amongst pineapple farmers in Ghana, SE has been found to differ depending on their ancestors´ crop cultivation, to raise household income, cooperation, contract farming, opportunity recognition, risk taking, and investment. Training by Western aid agencies can increase or decrease self-efficacy depending on the set-up.

Fortunately, the development of SE can be fostered by targeted policy measures. Better understanding how self-efficacy works and develops can increase the efficiency and effectiveness of economic development and modernization policies. Self-efficacy as the key to human behaviour change drives economic activity and social progress because positive change results from confidence in one´s abilities to achieve goals without reliance on force or manipulation. Moreover, a high degree of average self-efficacy in a population protects from destabilizing effects of modernization and helps to adapt to external shocks like migration and climate change.

Table of Contents

Foreword

Is there a correlation between the effectiveness and efficiency of a support measure and the self-efficacy (SE) of the target group? Is a political, economic and social system including the type of leader it produces correlated with different levels of individual and group SE? Why do exploitive systems and populist leaders work with SE-undermining fears? Do leaders like Donald Trump have high or low SE? What is the correlation between SE and natural resources, money, reputation, and institutions? Could there be a correlation between SE and the rise or decline of civilizations? What happens to people´s SE beliefs when they migrate? What are the effects of SE on economic performance and modernization of developed and less developed countries, and the question, who expects to profit or to suffer from modernizing change? And is there anything we can do about any of this?
(At the end of this foreword are my short answers; you will find more extensive ones in the context of this book.)

In Lomé, Togo, little girls, who were sold by their parents to work as house or market slaves, learn to read and write at the " Centre Kekeli pour la protection de l´enfant" (www.enroutepourlecole.com, Terra Mater 4/2018) as do grown women, some of whom might sell or buy children or were once sold themselves. The Carmelite Sisters of Charity running the center seem to know very well that a system of exploitation cannot be broken unless by exploiters and exploited both adopting a different way of survival and trusting in it. This example demonstrates that for modernizing changes to happen, losers as much as winners of a status quo need - aside of a material base - the faith in their own ability to get by or do well: this faith is self-efficacy.
Self-efficacy beliefs are fundamentally connected to our deepest human fears of survival. Am I able to make it here? And make it well?[*]

---

[*] This fear is a constitutive part of human existence and a missing aspect in money theory: as money is a proxy for SE, and a lack thereof a major cause for existential fears, utility from money does, in contrast to general belief, not have a

Though some might find it counterintuitive to help winners get stronger, they are often not strong but powerful, and can be expected to fiercely fight change that would endanger privilege unless feeling safe about their own ability to still do well under changed conditions.

I believe this fear of survival underlies most, if not all human activity. It accompanies us from before our first breath as prenatal research suggests. * We developed religious beliefs in a gracious deity to lift us out of it or give our eventual passing higher meaning. We developed ways to escape the fears with mind-altering substances or distracting activities. We developed fear-compensating power over other people and the material world to create the illusion of control in our actual total subjection to fate. The Canadian developmental psychologist Albert Bandura discovered the most powerful, healthy and socially compatible way to deal with our personal doomsday: self-efficacy beliefs in our abilities to get by on this planet, possibly well and in different and changing conditions.

Nature and quality of our behaviour hinges on the level and robustness of our self-efficacies: to cooperate, trust, abide to laws and norms, detect and pursue opportunities, take on risks, employ efforts, feeling responsible for their outcome instead of blaming others, adapt to change by learning and changing oneself – or in turn, our inability to recognize opportunities or need to shy away from them, retreat to lying, manipulation or force to get what we desire, distrust others and the course of things, making us unable to cooperate or plan in extended time frames, and possibly worst of all, prevent others from developing more SE than us.

Modernization means updating and adaptive learning (Pelikan), i.e. acknowledging new information and adapting behaviour, feelings,

---

saturating point. Depending on someone´s relative lack of SE, they will want and need ever more money (especially more than others in comparison!) and yet not feel safe enough to allow for changes in hierarchy, power, status, and profits. Lack of trust in their abilities to regain any of their privileges through own efforts adds greatly to make change a threat rather than an opportunity.

* The importance of psychological well-being of mother and child in pregnancy is probably dangerously underrated and more decisive for behaviour than genes and education.

convictions, methods and strategies to occuring change which initiates more change and more need to adapt in endless self-enforcing feedback loops of modernizing, or fighting it. The necessity to modernize is an integral, never ending part of life, for developed and developing countries, for any individual or group, be it a society, government, organization, company, school or family. Whoever stops modernizing fails to adapt to their environment, endangering their status and capability for well-being in the future; those who fight modernizing in fear of change fight against a ticking clock, increasing costs, often paid for by others.

Statistical data hardly convey information about the actual modernization process, but only its results; the "real thing" has to have happened beforehand, in the hearts and minds of people, often outside of the country in question. When they reflect foreign developments, modernization in the host economy and society can follow, but often it does not, or with immense time lag and destabilizing effects. If infrastructure, universities, hospitals, transportation facilities etc. are symptoms of modernization rather than initial causes (though they are necessary to keep up the process!): what does initiate modernizing of and within people, leaders and leading elites? My answer is:
Self-efficacy beliefs at every level of hierarchy and stage of development are the most important single factor determining pace and quality of modernization in society, polity, and economy because SE lifts people out of existential fears and enables them to self-determined action .
Modernization as a process of collective or individual learning, requires willingness and ability to change, and tolerate change in others and one´s surroundings. People embrace change as opportunity when they believe to have the abilities to profit from it; otherwise, depending on their status, they will tend to resist change as thread and defend the status quo for fear of losing however much or little they have, forming an unexpected coalition of haves and have-nots, as observable f.ex. in the treatment of women as threat to male privilege. Huntington warned that "modernization" causes destabilization and insecurity. This view confuses symptom and cause: we see destabilized, insecure societies and populations em-

bracing strongmen promising to end the instability that was caused by a *lack of actual modernization through self-efficacious agents.* Madeleine Albright rightly describes fascism not as an ideology for governing a nation, but rather as a method to gain power – preying on fears of people not to be able to survive well and securely in changing conditions.

For me, the present wave of insecurity, reconstruction, populism and aggression in the global public discourse exhibit a widespread and urgent need for SE fostering measures as part of the political agenda.

More developed countries usually try to calm people feeling threatened by modernization via aid or alimentation, but still lose out to fears-exploiting populists who offer myths of salvation from modern threads by return to a simpler and greater past. It is not the losers from modernization who are most attracted to their propaganda, but election analysis shows the appeal to middle class voters who despise change to threaten their position especially when they fear not to be able to regain it. (Note: objective hurdles are secondary for the subjective intensity of this fear.)

Companies and rent-seeking social elites of both more and less developed economies share property and income advantages not only based on merit, and therefore have an immanent interest in protecting exploitable grounds and profits from modernization changes. It is no contradiction that companies drive change through technology while the people behind the companies may fear changes in the exploitive hierarchy unless they feel certain to prevail – or be able to reinstall themselves.

Newly aspiring groups may be lured into traditional, exploitive methods of advancement. Corruption is a predictable outcome. Groups of aspiring people can develop a dangerous gap between their sense of entitlement and aspirations, and SE too low to attempt getting and doing what they want through effort and rules-abiding behaviour. In current migration movements, people flee not only from "traditional" wars, but also from an undeclared and asymmetric war of opportunities with domestic and international elites; and some may flee from and because of a lack of SE to achieve personal changes at home, and suffer further frustration of SE abroad when an actual lack of skills prevents the aspired.

Those profiting from the status quo and those suffering from it unexpectedly often share a lack of self-efficacy for change, and form a not-so-obvious alliance of resistance to modernization, leading to political populism, social violence, religious snake oil and economic downturns. And in the worst case, some kind of "-ism" as their nominal state order.

The fear to lose the status quo to novelty or other people is caused by a lack of self-efficacy to gain and regain through one´s own efforts and abilities and can lead to political, social and economic catastrophes!

As changes in circumstance and environment are part of life, adaptive learning enables people to cope with changes and purposefully initiate them as agents rather than victims. Empowering people by fostering SE is key to learning, behavior change, economic progress and political stability. Modernization must not be accompanied by instability, social tensions and existential fears, it can be a self-determined, peaceful, cooperative process of self-efficacious agents, lifting the rich and the poor, the more and the less developed countries.

The good news is that SE can be purposefully influenced. Its features, effects and malleability are well known and empirically tested in several domains. David Wüpper, whom I profoundly thank for this collaboration, collected data in Ghana that show three encouraging results for future policies: higher SE is found to be directly causally correlated with higher family income; higher SE is culturally transmitted in families and from "important others"; and a more supportive village leader is directly causally correlated with higher SE amongst village people.

I hope this book helps to spread information about the concept of SE as a potent tool for development workers, business leaders, policy makers and scholars to support people to create their own ways of development instead of following somebody else´s recipes. Self-efficacy only influences what people can purposefully enact and achieve. It does not replace the need for good governance, capital, protected and protecting institutions, infrastructure, fair terms of trade, protection from asymmetric exploitive corporate powers and human relations, or whatever else we have learned that a well functioning society needs in the political, social and economic realm. SE is not a silver bullet; it needs positive material conditions to work with. But SE can upgrade every player in the game for being better able to recognize and use their chances, create opportunities, cooperate and play fairly. I regard SE as the *fertilizer* that makes material "seeds" grow that would otherwise fall on desert ground, picked up at most by incidental passers-by.

Self-efficacy makes every other policy measure more effective, which makes it the single most important factor to initiate and stabilize modernizing processes. And that is a lot.

On above questions: Populations with high SE tend to exhibit higher rates of political participation, cooperation and norms conforming behaviour; their culture develops more inclusive and participative political processes and institutions with high-SE leaders; low-SE leaders and elites are threatened by high SE of others, aim to lower it, keep it low, and fight those with high SE. Mr. Trump acts like the prototype of someone with so little SE that he never seems to have trusted his abilities to achieve his ends in competition of effort and performance while observing the rules of law, civil convention and cooperation, all three of which mark high SE. Low SE can enter into an unfortunate alliance with compensatory entitlement: dictators, ordinary criminals and whoever else suffers from large demands and little trust in their abilities aim to get what they want by manipulation, lying and force. Money functions as a proxy for SE and enables people to get rewards without having had to develop the necessary SE. This proxy effect depresses evolutionary pressure on individuals to develop SE from abilities; a similar effect have natural resources on those who can obtain rents without personal achievement, and institutions which can grand power and profits beyond individual abilities. Societies (or any collective) with too many individuals profiting from such proxies are endangered of reaching a tipping point when too few people develop high and strong levels of actual SE to keep up the dynamics of modernizing change in economy, polity and society; this correlation could add to explaining long economic cycles and the downturn of civilizations. Sudden changes in circumstance through migration, climate change or change of political system can have a dangerous effect on SE. As part of one's identity SE develops in the context of habitat and circumstance over generations: when these change quickly, SE and identity are not adapted to the new conditions and require specifically targeted support, or else, massive problems of social alienation may occur. Similarly, aid projects offering new opportunities may not be used to full capacity when naturally evolved SE is too low to make best use of them. Fortunately, SE has been found to be malleable and can be fostered by targeted policies if political and economic insight in the necessity of empowerment and dangers of not doing so exceeds the lures of having it easier to exploiting and manipulating non-empowered peoples. And even though it may seem "unjust" to support the winners of the present system, building their self-efficacy (not self-confidence, arrogance or other compensations) as well as those of the people who suffer from it as in the above example from Togo, is vital for modernization to be sustainable; otherwise, an elite with access to a system's power instruments - money, media, military – will either prevent change from the start, bend it in their favor or roll-back it's effects as happened time and again throughout human history.

Barbara Drosten
Hamburg, January 2019

> *"Yet, only one thing has to be remembered: there is no effect without a cause, and there is no lawlessness in creation."*
>
> *Albert Einstein*[1]

1. Introduction

When Acemoglu & Robinson (2012) suggested that the single most important factor for poverty was bad institutions their conclusion was not only much applauded, but also criticized as oversimplification, ethnocentrism, reversing causality or ignoring factors like geography, culture, uncontrollable and/or external circumstance, and their history-based argumentation as suffering from hindsight biased.[2] The vital importance of well-functioning institutions has since been widely accepted, though recent developments have reminded us that institutions can only protect people and the system if people protect the institutions. In this discussion on institutions many other important influences on a nation´s prosperity and reasons for success and failure were called out, but to most of them counter examples could be found: there are successful countries with warm or cold climates, democracies and dictatorships raising countries out of poverty, countries of different religious beliefs and geographical locations being rich or poor. The lack of an imperative pattern that could include and explain the notorious exceptions to the assumed rule is mainly due to the lack of identifying a "general transmission belt". We simply have not identified an operative tool that actually and causally relates culture, environment, and geography to economic performance, the formation of the political process and to the shaping of institutions.

---

[1] Cited after Hermanns, William (2011).

[2] Acemoglu, Daron and James A. Robinson (2012), Why Nations Fail. The Origins of Power, Prosperity, and Poverty, N.Y. Engermann & Sokoloff, and North, Wallis, & Weingast had earlier found and suggested many aspects of what A & R later as a congruent non-complex explanation. Their critics range from Bill Gates to Jared Diamond, Jeffrey Sachs, William Easterly, Paul Collier et al.

This work suggests that this "missing link" which translates environment into culture and institutions, and all three to economic development and political participation is self-efficacy (SE). Self-efficacy is intergenerationally persistent, yet malleable by targeted measures. The psychological concept of SE was developed by Albert Bandura in the 1970´s, and has been extensively empirically tested in a multitude of domains and applications; it was found of high explanatory value for causally affecting human behaviour and decision-making. Here, I apply the concept of SE to the process of development and modernization, and trace its effects in an extensive appraisal of the existing political and economic development literature. I discuss if it could be self-efficacious agents whom Adam Smith[3] (1776/2000) describes as labourously, in rational self-interest, chances reckognizing and opportunities persuing producers of the Wealth of Nations; if it could be SE that constitutes Parson´s (1964) "evolutionary universal in development", and accounts for the differing adaptive and creative capabilities of populations. Indeed, when Tetzlaff (2017)[4] questions the possibility of development to produce Western benefactions like financial well-being, health, freedom, education, justice, individual

---

[3] Smith describes the detrimental results of preventing or destroying self-efficacy amongst workers by monotonous work and calls for stately protection:
"The man whose whole life is spent in performing a few simple operations, of which the effects too are, perhaps, always the same, or very nearly the same, has no occasion to exert his understanding, or to exercise his invention in finding out expedients for removing difficulties which never occur. He naturally loses, therefore, the habit of such exertion, and generally becomes as stupid and ignorant as it is possible for a human creature to become. The torpor of his mind renders him, not only incapable of relishing or bearing a part in any rational conversation, but of conceiving any generous, noble, or tender sentiment, and consequently of forming any just judgement concerning many even of the ordinary duties of private life. His dexterity at his own particular trade seems, in this manner, to be acquired at the expense of his intellectual, social, and martial virtues. But in every improved and civilized society this is the state into which the labouring poor, that is, the great body of the people, must necessarily fall, unless the government takes some pains to prevent it." , p.840.

[4] cmp. p. 10; see also discussion on theories, the nation state and systems of development, p.20

choice and security in any other setting than the (Western) economic and political system that brought these values about, the universally employable answer could be SE. It is constitutes a vital part of an explanation for the different pathways of development that the people of the world have taken[5] as it develops people instead of a system. With regard to those benevolent integrative institutions that accelarate and stabilize economic, social and political development in the sense of Acemoglu and Robinson, I view them as possible symptoms and result of an economic surplus in those cases where the environment fostered wide-spread self-efficacy and made exploitive institutions unprofitable.

SE is the belief to have the abilities and capability to cope and do well in present and changing conditions. It is not to be mistaken for self-confidence[6], self-reliance, hope or aspirations (f.ex. Lybbert & Wydick, 2016), or other concepts of the self. Many researchers are starting to trace the importance of human beliefs for behaviour and economic decision-making. In lacking a more widely accepted theory or model, new findings are given new labels, at times adding terms but not order. The present confusion should not prevent appreciating these findings and trying to reach a common vocabulary for this perspective. The concept of SE I am suggesting has been extensively tested empirically in a wide variety of human activities like sports, dieting, patient compliance, academic achievements and else since the 1970s; scales and methods for testing have been developed, and it is introduced here to modernization theory.

Naturally developed and culturally transmitted SE of a population, and their leaders and elites, can provide for the identification of causal relations between the different parameters of economic and political change. SE is the primus movens, the first drive of intentional human behaviour and thereby rational thinking as it links action to outcome under the limitations of environment and circumstance. It has been found to be well susceptible to altering interventions, positively and negatively. As SE is

---

[5] please see chpt. 5.4: Self-Efficacy is Not Genetic.

[6] ple see chpt. 2.4 on related concepts.

the main tool by which empowering and emancipatory policies work to enhance human agency, it can also enhance the effectiveness of other development and modernizing measures: a program that provides training, to f.ex. raise agricultural yield via mulching or fertilizing, can raise SE of its participants by raising their feeling of competence and potential, and being better equipped than non-participants; but participants can also leave the program with a feeling of inferiority or dependency whereby the enhanced technical information may not reap the attempted growth effects[7].

Modernization is an ongoing process of adaptation to an ever-changing environment[8]. This is a process of learning[9] by individuals in their different roles as individual, formal or informal group member, as member of an elite or as the leader of a group. Learning and adaptive change is necessarily a continuous process in any economic, social and political unit

---

[7] In researching self-efficacy in Ghana, the data contained the interesting effect that some people who had received more than three or more trainings showed less self-efficacy than those who received only 1 or two. Though it is possible that those who started out with particularly low se kept coming back for further training, it is also possible and important to watch out for in further measures that too much training might have the adverse effect of producing a feeling of incompetence and dependency on "foreign knowledge", and thus lowering SE.

[8] I agree with Goetze that modernization is a continuous process like "keeping the on-button pressed", but I do not agree that it necessarily means speeding up this process nor do I agree with the idea that the process direction is irreversible. Cmp Goetze (2004).

[9] Beinhocker (2007) differentiates between adaptation and learning. I suggest that adaptation usually happens via learning: any type of new or re-activated information requires a reaction of either ignoring, suppressing or actively processing its informational content – which is a process of learning that leads to adaptation, producing a new status quo; invention is not learning but an outcome of it. There is adaptation without learning as an act of imitation which can include a degree of implicit knowledge; imitated knowledge can get lost over time – as in the example given below of Tasmania. Imitation is an important part of collective or social in contrast to individual learning: watch the elders building a canoe, copy it and improve it. Lacking the necessary individual identity to claim individual achievements, social learning does not foster a similar degree of individual self-efficacy! (cmp chpt. 4.6)

regardless of its stage of development to prevent stagnation or regression. Modernization will produce ever more cultural, scientific, technological changes of the kind that brought them about in the first place. Like SE, modernization also develops in self-enforcing feedback loops once a certain stage of independence from the natural environment has been reached, and if these changes are not politically or socially inhibited.

SE makes the individual an agentic performer of intentional behaviour. It has been found and well tested for its role in human behaviour (Bandura, 1977, 1986, 1990, 1993, 1997; and Bandura, Barbaranelli, Caprara, & Pastorelli, 1996). SE is process- and domain specific; this means it develops with regard to specific activities or types of activity in varying levels from low to high, and different strengths, reflecting how robust this belief will be in adversity or contradicting experience. SE can also take on different degrees of generality reaching from one specific domain of activity to a wider range of similar activities to a generalized state of feeling able to cope with life: from selling cars to being a good business person to being able to cope in general. It affects inter alia aspirations, goal setting, motivation, persistence, effort, risk taking, time discounting, investment behaviour, and innovation responsiveness (see all literature above by Bandura and Bandura et al.), with higher SE increasing all of them. SE feedback loops lead to self-enforcing positive or negative processes: a person with higher SE will set more ambitious goals, employ more effort for a longer period of time, even in the face of adversity, and will thereby be more likely to reap positive results, which will then in turn elevate and strengthen her sense of SE even more. Similarly, low SE will lead to setting less ambitious goals, investing less time and effort, giving up earlier and quicker when problems arise, thereby being more likely to produce lesser results which will confirm low SE or lower it even more.

Self-efficacy refers neither to a task as Bandura points out, nor is it outcome-dependent but simply describes the belief to be able to do something well. Every child develops her self-efficacy from emotions she observes when people she identifies with carrying out activities in a certain domain. These emotions strongly influence her own towards these activities and eventually towards activities on a more general level, like having SE about one sport developing into a positive efficacy towards all sports, potentially spilling over into a high general SE of "I can do things that demand a lot of self-discipline, being persistent and working hard". The emotion-turning-belief become part of her identity, and thus her self- and world view. SE in different levels, strength, and degrees of generality develops naturally everywhere at all times as a reaction to the responsiveness of an environment to human intervention. It can be close to none and destroyed by trauma or degration.

Different environments request different levels of intervention in different planning time horizons, and react differently strong and differently positive to human action, maybe encouraging and rewarding it, or sanction and discourage it. The decisive factors here are rewards and reliability, allowing for long-term investment and planning, or arbitrary destruction and instability that both make for a high default risk. A natural environment with supportive conditions, like e.g. fertile soil, enough rain, and absence of natural disasters or infectious diseases will pay higher rewards to careful planning and farming work. A malaria-haunted or desert environment, with the odd neighboring tribe regularly raiding the adjacent meager fields, or harvests being destroyed by earthquake, flooding or locusts will offer very low rewards and incentives for investment in the land and planning. The former environment will foster higher SE than the latter as it "teaches" and "encourages" its inhabitants that their work and actions are good, and that they are sufficiently equipped for doing well. Modern policies should and can purposefully create a responsive, self-efficacy fostering environment to foster societal, economic, and political performance and modernization.

Economic activity used to reflect how much humans intervened in their natural habitat (Hodgson, 2003) and changed it – or nowadays possibly "re-nature" it. This relation also reflects if a habitat requested human intervention for survival, how responsive it was, and if it tended to react positively or negatively. Likewise, we can see culture as reflecting the sum of experiences of a group of people with norms, habits and rules they deduced from the survival lessons learned and developed in their habitat. This makes self-efficacy a direct result of the responsiveness of a specific habitat to human intervention, and an important determinant for the propensity of change. If we better understand how SE works to produce empowered, cooperative agents who set high goals, and with great persistence and ambitious investment work to achieve them, and how SE develops and can be effectively fostered, we can greatly enhance the efficiency and effectiveness of development and modernizing policies.

Geography, climate, disease or other environmental factors apparently do not directly influence economic performance[10],[11]. The answer to the question if or if not geography is linked to economy needs to identify an operative mechanism, tool or instrument of how exactly one factor would

---

[10] ..., or at least not in a country-to-country comparison; the data for interregional comparison is not unequivocal and may actually vary according to the chosen environmental variable. Thanks to David Wuepper for this comment. The African historian A.G. Hopkins argues that Acemoglu/ Robinson chose their data according to their thesis, while Hopkins in turn gets criticized by James Fenske for not embracing their work as important progress for the trait. Presently, we have to assume that we do not know how much direct influence is exerted by environmental factors but have to keep in mind that many of these existed in Europe too before and while it ascended. Cmp.: Hopkins (2009); Fenske (2010).

[11] In their critique of Jared Diamond and others who research environmental influence on economic and behavioural phenomena Acemoglu & Robinson decline the role of geography and climate stating a causal correlation had not been found. The reason for this lies in the failure to identify the mechanism or tool by which a factor like geography might exert influence on the outcome of economic performance. Also, while declining a link between geography, climate and even culture to the way people organize their community and activities implying human behaviour to be independent from surrounding conditions and beliefs, Acemoglu/Robinson do acknowledge that politicians in adopting wrong policies do not do so because of ignorance but because they react to incentives from their surrounding (p.65-67). Claiming these incentives to originate from political and economic institutions in their societies implies a profit/utility maximizing reaction pattern to incentives; and it leaves open the question, how culture and institutions, the “political process” and preferences (as decision parameter of utility) develop if not by adaptation to environmental or circumstantial stimuli. Cmp. Acemoglu & Robinson (2012), pp. 48-69.

work to influence the other. Environment, culture, institutions, and any other man-made or natural factor all influence human behaviour and thereby economic performance as limiting factors. But by which means and effect could these correlations work to form causal interaction?
I suggest that natural and social habitats with their different conditions react more or less positively, and more or less strongly and reliably to human activity, thereby encourage or discourage adaptive learning and change in humans. This interaction fosters different degrees of generality, levels and strengths of SE which in turn influence the way people feel about their potential to act, how they develop survival strategies and organize their lives in cultural adaptation to that habitat.

This potential for almost unlimited adaptation is what enabled the human species to populate every geographic and climatic zone of this globe, and to learn all the necessary abilities to survive here. The results of this adaptive process are "culture": culture comprises the pool of collective knowledge about the survival of a specific human group in a specific environment under specific circumstances which gets formalized in corresponding institutions that react back on individuals in that habitat (cmp. Hodgson, 2003). Culture functions as information filter for members of a group through taboos, norms, rules, roles, beliefs, and offers heuristics, all of which determine economic, social and political decision making.

The development of exploitive/extractive institutions is a result mainly of opportunity and profitability: if an environment offers itself for plantation agriculture it will lead to exactly that with the corresponding social, political and economic processes and institutions. Or as Brian Arthur (2014) titles in his work on exploitive behaviour: *"All Systems Will Be Gamed"*, and calls for failure-mode research for prevention policies.
These exploitive institutions persist even after industrialization of some kind has occurred as the profiteers of exploitation will have missed the chance to develop their own SE beliefs for other activities and other power-balances, and tend to choose exploitive survival strategies henceforth,

made possible by their institutionalized power[12]; world-wide gender issues may give more or less subtle evidence of this correlation.

Being a domain or process-oriented belief rather than a task- or goal-oriented one, the quality of SE in leaders and leading elites consequently influences the nature of the ruling ideology. Inspired by Schnaidberg (1994), the broad differentiation could be between an "impact-oriented" (or process) ideology in the case of higher SE, and a "profit-oriented" or rent-seeking (goal, task, Schnaidberg: *"production-oriented"*) ideology in the case of lower SE. The less SE a group of people or a leader has, the less will be the believe to be able to make it by one´s own virtue, and the greater is the incentive to exploit others and secure that status by segregating people, avoiding competition[13], or critique. Group or collective efficacy is the belief of individuals as members of a group in the collective abilities of all group members to achieve set goals together. In a group, you will therefore find two sets of self-efficacy beliefs: the respective individual efficacy as well as the individual´s belief in her group´s efficacy. The latter is a field of its own and mentioned here only where relevant for this work[14].

SE is culturally transmitted and was tested positively for being well susceptible for targeted promotional policy measures. It can be purposefully built as has been proven in several domains by different researchers (see below). This makes SE a promising tool for modernizing or development attempts that build on human capital: self-efficacy is the mechanism for empowerment. Its cultural transmission makes it suggestible, path dependent and accumulative. Even individual levels and domains of SE are per-

---

[12] There is a vast number of studies on the topic of persistence of culture in groups and institutions; comprehensive: Greif (1994); on institutional continuity: Gennaioli & Rainer (2007).

[13] An example of this mechanism can be found in sports or scientific institutions in early Nazi Germany who often dismissed Jewish members and rid themselves of competion *before* they were forced to do so: cmp: Martens (2016) on the treatment of Jewish athletes; on Albert Einstein and the Prussian Academy of Science: Grundmann (2004).

[14] comprehensive summary in: Bandura (2000, 1997).

sistent[15] over time without specific intervention. I suggest that higher SE can lead to more, more sustainable and wider spread modernization because it is likely to increase the inclination to learn by increasing faith in one´s abilities while reducing costs of learning for individuals as individuals, group members, members of an elite, and leaders. It can thereby foster higher economic growth, enhance effectiveness of modernizing measures, and enable more participative political structures, while lower SE tends to produce adaptation stagnation, thus less economic development, petering out of modernization and development measures, and political structures of lesser participation.

SE influences economic performance directly via four channels:
- Individual investment behaviour including financial engagement, plus effort, persistence, and ambition of the investment goal as well as cooperation to achieve it.
- Utility of learning and behaviour change for individuals, groups, and specific functions like leadership, all of which have deviating or antagonistic utilities that move towards greater congruence with growing SE.
- Culture and institutions of a given populace, which directly reflect living conditions and culturally transmitted survival strategies;
- Cooperation and participation. SE can increase economic performance and societal modernization in a ground-laying way via increasing the ability and inclination for cooperation instead of competition, and participative power division.

Cooperation is the actual core of the market system as Adam Smith (1776/2000) argued in his discussion on the division of labor by providing for peaceful exchange of goods and information which in turn is the prerequisite for a division of labor and specialization. Low SE hampers cooperation vial lack of trust in one´s own abilities, and lack of trust in others and the possibility that collective action could reach the desired

---

[15] In the enclosed study from Ghana, we found cultural persistence in groups and SE to be higher correlated to ancestral than to present conditions. This does not imply SE cannot develop in the short-term; the SE levels we found developed mostly naturally without supportive measures: Wüpper & Drosten (2016)

goals. High SE, on the other hand, fosters cooperation via higher trust in the abilities of all actors concerned, higher risk-taking for having more trust in one´s own abilities to cope with failure and setbacks, therefore higher openness to novelty, and longer planning horizons, again, as the trust in oneself to cope with whatever comes up enables people to operate in the uncertainty of not-knowing an outcome for much longer.

There are different possibilities for individuals to setoff a lack of SE[16] in a surrounding of high SE, but all of these come at a price for the collective in the form of increased risk rules-circumventing practices, crime, lack of cooperation, instability, unreliability, intolerance, defensive behaviour, rise of populism and leader-mentality, and rejection of novelty and change. These compensatory individual loopholes include institutions (bureaucracy, religion, organizations) with roles to fill in, rules to go by, signals of both via uniform, title etc., reputation not built on merit but self-marketing, money not earned through competence. There is no surrounding in which all individuals will develop the same (high) levels of SE, and do not need to because all of the above help a system to work anyhow as long as the ratio between real SE and its mimicry stays in sustainable ranges; future research may well find tipping points in historic losses of specific nations or cultures where too much compensation of and too little originary SE led to downturns.

I resume that it takes SE to acknowledge individual potential and boundaries as a prerequisite for being able to develop that potential, and be willing and able to limit oneself. This acknowledgement has deep consequences for a society´s order: if one cannot embrace one´s own humanity in strength and weaknesses, it is a much smaller step to dehumanize the humanity of others, and degrade them to functional units. It takes respect for oneself to build an identity that can take credit for her achievements to be able to build SE. Without SE, modernization is a threat; with SE it is a chance as Frank Pajares claimed. This makes SE a vital factor for development and modernization.

---

[16] ple see extensive discussion in ch. 5.2 on proxies.

1.1 Approach

By defining modernization as a process of learning, and SE the prerequisite and outcome of learning, I need to research who or what sparks this change, under which conditions, and who or what entertains the process. In the case of modernization and learning, Tetzlaff (2005) asks: *"Who is the historic learning subject?"* There are two kinds of candidates for the answer: individuals or collectives; non-human entities like states or institutions are not-learning constructs, changes are orchestrated by individual humans in the respective position on behalf of one or more collectives. Even if we answer Tetzlaff's question with "an elite", or "the avant-garde", these groups do not develop a super-personal common mind or sense; it is always the individual human being who learns, and does so in her individual roles as individual, member of whatever group(s), or as individual leader, according to her different benefits, including those developing from some kind of group dynamic, and biases. Though many of these benefits may be unobservable and often ascribed to biases, the individual is the historic learner who reacts to environmental and social triggers, and who entertains, hinders or stops the developmental process of learning. Her benefits and inclination to learn follow suit to her belief in her ability to learn, to profit from learning, to cope with change, and profit from it – which is the definition of self-efficacy. In their self-enforcing feedback loops these beliefs tend to be self-fulfilling prophecies through the successes they produce.

In the following, I employ a wide variety of literature from political science, economics, sociology, psychology, biology, genetics, complex systems modeling and physics, history, behavioural and cultural research, and even literature, and profited greatly from questions-inspiring discussions with experts from these fields. In my attempts to learn what learning actually entails and means for human beings, I reached the firm conviction that only concerted efforts of scientists from a wide variety of fields can tackle the upcoming problems of ever growing complexity and interconnectedness. Modernization is not limited to formalized parameters like institutions, infrastructure or industrialization, but a process that changes people in their inner structures and resonating cultural beliefs if it is to be supported and kept up by a population over time.

In detail, the structure of this work is as follows:
In chapter 2, I introduce what SE is, how it works and develops, and which role it plays in the political and economic process. I delimit the concept from other psychological or economic approaches or terms that could be mistaken for SE like aspirations, self-confidence, or agency etc.
Chapter 3 traces the path in development and modernizing literature that lead to the detection of the role of human environmental adaptation in the development process, and eventually SE. I introduce major theories and authors by grouping them in types of theoretical approach. The explanatory variables start with are materialistic and exogenous causes of underdevelopment. I then move towards culture and institutions that lead to the detection of SE as the adaptive human trait enabling learning for modernization and development. Pragmatic authors who are less concerned with causes but with designing efficient policies to reproduce elsewhere successful factors of economic growth like infrastructure, industrialization, and education are suggested to possibly have been unintentional but implicit promotors of SE.
In chapter 4, I define modernization as a learning process, and sketch learning as the evolutionary tool for adaptation to different and changing environments. This chapter shows the reciprocal relation between learning and self-efficacy: SE enables learning, and learning builds SE by increasing the (mastery) experience of success. There are different ways of learning and different ways for individuals and groups to react to new information. Collective and individual learning and their different effects on building SE are described, as well as the act of learning, and what it takes for learning to lead to behaviour change. I show different schemes of individual and group reaction to information by filtering them, and identify their respective different utilities of learning in relation to levels and domains of SE, which leads to differentiating between weak and

strong groups. Identity is stated as a necessity for anchoring SE, i.e. take credit for achievements and responsibility for failures. I discuss the prerequisites of learning to show that the more SE people have the more they can be expected to believe in their ability to cope with change. As these changes are brought about by learning and behaviour change, people who don´t believe to do well under changed conditions will develop little inclination for both learning and behaviour change by themselves or others. Higher SE, in contrast, makes novelty an opportunity rather than a thread[17]. Problems with negative forms of learning like pathological learning through failure, wrong-learning as misinterpretation, and non-learning as a complete refusal to change are outlined.

Chapter 5 addresses questions and misunderstandings around SE, namely those of asymmetries between self-efficacy, resilience and entitlement, and those of too much and too little SE. Attention will be paid to phenomena of low SE, and those of asymmetric appearance in concert with subsidiary or complementary traits like resilience and entitlement. This chapter will also discuss how institutions like religion or bureaucracy can compensate for a lack of individual SE or hamper its development, while the group has to pay a price of instability, risk and need for control or manipulation for it. Separately, I discuss the question of a genetic origin of self-efficacy opposed to Wuepper& Drosten (2015; 2016) suggesting culturally transmitted and purposefully promotable SE, empirical evidence following in the next chapter.

Chapter 6 is based on WP on the historic roots of current investment self-efficacy and its role in investment behaviour of small-holder pineapple farmers in Ghana, which I co-authored with David Wuepper, who conducted the fieldwork in Ghana and econometric analysis. Using an agent-based model and recent empirical data, we wanted to research if and how SE has an immediate effect on income. In the course of this research, we also found effects on the efficiency of development measures like train-

[17] cmp. on thread appraisal: Bandura (1997), pp. 116f., 140f., 148f., 347-349.

ing or the application of new methods like mulching, and interestingly, a correlation with more supportive leadership[18].
Chapter 7 embeds the challenges of developing a formal theory on self-efficacy in economics in the current scientific discourse on modernization and development. The discussion addresses problems of empirical research of self-efficacy, finding it in the data, formulating the right questions to detect and measure it, and how to econometrically control for it. The problems of often-claimed task-efficacy against domain-specific SE are addressed as well as fields for further research.

The conclusion calls for a culture of learning instead of knowing, and for supporting people to become masters of their own lot by their own virtue and chosing. It also underlines the fact that to avoid exploiting elites clinging to power and their exploitive base, all societal ranks need to develop high self-efficacy. It is a historically grounded but epic miscalculation that uneducated dependent masses were easier to keep in control than educated agents. The findings about SE do neither replace nor negate any of the many factors of economic and political under-performance identified by science so far. They rather offer a mechanism by which these findings can be put to more efficient use, and target empowering policies in any field more effectively targeted by knowing their operational functioning. They also offer a chance to identify sources of failure and instability that could otherwise limit success of or destroy the achieved. The long-assumed natural tendency towards liberal democracy, economic progress and universal human emancipation may not be an automatism after all, but rather one potential development that we provide for universally by promoting every human´s agentic emancipation through self-efficacy or seize to the dynamics of entropy and segregation.

[18] We could not include these in the WP, but I will discuss the findings in the course of this work.

1.2 Contribution

There are still many question unanswered about how modernization and development happens, how best to foster it by targeted policies, and how to avoid or handle the potentially destabilizing social and political effects. The main contribution of this work is to identify SE as an important tool and target for development and modernization policies in developing and developed countries alike. It introduces and applies the well-tested psychological concept of SE to economic, social and political questions of development and modernization, and shows how and why it is a vital factor for both. Specifically, I argue and produce data to show that SE develops naturally, that it is culturally transmitted, and how this can make its naturally evolved form maladapted to sudden changes in the environment or circumstance through f.ex. climate change or migration. I show how exactly SE affects people´s behaviour, their propensity for change, for learning and modernization, their adaptive capacity including i.a. risk taking and opportunity recognition. I discuss the influence of diverging efficacies amongst individuals and their reference groups, and develop how a lack of SE can lead to negative social and political effects in leaders, elites and the general public to stiffle modernization and change, and suppress its protagonists: particular interests need to be enforced with manipulation, force or circumventing norms if SE is not high enough for their regular pursuit. In this context and picking up on Akerloff´s general suggestions, I spell out potentially antagonistic utility functions of learning and modernization for individuals and groups, and develop corner stones for a formal model of SE in modernization.

By employing a strictly interdisciplinary approach, I transfer insights from a broad range of disciplines like psychology, sociology, agricultural economics, anthropology, political science and economics, and tie them together into one common search of how to best foster progress to show how SE influences the process and its results. I identify modernization as an individual and collective learning process depending on an individual benefit-cost-logic largely determined by individual SE and social conditions. This allows for further research on who profits from learning, who does not and who profits from keeping others from doing so. A better understanding of this can help to design better policy measures and help prevent destabilizing effects of change.

Empirically, the study from Ghana (chpt.6) shows that SE for agricultural investment is culturally transmitted over generations. Having historical roots explains why SE is so persistent. This finding is highly relevant for developing as well as developed countries as continuous modernization is a necessity for both and can be hindered by a lack of SE amongst the population or its political personnel and economic elite. The data also reveal a very important lesson for policy makers: as people tend not to update their basic self and world concepts without external shock or targeted intervention, SE tends to be information from the past, which is maladapted if context changes quickly as in migration, climate change or dramatic technological, economic or political melt-downs.

As SE has been found to be malleable, it can and should be fostered by intentional policy measures that I describe below. Building SE has several multiplier effects especially due to it functioning like a self-fulfilling prophecy that spreads through vicarious experiences. The empirical findings in Ghana also show that SE has a large, positive effect on investment behaviour and subsequently, on income, and it enhances the effect of other measures like training or financial support for mulching, fertilizers etc. which in turn raises investment and income.

A major contribution to the discussion on development and modernization is to suggest SE to be the primum movens (Rainer Tetzlaff with the author, Hamburg, May 2015) of intentional human behaviour and supporting rational versus biased thinking, which makes it not only a missing link in explaining historic roots of unequal development, but also a transmission belt for targeting empowering policies. SE is the mental factor that decides how much influence a healthy, free individual potentially can exert on her course of action under given circumstance. David Zilvermann likewise identified SE as the “prior of Baysian learning” (with David Wüpper, Berkeley, Sept. 2015).

By delimiting SE from the multitude of terms and (self-) concepts, which aim to capture what gives human behaviour its modernizing direction, I hope my work increases clarity in language and concept in the scientific discourse. Also, I suggest the concept of SE to be universally and interculturally[19] applicable. It is important for the understanding of development and modernization processes in developed and underdeveloped countries alike (Luszczynska, Scholz & Schwarzer, 2005; Luszczynska, Gutiérrez-Doña, & Schwarzer, 2005) thereby lifting the possibility of patronage from the discussion: same challenges, modernization traps, fears of losing out, same need to empower agentic behaviour to stabilize the process – through SE.

I discuss applications and relations that have so far not had much attention with regard to SE in economic and political modernization like integrating groups and individuals with different utilities of learning. By showing learning as the operational tool for modernization based on the self-efficacious belief in one´s abilities to learn and cope with change, this work adds to our understanding of modernization processes in general, and how to foster them: for example, not just by building schools, but by helping children gain SE about their ability to actually learn and do well, to believe in their abilities to carry out different activities successfully, to put to action what they have learned. I explicitly link this call for SE building with one for offering the experience of being trusted to cope and do well, as this is indispensable for building self-respect, which in turn is indispensable for positive identity building. A positive identity is what an individual needs to be able to take credit for one´s doings to build self-efficacy beliefs, and adapt them to changing cirumstances.

Different environments shape different degrees of strength and generality of SE in their populace, and thereby create different costs and profits of learning and change in individuals, groups and leaders. The closer a human habitat to natural conditions the stronger the influence of geography,

[19] ple see discusion on Henrich´s "WEIRD" people in my conclusion.

climate, and natural endowment on human behaviour and efficacy beliefs; the more developed, urbanized, industrialized and regulated by modern institutions, the less the influence of nature on behaviour and SE. In both cases, targeted policy measures can provide for SE "updates" where environment does not provide for the necesssary or desired incentives and experiences.

I identify self-efficacy as what operatively enables the different spheres of a larger community to communicate productively with each other: as an evolutionary tool for adaptive learning and innovations, the mechanism that translates environment and circumstance via survival strategies into culture, and culture into institutions, which then react back on the individual. This makes SE the translator of political measures into economic performance and activating agent of empowering policies. I also suggest that effects of SE have been implicitly found in a wide array of research on intentional human behaviour like time discounting (Galor & Özak, 2014), persistence, resilience, risk taking, cooperation, climate and agricultural development, political participation, corruption, crime rates, and several others that display performance based on human trust in conducting an activity[20]; additionally, I draw attention to the fact that SE can

---

[20] Studies for example on risk attitude in general or in entrepreneurial decision making seldomly spell out SE, eventhough that is what they are implicitly also treating; cmp. for example: Weber, Blais, and Betz (2002), who basically research the same as Krueger & Dickson (1994) but only the latter spell it out.
An example for the wide applicability of the concept of process and domain specific SE can be found in the sociological study of Orna Donath (2015) on women resenting motherhood, who found that these women usually love their children (goal, target) but despise the process of motherhood, which Christina Mundlos (2015) ascribes to the lack of confidence in their abilities to be a good mother, i.e. to master the process well – which is the definition of low SE for the process of mothering. This latter effect is at least true for the one third of interviewed women who said they had consciously made the decision to have children and then did not feel up to the task.

take on the function as a prior in Bayesian learning, and influences cooperation and risk taking in game theoretical experiments[21].

An important contribution of this work is to show why programmes that increase SE also enhance the efficiency and effectiveness of traditional policy measures targeting material conditions like availability of capital, improving infrastructure, or reframing institutional settings and make substantial and sustainable differences in economic performance. Individuals and groups with stronger and more general degrees of SE are more able and willing to identify and incorporate new opportunities into their social relations and work life. In the face of novelty, people have to be able to change their habits, beliefs, behaviours with regard to work, investing, methods and technology, planning, risk taking, reaction to and seeking of new information, and eventually change their self-image and social relations. This will only happen if people believe they have the necessary abilities to profit from change. People with higher SE have been found to be more empowered, emancipated, independent, more agentic. High SE is an important trait also in reference groups, elites and leaders as their decision to allow or restrain learning and behaviour changes amongst their members or clientele, and decisive for the success of modernizing measures. In sum, all questions that touch upon good governance and institutional support, as well as the learning culture of informal reference groups like family, clan, village, friends, contain an important aspect of functional SE. Groups and leaders have to have enough SE to believe they will be able to keep their positions, gain new ones or make it as well without them[22] to allow for change.

This work aims to add to a better understanding of the workings of SE as important for the less developed, poorer countries of the South to foster

---

[21] F.ex. in spontaneous cooperation when non-cooperators fair better in a group of cooperators; Kabalak, Smirnova, and Jost (2014).

[22] On specific development hurdles for especially African countries, some authors show that it is first and foremost the lack of institutional and policy support that limit successful entrepreneurship, f.ex. Kappel (2015), Kappel & Ishengoma (2011).

development and economic growth, empower democratic participation and elites for better governance, and increase the efficiency of financial and political measures. But a good understanding of SE and how to foster it is actually equally relevant for the richer, democratic, industrialized countries which now face modernizing pressures internally, and externally, and from past modernizing failures. Western economies experience growing domestic modernizing pressures in their transition from economies driven by industrial production to digitalized ones. This transition happens as national populations are aging and declining, and in the presence of new pressures from social media out of reach for traditional politics, changing self-images, gender relations and roles, immense household deficits, financial markets that have been robbed the intervention possibilities of monetary policies, political and social omissions from the past, and rather fixed proportions of populations that have been difficult to integrate into an industrial labor market and dim outlocks for a digitalized one. High degrees of self-efficacy are required and helpful in individual and collective transitional processes. External pressures caused by inequalities in the distribution of wealth and well-being around the world increasingly add to the challenges at home through large numbers of refugees and poverty migration, terrorism and wars, which have reached the doorsteps of the developed countries. It is in their best interest to help the less developed to close the gap a good bit. While at the end of colonialism, the question of a more evenly developed world was very much one of morality and ethics, the incentives for prolonging pseudo-colonial relationships to a business-as-usual remained high. Using their best knowledge to assist every nation into peaceful stable modernization has now become the best strategy to preserve one´s own security and wealth for the developed countries.

Institutions and elites must withstand the seductions arising from a lack of SE amongst elites and leaders that support corruption, manipulation and retreating to reducing democratic participation. This is true for developing as much as for developed countries. Every individual and every group of people in privileged positions with a greater access to power and

income has a lot to lose from change. The industrialized world may believe their institutions were immune against these lures but democracy is a process, not a state, and has to be continuously reproduced:
"We have to imagine Sisyphos as a happy man" (Camus, 1942).

Acemoglu & Robinson (2012, p.41) write: *"the inequality doesn't just have consequences for the lives of individual people in the poor countries; it also causes grievances and resentment, with huge political consequences for the United States and elsewhere."* Kappel (2015a) adds: *"it is not just about refugees and migration; Africa is in a broad process of radical change with crumbling states, which will have clear consequences for Europe and Germany"* (transl. bd). At the same time, as migration and terrorism carry the pressures of underdevelopment from the outside right into the middle of the developed world, the necessary adaptive measures here and helping the poorer countries more effectively there make understanding how to foster increasing SE of all parties involved highly desirable; it may carry the key to modernizing toward better governance for all.
As Eric Beinhocker (2007, p.52) writes: *"Time waits for no one"*.

"Beliefs Are Rules For Action"
Charles Peirce[23]

2. What is Self-Efficacy?

2. 1 Concept

Self-efficacy[24] is the belief to have the abilities to act according to one´s own decisions and to achieve desired goals, and to have the capability to cope with future changes. SE is also important for rational thinking as it links one´s actions to outcomes under given limitations of environment and social circumstance. Experiences "teach" causal thinking when one does not only regard oneself as locus of control for decision making but as the one whose actions have a decisive influence on the results, that one´s actions matter. This effect accumulates and is self-enforcing.

Bandura (1996), identifies its development as reason for the revolution of knowledge and growth: *"This change in human self-conception and the view of life from supernatural control to personal control ushered in a major shift in causal thinking, and the new enlightenment rapidly expanded the exercise of human power over more and more domains."*
Because SE assures and motivates people, it increases their persistence and time planning horizon while decreasng risk aversion. As it also increases their openness to learning, it form the base for entrepreneurship. SE develops at all times and everywhere in interaction with the surrounding environment. Its evolution is not limited to specific circumstance, but its quality is: the more positively an environment reacts to human intervention like granting greater harvests after fertilizing, the higher the respective SE people develop. In environments with f.ex high disease pressure or low agricultural potential, a lower average sense of SE is the natural outcome. In these cases, low SE feeds back in lowering the pro-

[23] Cited from an interview between Frank Pajares and Héfer Bembenutty (2007).
[24] The first part of this chapter is a revised version from Wuepper & Drosten (2015), pp.25.

pensity for effort, risk taking, and openness to novelty even further and thus future successful interventions even less likely. Whatever features of individual effort and collective organization are needed for survival or bring the greatest profit will be key to the level of SE and cultural traits developed in that habitat. The ideal environment to develop a high sense of SE is one that is challenging, yet can be mastered with effort. Many environments in the temperate zone fulfil this criterion. Europe f.ex, where diseases were mostly weak enough to successfully fight them and where soils and climate allowed the development of intensive agriculture to feed a growing population was more supportive for developing SE, while tropical and polar regions were less so.

Bandura[25] started to experiment with SE in the 1970´s after having been working on social learning theories (1963, expanded 1977). In his famous Bobo doll experiments (i.a. Bandura, 1965) he had shown aggressive behaviour to not only result from drives and frustration, but from observation and vicarious reinforcement (watching behaviour of relevant others being rewarded or punished). Bandura discovered that learning was done differently than had long been assumed in behaviouristic thinking. Learning, he stated, could therefore not be fostered in traditional ways through incentives, rewards and retaliation but needed a different approach. He went on to develop a theory of self-efficacy and widened his approach into his Social Cognitive Theory (1986)[26], subsuming his research on the different aspects of learning and behaviour change. He defines people as agents of their actions, not in the sense of being the sole conscious determinant of a specific outcome, but as contributors (1997, pp.3, 227ff) by being self-regulating, self-organizing, self-reflecting, and proactive: *"Beliefs of personal efficacy constitute the key factor of human*

[25] Bandura published his theory and empirical findings in an extensive number of papers. A comprehensive overview, containing revised versions of several earlier publications, offers: 1977, 1989, 1997, 2008/1995.

[26] Bandura (1986); unfortunately, some of his important ideas have reaped misunderstandings and misinterpretations, which may have prevented a wider-spread acceptance and application so far.

agency. If people belief they have no power to produce results, they will not attempt to make things happen (1997, p.3). Bandura (1994) identifies four basic processes[27],[28] through which belief in one´s SE determines how people think, feel, motivate themselves and act, all of which constitute the framework for self-regulation:

1. Cognitive processes are influenced in several ways via goal setting, self-appraised capabilities, anticipations and visualizations, conscious commitment: *"The stronger the perceived self-efficacy, the higher the goal challenges people set for themselves and the firmer is their commitment to them"* (p.3).

2. Motivational processes as outcomes mainly of cognitive processes build anticipatory forethought and determine what people believe they can do. There are three known cognitive motivators and respective theories:

i) Causal attribution and attribution theory: high SE beliefs attribute failures to insufficient efforts, while low SE attributes failure to inability. "*Causal attributions affect motivation, performance and affective reactions mainly through beliefs in self-efficacy"*(p.4).

ii) Outcome expectancies and expectancy-value-theory: "*motivation is regulated by the expectation that a given course of behaviour will pro-duce certain outcomes and the values of those outcomes. But people act on their beliefs about what they can do, as well on their beliefs about the likely outcomes of performance...There are countless attractive options people do not pursue because they judge they lack the capabilities for them*".

Expectancy-value-theorists criticize that the concept of SE becomes useless if is to explain the goal as much as the behaviour that leads to

---

[27] following is a summary of Bandura (1994) on efficacy-mediated processes; I cite from a reprint of his wp, retrieved online 10/5/15, www.uky.edu/~eushe2/Bandura/BanEncy

[28] cmp. discussion in Hulleman et al. (2010) on "Different labels for the same constructs or different constructs with similar labels?".

reaching it. Bandura calls for including SE as an influential factor to enhance the predictability of expectancy-outcome-theory, not replace it.

iii) Goal setting and goal theory: Bandura interprets goal setting as an important factor of self-influence rather than directly influencing motivation and behaviour. To avoid cognitive dissonance and aim for self-satisfaction from achieving set goals, efforts would be intensified: "*Motivation based on goals or personal standards is governed by…self-satisfying and self-dissatisfying reactions to one's performance, perceived self-efficacy for goal attainment, and readjustment of personal goals based on one's progress. Self-efficacy beliefs contribute to motivation in several ways: They determine the goals people set for themselves; how much effort they expend; how long they persevere in the face of difficulties; and their resilience to failures. When faced with obstacles and failures people who harbor self-doubts about their capabilities slacken their efforts or give up quickly. Those who have a strong belief in their capabilities exert greater effort when they fail to master the challenge. Strong perseverance contributes to performance accomplishments.*" (p.4)

3. Affective processes relate to how people feel about themselves, their activities and capabilities, and their surrounding. SE with regard to coping abilities determines the level of stress, and disposition for anxiety and depression. The belief in one´s ability to cope not only with a given or potential situation, but also with exercising control over stressful thoughts and feelings has great influence on the question if a challenge is regarded as stress/thread, or as a challenge/chance.

4. Selection processes constitute the interface between individual decisions and environment: people make decisions, selecting between choices, thereby selecting and influencing possibly their natural, most certainly their social environment, which predetermines future selection possibilities. "*People avoid activities and situations they believe exceed their coping capabilities*" while "*readily (undertaking) challenging activities and (selecting) situations they judge themselves capable of handling.*

By the choices they make, people cultivate different competencies, interests and social networks that determine life courses... This is because the social influences operating in selected environments continue to promote certain competencies, values, and interests long after the efficacy decisional determinant has rendered its inaugurating effect. The higher the level of people's perceived self-efficacy the wider the range of ...options they seriously consider, the greater their interest in them, and the better they prepare themselves ... and the greater is their success." (p.6).

Bandura stresses a point that is amongst the most misunderstood about the whole concept: SE refers exclusively to domain and process specific issues. It does not refer to tasks or goals, i.e. it does not refer to the end result of a process. SE ist the belief in being able to *conduct*, to *act* in a way that is apt to reach a certain goal. When researchers find outcome, task, goal specific aspects, these do not directly show SE but its effects.

Self-efficacy develops in different levels of strengths for different domains. Domains describe the kind of activity for which one perceives self-efficacy. Any person will have many very different levels of SE for her different aspects of life: she can feel very high SE with regard to her work as a farmer and feel very low SE with regard to the business side of her work, even lower for playing in their village soccer team, and the highest for preaching on Sundays. Even if you could know the individual level of SE for each activity, it would not give you information about which harvest, profit, number of goals or rescued souls to expect. But it does give information about the expectable effort, persevearance, and resilience if you wanted to know which trait to support to improve the results. As people have SE for different domains, they will also develop different levels of generality of SE. While there are innumerous domains, many of them demand similar abilities and capabilities. People with high self-efficacy in major fields of their life will tend to develop SE in a more general sense, not just for foodball but sports, not just for selling sunglasses but doing business, not just for preaching but to dealing with people in general.

"The best thing a good fairy could put into a child's cradle is challenges it must master."
Alfred Adler (1920)

2.2 Development of Self-Efficacy and the Question of Identity

For the sake of this work, the citation from the individual psycholigist Alfred Adler should read "challenges it must *and* can master": self-efficacy develops naturally if challenges have to be met that are just hard enough to demand effort, learning, work, persevearance, planning, courage and risk taking, cooperation; which entail a high or painful price if they are not appropriately met, and which *can* be met if effort is sufficient and right. This is, in a nutshell, what intended policy measures would have to mimic to help people raise their self-efficacy.

Wuepper & Drosten (2015) researched how SE develops naturally as a result from interaction between humans and environment. We found how a responsive, stable natural environment which gives much leeway for human intervention, and rewards it with good harvests, good hunting, good trade, naturally builds higher levels of SE; these specific self-efficacies are culturally transmitted in groups and to offspring, and they are persistent! The more developed a group of people the more independent from their natural environment they become, the more important become the social and man-made influences on self-efficacy.
Bandura (1994) researched the social process that led to higher levels or more general SE to be able to intentionally foster their development by targeted measures. He identifies four main sources of influence on how people develop self-efficacy:
"*...mastery experiences, seeing people similar to oneself manage task demands successfully, social persuasion that one has the capabilities to succeed in given activities, and inferences from somatic and emotional states indicative of personal strengths and vulnerabilities...*" (p.13).

Incidentally, these four sources of SE represent exactly the same mechanisms by which natural environments foster the development of SE: experience of mastery and success in agricultural work through planning, investing, hard work, choosing the proper crop, for example; seeing other members of the village or clan succeed in their interventionist work; being told by elders personally that one was a good a hunter, fisher, farmer or by identifying with a "story" and "myth" on special capabilities that built the community´s social web, and the excitement and physical arousal of succeeding in whatever activity one then would chose to do.

Bandura suggests the most effective way to build SE is by mastering experiences. Taking on a task or challenge and succeeding in it, creates a robust sense of SE. Once a certain level of robustness has been reached, failures can be attributed to objective circumstances, planning mistakes or lack of effort and initiate another attempt with lessons learned from the last try. Before this stage has been reached, failure is likely to provoke scapegoating or self-doubt, undermine SE, and attribute misconduct to one´s own – incurable – inability. In order for failure to be overcome by more effort in another try, one has to have strong trust in one´s abilities. Vicarious experiences from social models, which succeed in their efforts lead to higher efficacy beliefs in those who can identify with them. Humans learn from others by imitating, identifying, watching and repeating. In growing up amongst a group of people, culturally transmitted self- and world-constructs and collective knowledge and beliefs will be transported with corresponding levels and magnitudes of SE. As culture has been found to be highly persistent, "inherited" self-efficacy is too. This does not mean it cannot be changed! It means that people are endowed with very different levels on which one has to build.

Important to notice is Bandura´s observation that by verbal persuasion, SE can be quickly improved but not necessarily to robust stages unless it is supported by positive experience. And worse so, verbal persuasion is very effective in destroying SE. The logic of this lies in the functioning as a self-fulfilling prophecy: verbal persuasion may boost somebody´s SE enough to make him exercise more and harder effort for a longer period

of time and truly produce the attempted success, thereby promoting a stronger, more robust sense of SE. If, however, instead of success failure is reaped, this only verbal stimulation will easily produce the opposite effect by lowering SE again, not necessarily to realistic, but possibly to even lower than appropriate levels. The worst case is to discourage people´s SE by verbal attacks on their abilities to do well or cope: these latter two cases are difficult to overcome as people with low SE will avoid any challenge and situation that could lead to failure or, in turn, success:
"But people who have been persuaded that they lack capabilities tend to avoid challenging activities that cultivate potentialities and give up quickly in the face of difficulties. By constricting activities and undermining motivation, disbelief in one's capabilities creates its own behavioural validation." (Bandura, 1994, p.2) This effect, even coupled with group identification, was found by Steele & Aronson (1995) in their work on cliché: in a cycle of aptitude tests, Afro-American students did worse when they had to indicate their race in the beginning of the test; when they were not asked to tick the respective answer, they did as well as all others.

Self-efficacy cannot develop if it does not have an "anchor": self-respect as part of individual identity. The individual has to be able to give herself credit for her achievements through her own actions and by her own virtues. Her identity must include enough self-respect to claim and accept this credit. The child builds her identity by differentiating herself from her surrounding, later to decide how much she wants to be similar and how much she wants to be different from it. This process of individuation determines her identity, which is really another layer around her self-construct (see below chpt. on learning), but while her self-construct is believed to be stable for her lifetime, her identity is not as it undergoes several phases of transition. The experience of respect for one´s being, *not* one´s achievements, is indispensable for building self-respect. Without an identity that respects herself, one cannot build self-efficacy at all, one can only create compensatory coping strategies: like trying to evoke fear or praise for action instead of respect or love for being.

If a social or natural environment does not request or reward human intervention, SE cannot develop; well–adapted behaviour in this case could at best foster entitlement or resilience as survival strategies, but not SE. They can occur simultaneously but are independent, their asymmetric occurrence offering ample cause for societal problems. Think of nomadic groups surviving an inhospitable, barren environment only by regular raiding, without ever being able to develop a sense of SE as their habitat does not react to intervention of their own capacity and cannot be sustainably changed through work, planning, investment etc. Or consider communities whose achievements are regularly destroyed by natural catastrophes or lives cut short by uncontrollable diseases like malaria. It is the experience of successful undertakings, like choosing the right crop, employing the right amount of work and capital, doing the right kind of planning for storage, cooperation, and trade, that gives people a higher perception of their own ability to reach their goals, to influence their livelihood. Another example is the current discussion in the U.S. about universities and colleges having to deal with growing numbers of students with psychological issues that impede their studying success and potentially endanger successful professional lives. These issues originate from lack of resilience and lack of self-efficacy with regard to handling adversity and ordinary everyday challenges. Growing complexity, performance pressure on the one hand and insecurities on the other not only pose social and political problems but economic ones, when growing numbers of youths lag behind their potential because their belief in their capabilities is too underdeveloped to tackle their future.

2. 3 Self-Efficacy in the Economic and Political Process

It is important to note that the concept of self-efficacy concerns only those aspects of one´s life that one can intentionally influence. Having self-efficacy does not change someone´s material conditions by itself; one needs a material base to start of with, but self-efficacy will increase a person´s ability to identify opportunity and try it, and use the given material base more insensely and more effectively than people with less SE, making more of what one has at hand. The idea of self-efficacy does not shift responsibility from political decision makers, international corporations and aid agencies to the poor or less developed. Neither does it make good governance and inclusive institutions, or any other structural policy measure for building modern industries, infrastructure and finance sectors obsolete. And it certainly does not shift responsibility to develop higher self-efficacy to the poor and those who have less of it as SE typically develops naturally over generations according to the surrounding. In a low SE environment, one cannot develop SE in isolation and without impulses, examples, encouragment or survival need. If SE turns out to be insufficient for changing circumstances and requirements, it needs specific measures of support to increase SE quicker than it would naturally do without targeted policies. Once you have acquired high and strong SE beliefs, and have become a self-educating, self-regulating master of your own lot, you may build on your stock to add more. But in order to increase individual SE from a natural low and weak to higher and stronger, one needs indispensable triggers and entertainers as described above, i.e. first, a stimulus from the environment or social support to make you believe you must and can exert purposeful action, and secondly, recurring confirmation over some time and enforcing mastery experience. If you live in an environment that does not support the natural development of individual SE you depend on social intervention to create this support.

Bandura placed his concept of the individual in context with her surrounding in a triadic reciprocal (1997, p.6ff) causation, which reflects the connections between human behaviour, environmental factors, and personal factors. Human behaviour is exercised under personal cognitive, affective, and biological conditions in a natural and social environment, and circumstance. This interconnection is governed by reciprocal limitation, which means the different aspects set limits to each other and thereby define and determine each other. Each aspect influences the other two and is influenced by them. The respective influences are neither equally strong nor constant in their ratio, nor do they develop at the same

time; the whole system is a complex dynamic one with self-enforcing feedback loops, producing unintended, unobserved and long-term effects, but can be tested for at least with regard to the produced efficacy beliefs. Over three decades, this concept was empirically tested by Bandura and other psychologists who found SE to affect almost every field of human endeavour. It has been mostly tested with regard to medical compliance, risk behaviour, sports and diets, and academic achievements, i.e. those human fields that refer directly to acute behaviour change and learning new arguments, explanations, action and reaction patterns[29].
Based on Bandura´s conception of triadic reciprocal interconnectedness and influence I suggest that self-efficacy is the key factor of individual economic and social performance, naturally originating from long-term environmental stimuli[30] and malleable through intentional intervention.

SE is a "mental model" with some degree of independence of the actual competence of an individual in a given moment (though competence will reap more success and foster higher SE in the next period and vice versa), her immediate environment in the moment of decision making and of how realistic her judgment is. What is decisive for setting ambitious goals and calculating the chance of reaching them is the belief to have all what it takes to reach them. It is this belief that enables people to dare to learn new information, try new inventions, set high goals, keep trying for a longer time even when problems arise. Having a high degree of SE

---

[29] There are innumerous studies in these fields. Bandura gives a comprehensive list of studies in his 1997 book; good overview also: Pajares (1997, 2002); Stajkovic & Luthans (1998); Bandura (1990), Bandura, Barbaranelli, Caprara, & Pastorelli (1996). An interesting study unfortunately states that "self-efficacy is not only of a task-specific nature": Luszczynska, Gutiérrez-Doña, & Schwarzer (2005); a similar, in my opinion wrong, interpretation about SE being task-specific give Woodruff & Cashman (1993). Bandura has written several papers to answer his critics and misinterpretators, the latest being: Bandura (2012, 2015). On measuring general efficacy via scales: Schwarzer & Jerusalem (1995), Luszczynska, Scholz, & Schwarzer (2005). And in general: Schwarzer (1992/2014).

[30] On persistence of culture and human traits see f.ex. Boyd & Richerson (1985, 1995); Nunn (2012).

means that a person believes she has influence on her life, she has the internal locus of control and can move from there to act. She is able to be persistent in her endeavours, master difficulties and keep on trying for a longer time.

Note that while persistence describes the time aspect of SE, resilience does not. Resilience is the ability to spring back after an external shock and is an independent trait, which may or may not, and more often than not does, occur in conjunction with SE. Persistence and resilience are often used synonymously in the literature; it is important though to differentiate: persistence is an integral part of SE. Resilience is independent: you can find cases of resilience without SE as an ever-enduring in adverse conditions as in war times, and SE without resilience, as in the odd case of failure that a self-efficient agent will ascribe to his lack of effort or circumstance instead of any condition that would require resilience to cope. One could say, that self-efficient people have less need for "springing back" from setbacks as they are protected from many adverse feelings because of their mental interpretation models for failure.

Self-efficacy is the core prerequisite of human agency as it is this belief that enables people to act as an agent for herself and others. It may occur in concert with resilience and entitlement, but while SE is part of the inward-oriented self-construct, entitlement is outward oriented and part of an individual´s world-view. Asymmetric occurrence of these three connected traits leads to social stress that may adversely affect economic performance: without the respective SE to earn the rewards one feels entitled to, may lead to a feeling of deprivation which in turn may lead to adverse or maladapted social behaviour and to shortcomings in economic activity. Having resilience without SE may lead to suffering through endurance instead of activity to get out of the adverse situation, again potentially harming inter alia economic performance.

Research showed that people with higher SE are more persistent, have a lower incidence of angst and depression, and are more successful in their education and training. Locke & Latham (1990) found what they called a "high performance cycle" in that people with higher SE tend to have higher expectations, which lead to setting higher goals. In a kind of self-fulfilling prophecy, they will then put in more effort to reach their higher goals which, when accomplished, increases their sense of SE even more. Wuepper & Drosten (2015) identify historical, environmentally shaped, and subsequently bequest self-efficacy as the source of entrepreneurial traits. From Schumpeter (1934/1983) to Galor & Michalopoulos (2012), entrepreneurial behaviour has been linked to economic development. Entrepreneurship is usually described by its aspects: openness to novelty, being explorative, longer planning horizons, greater risk taking, faster in innovation adaptation and others, all of which have been found to be directly influenced by the strength of SE beliefs and suggests self-efficacy to cause and enable a person to be and act entrepreneurial.

SE as the belief in one´s capabilities to *act* successfully refers to conducting the process, not directly to achieving the goal as its end product. In their study on Ghanaian smallholders, Wuepper & Drosten (2016) identify SE to influence investment behaviour and thereby household income. The goal of bettering one´s livelihood by increasing income could be realized through the belief in one´s ability to invest better or more with regard to money, work, fertilizer, learning etc. We researched how different environments gave different signals to their inhabitants, either rewarding or discouraging entrepreneurial behaviour, thus shaping culture and human traits. We found that historically developed and culturally transmitted SE indeed affects today's farming income.

SE was recently discovered by management researchers for motivating employees, recognizing opportunity by entrepreneurs (Tumasjan & Braun, 2011), risk taking, time preferences, perseverance and resilience in crisis. The relevance of SE in a modern agricultural value chain by the example of Western Africa has been shown by Wuepper & Sauer (2016). As an important determining factor for intentional human action, SE contributes to a range of phenomena vital for economic performance (Stajkovic & Luthans, 1998) such as self-control: e.g. when tempted, individuals with low SE may convince themselves that their effort is hopeless anyway and thus consume their capital instead of saving/ investing; time preference: e.g. low SE makes individuals discount their future stronger; and possibly trustworthiness: low SE may mislead individuals to justify dishonesty as their only means to get what they want. Trust plays a vital role in cooperation and in economically relevant investment of effort.

When Nathan Nunn researched today´s causes of poverty in Africa, he identified, amongst others, human factors (which he called "internal factors") which were reflected in local cultures and institutions. He found that these internal factors, and especially detrimental the lack of trust, was an outcome of slavery: "*... that most of the impact of the slave trade works through factors that are internal to the individual, such as cultural norms, beliefs, and values*" (Nunn & Wantchekon, 2009, p.46; Nunn, 2007). In his examination of the Engermann-Sokoloff-Hypothesis which asserts that slavery and plantation economy in Latin America and the Southern States of the United States had produced inequality as the present source of economic dysfunction, Nunn did find the correlation between slavery and economic failures not with regard to inequalities, but again to trust (Nunn, 2008). His findings correspond with those of Wüpper & Drosten (2016), and Wüpper & Sauer (2016) in West Africa with regard to self-efficacy: trust in one´s abilities goes hand in hand with a more optimistic, in general more trust-inclined attitude, trust in oneself, trust in others including one´s reference groups, and trust in the course of things. I suggest that Nunn´s findings of the trust destroying effects of slavery reflect the destruction of SE and more, the destruction of the base for self-efficacy building, i.e. self-respect and a positive identity for anchoring success, amongst many of the governing elites and the general public, and thereby the fundamental base of today´s poverty in former slave economies.

Belief in one´s SE fosters not only innovation diffusion, but also risk taking, long-term planning and cooperation, all of which are outcomes of trust (f.ex. Weber et al., 2002; Krueger et al., 1994; Tumasjan et al., 2011; Stajkovic et al.,1998). By the same token, will trust and its outcomes develop a more collaborative culture and respective institutions that reflect it.

If SE is low, the requirements for trust in the potential cooperation partner are unproportionally high. The same is true for the stakes to any kind of risk taking: with low SE, the subjective costs will demand unproportional rewards or trust in circumstances. Sokoloff & Engermann in their study on the correlation between slavery, plantation economy and today´s lesser economic performance in the Americas found the same economic data but attributed them to inequality. Again, I suggest it is SE that was destroyed in slave trade, and through working and living conditions on the plantations, and in the rich households. And not only amongst slaves, but just as much amongst slave traders and owners who learned to live well off exploitation, missing out on developing self-efficacy on behalf of their own virtue. I suggest this combination: high sense of entitlement and material profit with a low sense of SE as trust in one´s capabilities to succeed, as - aside of availability - a major cause of exploitive political and economic systems. If the reason for one´s well-being lies within oneself, change and novelty offer chances for new endeavours, but if one´s well-being depends on factors *external* to the actor and over which she has conquered some control and power, these will not be easily given up, but be defended. This can be observed in former plantation economies that seem resistant to modernization while being prone to corruption amongst the old elites who jealously protect their privilege: they may not have developed the self-efficacy to trust their abilities to do as well in a competitive system that is based on merit.

This is certainly a problem in all countries and systems at any stage of development: once the troughs of power and riches have been reached, few have the SE beliefs that whatever may be available for them after their present position will be as profitable. This is where the vital importance of institutions comes in, and the reason why lesser egalitarian countries may have greater difficulties installing them in the first place.

Culture and institutions, developed in a given environment, directly reflect levels and domains of SE of the respective population, i.e. individuals, groups, and leaders. Deducting from the innumerous studies on how SE affects human behaviour, we can assume that Individuals with low SE and a perception of entitlement living in environmental conditions apt for it, will have incentives for building exploitive institutions to redistribute and gain some kind of power position, whereas individuals with high SE would have a much greater incentive to build inclusive institutions to safe on the social and material costs of power struggle and hampering development. High SE individuals can trust to get what they want by their own virtue; these individuals are better equipped and motivated for cooperation as they don´t need to forego regular ways to achieve their goals. Low SE individuals however, cannot trust their own abilities in the same way and are thus more susceptible for passive, resignative attitudes, or to the lures of manipulation, control or force to gain more of what they aspire.

Higher levels of SE help people to successfully go through different transitional phases in their lifespan as children have to enter into adolescence; adolescents have to grow into adulthood; young adults have to face the transition into partnership and parenting; and ever more people are growing older. Indeed, as more people live longer and at better health, more people in Western societies need to adapt to more different phases in their lifespan than before and will do so more actively with higher SE (Bandura, 1997, pp.168ff).

Self-efficacy has been found to foster political participation and more supportive democratic organizational structures. Lanning (2008) notes: "*...at the level of the individual, democracy implies both self-efficacy and engagement. With respect to self-efficacy, it is not enough that individuals are in fact self-governing. We must* ***believe*** (highlighted by b.d.) *that we are self-governing as well (...). With respect to engagement, citizenship, like all forms of group membership, ..,.may be understood as a feature of the self-concept. To the extent that this feature is prominent within the self-concept, the actor may be said to identify with the state. The role of identity in democracy is important in understanding individual differences in political participation, which do not derive only from differences in resources and abilities (Dahl, 2006), but also from differences in what Allport described as "ego-involvement."* (p.433)

Basically, there are two sets of political efficacy: the first one refers to the above described belief of a citizen to be able to exert some kind of influence in political surrounding and onto its procedures, which could lead to different degrees of engagement from thinking about political issues to running for political office. In a study on how to promote democratic citizenry with high degrees of participation, tolerance and involvement via school education, Solhaug (2006) found SE to be more important than knowledge for actual participation as it increases motivation. In a study linking human traits to political participation, Vecchione & Caprara (2009) found *"Openness and Energy/Extraversion accounted for significant variance in political self-efficacy beliefs, which in turn accounted for political participation"*. In a commentary on the roots of participation, Caprara (2008) prior remarked: "*People have reason to participate if they have a voice in the in the choices of those entitled to use power, if they believe that authority considers their interests as valuable as others', and if they judge that their arguments are influencing decisions. Thus – both voicing one's opinion and exerting control over one's representatives are crucial features of democracy that unavoidably have an impact on self-concept and identity.*" This experience represents an originary efficacy-building mastery experience of political efficacy.
Vital for social, political and economic ability for cooperation, Caprara underlines: *"As voting outcomes depend on aggregation, voting is a cooperative enterprise that turns personal efficacy into collective efficacy"*, which applies to every successful constructive action in a collective framework.

There is second form which is often mistaken for political efficacy, as it happens in the political sphere, also aiming at political office, but of which I would argue to actually be non-political by origin: aspiring political office as part of another personal self-efficacy belief refering to those abilities that could gain political career, and a sense of entitlement. This is the same kind of efficacy belief that can also be found outside of politics: in business and management. As Chamorro-Premuzic (2013) points out about the latter with his provocative question: "*Why Do So Many*

Incompetent Men Become Leaders?", we tend to *"misinterpret displays of confidence as a sign of competence"* (ibid*)* while the competence and corresponding efficacy belief is really only about this display, about the ability to gain a position, not about the actually needed business, management, intellectual, ethical, human, and political compe-tencies for leading. This "hubris efficacy" belief is therefore about having the charisma, reputation building, networking, (military) power exertion abilities to gain office/job position, and in principle undemocratic, unparticipatory, and unpolitical.

Bandura (1997) observes an erosion of real political efficacy when trust in political institutions to solve human problems, their perceived efficacy, decreases (p.520). It is a good example for the interdependency of individual and surrounding: the human being exerts some influence over his life and surrounding, and is influenced by it, both limiting and determining each other.

2.4 What is Not Self-Efficacy: Related Concepts

There is a range of seemingly similar, from psychology adopted economic concepts, that might be mistaken for self-efficacy or contain self-efficacy under a different name. Bandura differentiates SE explicitly from confidence, control beliefs, effectance motivation, expectancy-valence theories, intentions, locus of control, means efficacy, outcome expectations, perceived control, potency, self-concept, self-deception, self-esteem, skills (1997). Likely for confounding are all concepts that carry a "self" in their name. Self-esteem, self-confidence, self-concept, self-reference, self-appraisal and all other self-beliefs carry a part of this one aspect of self-efficacy in them that refers to belief in one´s abilities to act, including deciding and setting goals. But they are all more general concepts that refer to evaluating, judging and attitudes toward the self as a whole. Bandura´s Stanford colleague Carol Dweck developed a similar concept of "growth mindset" as a teachable self-optimizing program while Angela Duckworth developed the concept of "grit" which concentrates on personal character and the effects of persistence. These ideas border on aspects of SE, but basically through its symptoms, not its causes and are thereby limited in explanatory scientific capacity and in the potential positive effects of respective training programmes.

Self-efficacy is about empowerment and liberation, helping people to become agents of their life, not training anybody to be more "successful" under a set of rules with a set of possible outcomes. Especially self-confidence is often mistaken for SE. Bandura describes it as a *"colloquial"* and *"non-descriptive term that refers to strength of belief but does not necessarily specify what the certainty is about. I can be supremely confident that I will fail at an endeavour. Perceived self-efficacy refers to belief in one's power to produce given levels of attainment."* (1997, p.382)

Self-reliance includes the aspect of independence and is used in sociology, linguistics, data processing to describe a state of self-sufficiency. (In political science, it was part of a dissociative theory for developing countries to end dependency and the dictate of terms of trade in the 1970s (ple see below Nyerere, Galtung, Senghas)).

Locus of control refers to a person´s notion of being the one who makes the decisions, and is in control of her own matters; it does not refer to the achieving process, but to the decision to start it - which is a result of self-efficacy and circumstance.

Aspirations as a concept for expanding human capital has been shown to have large impact on short-term performance, low aspirations being a factor of poverty in poor families through beliefs that serve stereotypes[31]. Bandura et al. show that SE can be a decisive factor for developing aspirations and actual goal setting[32],[33] while these are not identical: as

[31] f.ex with regard to development of aspirations and social groups: Gottfredson (1981); with regard to race, class and environment: MacLeod (1987).

[32] in children: Bandura, Barbaranelli, Caprara, & Pastorelli (2001); on social programs and poor families: Chiapa, Garrido, & Prina (2012).

[33] on lack of investment aspirations, and how to raise them through vicarious/

aspirations refer to a wish like "I want to be a doctor", a goal is the end result of a specific process that causally links one´s own actions to the desired result of that process: "I want to be a doctor because I can and will work hard in school which will earn me the degree and the well-paying job". This linking of one´s actions to the attained results is what people lack who lack SE. Aspirations are much easier to evoke than to develop SE especially in cases with clearly defined targets like education: the wish to become a doctor says nothing about the willingness to work hard and consistently, or having the persistence, resilience, frustration-tolerance, and adaptability every school system demands. When short-term simple measures like exposing people to a vicarious experience via film showings find quick success in producing wishes for higher education in children and parents, they are likely finding only aspirations without and instead of SE. People with low SE may have high aspirations, but low success expectation in proving oneself: why should I try harder, if I will probably fail anyway. And if they do, they may still lack the persistence and resilience that is necessary in most processes and which come with SE. Aspirations take only a wish for more or better which is easy to install by basically marketing and advertising something, building SE indispensably requires sufficient self-respect to even be able to anchor SE.

Even believing to have the internal locus of control and aspirations is not sufficient for actual goal setting (or achieving them). Having aspirations and locus of control but lacking self-efficacy for the necessary process can foster a problematic, frustration or aggression producing sense of entitlement without achieving competence. This unfortunate effect can presently be observed in the Maghreb (Müller, Sievert, & Klingholz, 2016) as a result of maladapted education programs that were able to produce large numbers of university graduates without being able to offer

---

video observation: Bernard, Dercon, Orkin, & Taffesse (2014); on raising investment behaviour and aspirations through social interaction, encouragment and supportive leaders: Macours & Vakis (2009).

appropriate jobs. While many students underwent their education in the strict belief to be rewarded with good government jobs afterwards, many developed high aspirations. But their education according to the French system of hautes écoles (Hessel, 2011, p.205ff, 235ff) ignored the necessities of catch-up economies: people with entrepreneurial SE to create opportunities for themselves and others.[34]

Hope (f.ex. Lybbert & Wydick, 2016), sometimes combined with aspirations, is another attempt to capture human drive, but like aspirations it is an unspecific notion, easy to evoke and easy to destroy, susceptible to manipulation and without clear reference to a person´s own action; hope does not lead to a long-lasting robust state on which to found policies.

Theodore W. Schultz (1972, 1993) used the term allocative ability to describe the underlying necessity to allocate whatever someone owns and can do in an optimal way to achieve his personal optimal result – here,

---

[34] This problem exists in many developing countries adding to migration pressures as well as possibly to a reservoir of potential militants amongst entitled feeling, but not very self-efficacious (male) youths in countries with archaic male role models, and possibly amongst second and third generation immigrants who have not been able to build a new identity which they themselves and others respect. The usually employed religious and anti-Western rhetoric appears like a justifying construct when delinquents are found to be unsuccessful drug-dealers, petty criminals, and otherwise failed but aspiring young men. A Western variation of this lack of SE combined with maladapted self-images may manifest itself in the orbit of Brexit, Trump, and right leaning populist movements where those, often white men, with disappointed aspirations or as such perceived, frail status make their fears and anger noticed with a justifying, but constructed anti-immigrants rhetoric. Asymetries between SE and aspirations, or self-construct in concert with the experience of (so felt) humiliation as a result of this asymmetry is in my opinion the actual cause of several of these phenomena. I do not follow the argument of modernization losers; most inflicting men did not emerge from marginalized backgrounds, the respective organizations were founded and led by studied men who could have led a company or hospital instead, but apparently suffered from more desires than having belief in abilities. Cmp. findings in: Tetzlaff (2016), and cited newspaper articles in fn. 100; also cmp. fn 61 here: discussion on low SE in poor white men in America and class conflict as race conflict.

with regard to his harvest. Allocative ability is a summary of a several abilities that enable a person to make the proper decision, which Schultz showed to increase with education. It does contain the aspect of SE as the necessary empowering factor: one has to belief in one´s ability to act before making the decision to act. Self-efficacy empowers to exercise agency and develop allocative ability.

In an important attempt to formulate a general theory of psychological influences on economic behaviour and decision making, Akerloff & Kranton (2010) developed a concept of "Identity Economics" which aims to include all major insights of behavioural economics, building on a general definition of identity, and expanding it by a number of different concepts like biases, reputation, self-efficacy, different identities in different reference groups, clichée, and several others. Probably due to its generality, it has not received general acceptance (yet?); scientists are still searching for the connecting factor that could be self-efficacy in the end.

" An unfortunate tendency of some politicians and economists is to use the terms "underdeveloped" and "developing" inter-changeably, with the latter regarded as a more acceptable euphemism for poor. *Clearly*, level *of income and* rate of change *are different things."*

Lipsey, Sparks & Steiner (1976)

3. How Self-Efficacy Fits into the Theoretical Framework

A wide array of theories aspires to capture the causes of today's differences in economic, social and political development to gain insights on how to overcome them. Below, I trace major theoretical strings to embed the concept of self-efficacy in our present explanatory approaches.

3.1 Modernization and Development[35]

Both terms describe a process of change over a period of time, from a state of lesser to one of higher complexity and order. There are no equilibria to be reached, and therefore no end to the necessity of the process. In analogy to the process of democracy, which continuously needs to reproduce the conditions that bring it about, modernization and development are civilizing processes that need to produce material and human growth in a continuous process of self-limitation and self-empowerment that brings these advances about.

According to the Encyclopedia Britannica "***Modernization,*** *in sociology, (describes) the transformation from a traditional, rural, agrarian society to a secular, urban, industrial society. Modern society is industrial socie-*

[35] in the following chapter I have neither directly used nor cited Allen Schnaidberg (1970), but found his work inspiring for asking questions about the concept of modernization.

ty. To modernize a society is, first of all, to industrialize it. Historically, the rise of modern society has been inextricably linked with the emergence of industrial society. All the features that are associated with modernity can be shown to be related to the set of changes that, no more than two centuries ago, brought into being the industrial type of society." (Kumar 2014)

The welfare and development economist Hla Myint (2014) answers with his definition of economic development as being "*the process whereby simple, low-income national economies are transformed into modern industrial economies. Although the term is sometimes used as a synonym for economic growth, generally it is employed to describe a change in a country's economy involving qualitative as well as quantitative improvements. The theory of economic development - how primitive and poor economies can evolve into sophisticated and relatively prosperous ones - is of critical importance to underdeveloped countries, and it is usually in this context that the issues of economic development are discussed.*"

Both definitions describe the same kind of process equally ideologically burdened and limited in its suitability for describing the ongoing challenge for every economy and polity to provide for stability while continously adapting to and producing technological novelty, demographic changes, and the necessary institutional update. This never equilibrium-reaching[36] process does not stop with industrialization or any other stage as far as we can know now.

The German historian Hans-Ulrich Wehler (1975) broadened the term by developing an analytical system of levels for

- economic growth,
- developing differentiation of life spheres in public, private and work (specialization) life,
- developing of universal rather than group-exclusive values (!; b.d.)

[36] "...in fact, if the system ever does reach equilibrium, it isn´t just stable. It´s dead." John Holland at a Santa-Fé-Institute meeting, cited from: Beinhocker (2007), p.70.

- spatial and social mobility
- growing participation in the political process
- institutionalizing of conflict and committing the monopoly of force.

The sociologist Ulrich Beck (1996) expanded the concept even further into what he called "reflexive modernizing" or "second modernity" to include post-modern developments in industrialzed countries, acknowledging that the need for modernization never ends, but also, that pre-modern and anti-modern phenomena continue to exist and exert pressure. Beck hereby rejects the notion of Wehler and most other authors that modernization was irreversible - which many examples in history have shown[37]. Based on Wehler and Beck, my concept of modernization most resonates with the approach of Hans van der Loo and Willem van Reijen (1997). They identify modernization as a comprehensive process including social change, and differentiate four stages and spheres of change that are entangled and affect each other in feedback loops so that each one causes status and change in the other, thereby creating paradox effects that need to be addressed by politics and the social community. According to Loo & Reijen:

- Modernizing is a result and cause of specialization, and exploitation of natural resources, and offers as much opportunity for individual liberation and development as it demands civil self-limiting in cooperation and natural resources management.
- As complexity of communication and interaction grows ever more complex, "markets" develop for self-regulating, which demand ever greater specialization and ever greater, potentially worldwide exchange.

---

[37] While the loss of structure, cultural achievements and wealth after the end of colonialism may be ascribed to the rejection of anything connected with the hated colonial rulers, the collapse of former high civilizations like the Mayan demonstrate how within one generation crafts were lost to other still disputed reasons like ecology and/or population pressure combined with sunk-cost effects f.ex.; similarly, at the end of the Roman empire, in one generation the ability to read Greek was lost. The detrimental effects of possible crowding-out of self-efficacies in this context will be discussed later.

- Increasing individualisation comes with emancipation of old constraints. But these are replaced by more anonymous bueraucratic ones which, as much as the nation state has to yield to supranational organizations, come with growing alienation and lack of identification.
- The latter increases the loss of culture in favour of ratio; rational, normative analysis replaces tradition and authority; the rule of science ends the rule of religion, ending the dominance of the collective in favour of individual freedom, social and geographical mobility, and ever rising insecurity and risk.

Van der Loo & Reijen spell out what modernization processes do to individuals and societies, and what I consider the dilemma of modernization: While in a natural environment the conditions of existence of anything are limited and defined by circumstance and everything else that exists, civilization lifts man out of many of these external limitations and thrusts upon him the levies of self-limitation. Modernization as the updating of the civilizing process reduces collective, social limitations while simultaneously increasing the normative demand for self-limitation under growing individuation, economic pressures and lures, and ideologies. Where this is not answered by compliance, bureaucratic rules step in, without the emotional and social bonds to back them as in traditional settings. It leaves behind an individual with the need to limit herself according to self-set norms and a self-constructed identity in transition. This is a burden and great cause of insecurity leaving anybody in the need to develop individual survival strategies between total merging and rebellion. Self-efficacies determine a great part of the pathways chosen.

The term "modern", from the Latin modernus or modo, means "just now", "contemporary", "related to the present or immediate past" (Webster´s, 1965) cannot describe be a permanent stage. Modernization therefore is a necessity that puts less and more developed countries into the same boat, which could offer new possibilities of cooperation or another uneven race with one decisive difference (that will be discussed in the chpt. on learning): knowledge is the one "commodity" with increasing utility[38]. The more you have the easier it is to acquire more. One part of the explanation is growing SE that helps not only developing countries to dare modernization, but also industrial countries to not lose larger parts of their population to unemployment and social disintegration on their way to ever more complex systems, and the elites of developed and less developed countries to fighting progress and corrupting institutions.

The terms "modernization", "development" or "underdeveloped" imply an evaluation about the economic, social and political asymmetry amongst the countries of the world. Those that are more modern are presently more developed, richer, exercising a greater degree of individual freedom, opportunities and guaranteed legal rights, societal participation, and gender equality; those that are "underdeveloped" are thought to have a potential for similar development. This evaluation thus sets a kind of standard of modernity and determines in which direction and towards which normative values the process of modernization should lead. We have not seen any other way of modernization than the one the presently developed countries have chosen, though Bhutan is trying, and New Zealand has currently announced to attempt a variation of it. We do not know if underlying this process, there is some kind of predetermined chronological order or universally applicable natural regularities, like necessary steps or stages of f.ex. a collective to develop from granting loyalty and human rights only to members of their direct group (family, clan, tribe) to the final stage of including all of mankind as their equals. We do know though that these steps and stages can come to a halt and be reversed: normative progress is not an automatism. While a state of developed and modern is a transitory one that requires continuous updateding for not falling back into anachronisms, the question remains if there are fundamentally different ways and goals of modernization than teh present Western model.

---

[38] according to Brian Arthur, this and the critique of Krugman, and the defense from Kenneth Arrow, in: Beinhocker (2007), p.57 and 464.

Both terms, “modernization” and “development”, are easily ideologically coopted. Huntington´s “Political Order in Changing Societies” (1968)[39] is an example of connecting the complex processes of modernization with political agenda leading to a problematic further use of the term. He identifies modernizing economic measures to neccessarily cause political and social instability, and calls for authoritarian control to prevent social unrest; U.S. policy should discourage modernization attempts in poor countries for this destabilizing reason. Alesina & Perotti (1996), however, show in their analysis of 71 countries in the period between 1965-1985 very clearly, that the instability Huntington ascribes to modernization is rather caused by the evoked inequality, which not only hampers further modernizing investments but also calls for measures that cushion or limit the developing inequality, instead. One could add it also produces a decrease in coping SE if conditions change quicker than adaptation SE can be build up.

Here, I use the both terms without reference to any theory or ideology, and refer solely to the process of adapting to changing and new information from within or outside an economic, social and political entity, basically without regard of its status of development. Rather, modernization is understood as necessary and ongoing for any developed or less developed social unit, which by reassessment of old, or learning of new data adapts her existing knowledge, regularly leading to higher order (e.g. via differentiation) and complexity. These processes are naturally more obvious and therefore easier to detect in less developed countries, which thereby offer themselves for research.

A number of scientists found a multitude of symptoms, causes, influential factors, phenomena, impeding development and causing *“underdevelopment as a sum of problematic development areas”* (Nohlen & Nuscheler, 1982, p.30, transl. bd). They identify seven basic *“problem areas”* (“Problemfelder” as they call them) that are as much symptoms as causes

[39] cmp. discussion on Huntington´s “Clash of Civilizations” below.

of reproducing slagging development, and so intertwined that the following seven areas are not fully independent categories:

- Population Pressure; while Nohlen/Nuscheler here address the problem of population increases with the following pressure on all social institutions like medical care and education as well feeding the growing numbers, and employing them, the problems of a quickly growing population also touches upon the problems of ethnic and religious diversity that was so unintelligibly created by colonial bureaucracy.
- Food Shortage; this problem has been somewhat relieved between 1982 and today – 2016 - through the millennium project, though one billion people must still be regarded as poor enough to not live in a secured food situation. The question of healthy, clean food and water and a balanced diet in sufficient reliability is still unreached for many more people.
- Paid Work; sufficient fairly paid employment has been identified as a major driver for development while the lack thereof causes all of the above problems on top of the immediate social and human ones ranging from crime to depression and substance abuse to black markets that divert economic activity from the stately sphere and thereby getting lost for a nation´s growth and development. (Even though there might be some impulses from heavy black market activity if human, monetary or technological gain get rechanneled into the official market, but it has to be regarded as highly inefficient as most of it will get lost and resources tied up in this inefficiency).
- Health Problems; between 1982 and 2016, great progress ahs been made through vaccination and malaria prevention programs, but poverty must still be regarded as one of the greatest health hazards which is therefore inseparably tied to all of the above and the basic condition of underdevelopment. Clearly, unhealthy, mal- or undernourished, badly paid workers in bad working conditions will only achieve a proportion of their working potential which on top of its immorality is an immediate loss for the national economy and its development potential.
- Education: Nohlen & Nuscheler point out education and health as key indicators of underdevelopment. Moreover, both are key causes of it.

- Natural Environment; again, symptom and long term cause of underdevelopment, the exploitation of natural resources and destroying of parts of the natural environment while poisoning others, is causing social, political and economic results of incalculable dimension. Their outcome lies in an unknown future while any reconstruction or repair of natural damage may prove impossible or demand time stretches beyond human planning horizons.

Nohlen & Nuscheler´s "problem areas" allow for identification of the complexities of underdevelopment. They can cause a constant reproduction of slow development that was later to be described as causing a poverty trap (Sachs, 2006; Collier, 2007), a vicious cycle where tackling one of above problems could unintentionally cause several others to deteriorate even further. But they do not shed light on the question what had caused these problems to begin with. Their validity for policies aimed at interrupting the recurrent reproduction of poverty, nevertheless, remains acute.

Materialistic schools of thought on the origins of slagging development can be grouped in two rough categories: those who would locate these originating causes exogenously, while others identify endogenous ones. Nohlen & Nuscheler disregard the categorization of exogenous and endogenous causes of underdevelopment as they claim this differentiation to be "*analytically fruitless*" (1982, pp. 25-47), and rightly so cite the example of exogenous influences having actually affected the social and economic structures of developing countries, and thereby having been *"internalized"*. I agree with their view, but to trace the path leading to the discovery of psychological aspects in development theory, I find it helpful to apply this differentiation. I am looking less at the results of dysfunction but at its root causes, and therefore stick to the differentiation of exogenous/endogenous factors, but extended by the aspects of materialistic and psychological ones. The difficulties here lie in institutional factors, which are as much materialistic as psychological in their materialized manifestation of culture. I attempt to solve this conflict by splitting up culture (psychological reaction to materialistic causes, becoming psychological cause) and institutions (materialistic result and cause), analogue to colonial economy (being the exogenous cause) and national elite (endogenous result).

3. 2 Materialistic Approaches

Major development researchers searched for material causes of lesser development that could be targeted with specific economic measures and an active development policy. Over time and with the recession of white supremacy ideologies, a great number of factors and circumstance where identified that clearly contribute to poverty, lack of development, and lack of potential and hinder modernization of economy and society, some of which were exogenous, some endogenous, and some a mixture of both developed over time. The origin of the multitude of negative factors, the exact causalities and how they could be tackled, was therefore not quite clear in many cases, and object of ideological and scientific dispute. Especially, why and how European countries as the global measure for successful development had overcome their own historic underdevelopment while other regions of the world had not, could not be agreed upon, thus, lessons not be fully drawn from Europe´s rise.

While colonialism had clearly left a scar field of artificial nations with ahistorical boundaries, multi-ethnic, multi-language and multi-religions populations, and inappropriate economic structures that should prove a detrimental legacy reproducing underdevelopment potentially infinitely, it had not caused the lack of development that they had met when the Europeans first arrived on foreign shores. The damage left behind by the colonial rulers not only in the political and economic structures, but also in the social settings of collaboration between the new national and old foreign elites were prone to hamper successful catch-up development and a group of scientists, partially from the countries in question, concentrated on identifying these aspects of distortion to demand their abolition for an independent economic and political development.

The materialistic exogenous view locates several detrimental factors: dependency on the former colonialists; a world market dominated by their needs and wishes as reflected in unfavorable terms of trade; keeping of colonial economic structures like monocultural agriculture, sometimes on the basis of imported and non-food crops; and focussing on natural resources to serve the needs of the former colonial powers instead of developing a modern processing industry. These explanatory approaches revolving around imperialism, dependencia, periphery, and asymmetric international division of labor/terms of trade (Prebisch, 1976; Amin, 1974; Senghaas, 1974, 1979; Elsenhans, 1992; Wallerstein, 1974) identify todays poverty and slagging development as caused by colonial distortions in economic, social and political structures that are being ever reproduced by the problems they cause; corrupted political elites periodically employed and employing in ideological proxy wars who continue in their old spirit to prevent political and social change that could break the vicious circle; the industrialized Western former colonialists having built a world-wide economic and financial system based on the inner logic of imperial colonial ideology, thereby updating the exploitation of the so called Third World basically forever. Consequently, disassociation and more independence from the world market mechanisms were prominently suggested solutions (f.ex. by Wallerstein, 1974)[40], inter alia, to gain greater bargaining for the following demands for a New Economic World Order (Tetzlaff, 1975; Amin, 1979). While over the course of some 45 years, considerable international political changes have helped to levitate some countries out of the worst poverty and some into the ranks of semi- or less industrialized countries, globalization of the past two decades has possibly widened the extent of exploitation from natural resources to large fractions of populations employed in semi-industrialized marginal jobs. Progress in the international political sphere is counter-acted by growing Western corporate and nationalistic interests (f.ex. land grabbing).

---

[40] For discussion of the proposed causal relationships see f.ex. Sautter (1985); Tetzlaff (1975, 1982).

Exogenous explanations leave the question for the asymmetric state of development at the time of European arrival on foreign shores unanswered: Colonial seizure was possible because the to-be-colonies were in a state of pre-modernism when the Europeans arrived. Question is, if this was due only to an asymmetry caused by chance, suggesting, the Europeans had simply arrived too early, before a modernizing development had reached similar states, or if endogenous factors had been preventing timelier development.

From Malthus (1798) to Dennis Meadows (1972), population pressure has been identified as one of the greatest threads to development: ever growing populations consuming whatever excess gain was being achieved, exhausting the state´s leeway for any type of modernizing investment like the introduction of new technologies, infrastructure or mass education. This could lead to pauperization of large parts of the population, dependency on Western aid and political instability. While indeed a great present strain on development, political stability and economic growth, population growth cannot be a counted as a root cause of early underdevelopment. It is now, but was not until Western intervention created it in modern dimensions without equally raising food production and other economic prerequisites like education and jobs that helped to create Europe´s rise in a natural and chronological order. Since the early times of Mesopotamian civilization, urbanization and population growth were a result of rising productivity and excess food production (Harari 2014; Diamond 2005), not the other way round. High population growth rates without respective food production are symptom and result of underdevelopment rather than its cause (Demele et al. 1989)[41].

The aforementioned – externally caused - distortions of colonization (for Nunn: slave trade, see below) led to endogenous distortions in the social, political and economic structures of the former colonies that were regarded as reproducing themselves and their detrimental effects in "*vicious*

---

[41] Specifically on birthrates, female education and female opportunity costs in developing countries: Akman (2002); Lim (2002).

circles of poverty" (Nohlen & Nuscheler, 1985, p. 35) Low incomes would lead to low savings rates which would necessarily lead to a low investment rate keeping productivity and incomes low. Hernando de Soto Polar (2000) identified indeed a lack of capital as one of the major inhibitors of development, but differing from German authors like Hesse & Sautter (1977) ascribed it not to an absolute lack of capital due to f.ex. export structure and terms of trade, but to a lack of institutional structure like property rights that would allow for sufficient endogenous capital accumulation and exogenous capital attraction.

Demographic structures (not absolute population growth) as root cause for poverty and underdevelopment were identified by several scientists pointing at what Boeke (1953) in researching the Netherlands East Indies as early as 1953 called "dual society": societies being divided into a modern and an traditional part, with two parallel existing social systems, value sets, behaviours and habits, even ways of production and social organization; one, Westernized in self-image, consumption and aspirations to the point of what Nohlen/Nuscheler (1985, p.38) call "partly capitalistic", while the other remains traditional, poor, unaspiring and, most importantly, non-entrepreneurial. This idea of a divided, disintegrated society, which also reflects patterns of exploitation and a political power divide, was, though criticized, partially adapted and enlarged developed into a theory of structural heterogeneity. The latter is regarded as a stable form of capitalism in underdeveloped countries, sometimes called peripheral capitalism leading to marginalization of the traditional segment without developing any modernizing dynamics (Tetzlaff, 1975).

Other scientists tackled the question why some countries are poorer and less developed by trying to identify why Europe was richer and thereby, track down possible causes to be found within the respective countries. Which factors helped the inhabitants of the European continent with its unfavorable climate in the North and infectious diseases in the South to leap from moor wading hunter-gatherers and mosquito plagued swamp inhabitants to colonizing the whole rest of the world? Many first turned to questions of geography before looking at human factors, tainted at times by an ideological lens.

Climate and ecology were long treated under limiting premises. Researchers identified flaws in proper adaptation of western technology or methods to developing countries′ ecology as causing further deterioration of soil quality and groundwater levels, but failed to research the interaction between environment and human behaviour, and its translation into culture and institutions. Even worse, under the heading of social anthropology climate theories, inherently racist explanations on temperature and work ethics (Alatas, 1977) were developed, justifying and establishing the image of lazy, apathetic, hedonistic, undisciplined southern people (Nohlen & Nuscheler, 1985, p.33ff), the laborious Asian, the Weberian protestant. Not until Diamond (1997) researched the differences between Europe and others, starting at the beginning of divergence about 13 thousand years ago when a rather similar state of development could be assumed worldwide, climate and ecology were given the focus of ground-laying importance. Diamond identified natural environment: i.e. climate, geography, flora, fauna, as causal factors for small differences at the starts to initiate a process of self-enforcing feedback loops that created results by taking Europe from stone-age to artificial intelligence (Beinhocker, 2007; Epstein et al.,1996; Arthur et al., 1987)[42].

Diamond differentiates between initial *"ultimate"* causes that define varying starting conditions, and proximate causes that produce immediate differences in action outcome. He identifies the naturally given possibility to produce excess food as the one ground laying factor on which all others are founded: the presence of domesticable plants and animals, and the absence of insurmountable transportation obstacles that could hinder exchange of produce, knowledge and natural resources. This special po-

[42] Beinhocker (2007), pp. 79-97. Beinhocker describes a computer simulation where small starting differences in resource endowment will, under every possible test set-up, lead to unpreventable divisions of poor getting poorer and rich getting richer. The experiments were done by Epstein & Axtell (1996). They confirmed earlier findings of Brian Arthur at the Santa Fe Institute from 1987.

tential for high yield agriculture in Eurasia offered the chance for sedentary life, leading to ever denser population and hence complex administrative and governing structures which relied on the development of a scripture which was the then used to store and communicate ever growing knowledge over geographical distance and time, both of which were the prerequisites of technological progress. All of this led to Diamond´s proximate causes: many people living closely with their domesticated animals catching their "germs" – zooanthroponoses – made Europeans pretty much immune to what should later kill many of their colonial encounters (germs/disease); excess food production enabled urban societies with central governments, armies, specialization, all of which let to complex social structures with respective culture and institutions; technological progress, central organization, and exchange with others in knowledge and resources led to trade, scripture and new products (steel); and the will to expand (guns). While natural endowment caused excess food production, Diamond identifies the four proposed proximats: writing, disease, technology and complex social organization, as the causing forces behind the allocation of the thereby created wealth and power (Venkatachalam 2001), and thereby laid the groundwork for the discovery of the connection between environment and culture.

A wide-ranging theory in this context was developed by Welzel & Inglehart (2013) who identify the necessity of a certain climate and availability of natural transport systems in their Cold Water Theory as prerequisite of modern development, making a difference between development until and after the Middle Ages. They also argue for human empowerment as a multi-factor syndrome of development that will be discussed in the next chapter, but their material endogenous fundamental cause of development is *"`cool water`(CW) environments. These environments combine (1) fairly low average annual temperatures with (2) continuous rainfall over all seasons and (3) the presence of permanently navigable waterways."* (p.8) They argue that the lagging of Northern Europe and Japan behind eastern countries until the Middle Ages was owed to basically exact these features as they prevented early spreading of an excess-producing agriculture and its resulting in specializing/urbanization with all the positive results discussed above: *"Importantly, the Eurasian fringe location placed Northwestern Europa and Japan at a large distance from the early centres of agriculture stretching from the Mediterranean to China. The diffusion of advanced agriculture and urban civilization reached Northwestern Europe and Japan late for this reason.*[6] *Indeed, the data of Putterman (2008) show that the flank civilizations adopted agriculture millennia after the older civilizations of the Middle East, India, China and the Mediterranean. Likewise, Maddison's (2007: 40) estimates suggest that levels of urbanization known from the older civilizations since long haven't been reached in Northwestern Europe before the 15th century BC and in Japan before 17th century BC. The overseas CW-areas were even more isolated: no advanced agrarian societies were in the vicinity of the Northern coastal areas of today's US, the southern coastal areas of today's Canada, the Southern tips of South America and Africa or the Southeast of Australia/Tasmania and New Zealand. Accordingly, advanced agriculture did not emerge in the overseas CW-areas until settlers from the European CW-areas imported it.* " (p.9) (fn 6: "*The flank position of these two civilizations saved them from foreign imposition of despotism by Eurasia's recurrent land empires. Thus, the potential that resides in the CW-condition could unfold undisturbedly from foreign despotic absorption in Northwestern Europe and Japan. This was the exact opposite for the more inwardly located CW-areas in Eurasia, like Russia's Northwest or China's Northeast: they fell victim to despotic absorption.* ") (p.9) The rise of northwestern Europe and Japan since the Middle Ages is consequently attributed to the material endogenous causes of a natural environment unsuited to central and large-scale exploitation, but produced material and psychological human capital effects that Welzel/Inglehart call "*plural autonomies*". This "*existential* (environmentally driven, bd) *autonomy orients groups towards the asser-*

tion and defence of derivative autonomies, including control over their produce (Braudel 1987, 315ff). "[43]

- "*...widespread autonomy orientations provide a continuous source of resistance against unchecked rule and, hence, feed a pluralistic power structure. With such a structure in place, competing local, regional and national rulers must grant concessions in return for the tributes they wish to take*".

-"*...a multitude of local, sectorial and corporate autonomies and a concomitant pluralistic power structure in pre-industrial Northwestern Europe and Japan with an apparent lack thereof in all of Eurasia's and Mesoamerica's pre-industrial civilizations (McNeill 1968; Jones 9185; Braudel 1987; Powelson 1997; Landes 1998)* (p.10)

The result was the demographic root for technology and innovation: reproductive autonomies over fertility decisions (p.10) in a healthier environment leading to less child mortality, allowing for lower birthrates, and an "emerging markets" logic: investing in skills and ideas in children and oneself instead of into maximizing the number of offspring. Some aspects of the above theories were recently found by Burke, Hsiang, & Miguel (2015) in a meta-analysis of economic data from 166 countries between 1960-2010. They found strong indicators for a worldwide causal interconnectedness of climate and economy: "*We show that overall economic productivity is non-linear in temperature for all countries, with productivity peaking at an annual average temperature of 13C and declining strongly at higher temperatures. The relationship is globally generalizable, stable since 1960, and apparent for agricultural and non-agricultural activity in both rich and poor countries. These results provide the first evidence that economic activity in all regions is coupled to the global climate...*" (p.1) Burke et al. do not identify the mechanism that ties temperature to productivity, and offer no explanation for outliers like Singapore. They extrapolate with regard to global warming: *"If future*

[43] the study by Braudel referenced here is probably (missing in original): Braudel et al. (1987), Die Welt des Mittelmeeres: zur Geschichte und Geographie kultureller Lebensformen, Frankfurt a. M.

adaptation mimics past adaptation, unmitigated warming is expected to reshape the global economy by reducing average global incomes roughly 23% by 2100 and widening global income inequality, relative to scenarios without climate change". (p.1)

The data and effect that Burke, Hsiang, & Miguel identify, may show an effect that seems to be of temperature influencing economic activity, but may rather be environments providing different environmental stimuli in the form of demands, rewards and detrimental effects for human intervention in their habitat. High temperatures are one symptom of a certain tropical biotope of soils, precipitation, animals, bugs, diseases, cultivatable crops, threads like harvest destroying floods, droughts, heavy storms etc., which influence possibilities and rewards of interaction between humans and their habitat. I argue that the effect Burke et al. found could well be that climate zones with differently responsive natural environments produce different psychological conditions fostering different cultures with regard to levels, domains and grades of generality of SE, and that is what influences economic performance.

> *"The foundation of political economy and, in general of every social science, is evidently psychology. A day may come when we shall be able to deduce the laws of social science from the principles of psychology." Vilfredo Pareto(1906)*

3. 3 The Human Factor

Several approaches have focused on human behaviour in relation to economic performance and political organization. The concept of self-efficacy is an especially promising instrument to do this. Nobody has yet produced unambiguous evidence that and how culture and institutions are decisive for economic success yet. One of the main reasons for this is that the operative means that influence either or both had not been identified. There is a widespread understanding that economic models of the past have been too remote from human existence to still be viable; as Hoff & Stieglitz (2016) write: "*Just as economists have had to come to terms with the fact that individuals act in ways that are markedly different from those predicted by the rational actor model, economists will have to come to terms with the fact that preferences and cognition are shaped by those surrounding us, and that these social interactions may be as important determinants of economic outcomes as the variables upon which economists have traditionally focused. The social influences on the nature of the individual are no longer beyond the boundaries of economics. Instead, social determinants of preferences and cognition are increasingly demonstrated in empirical work on individual choice and societal change. The broader perspective expands the explanatory power of economics and the accuracy of economic predictions. Most importantly, this perspective identifies sources of societal rigidity that the standard model takes no account of, and identifies new instruments that can influence behaviour and long-run social change.*"[44] (p.27)

The most widespread consensus on the matter seems to be Weber´s identification of the religious belief of Protestantism that as a cultural factor would shape people perfect for capitalistic production: hard working, determined, frugal, resilient to hard ship, disciplined. This notion is questioned by Cantoni (2014). He used population figures of 272 cities from between 1300 and 1900, and found no effects of Protestantism on economic growth, though Weber and his basic concept is referred to in almost every study on culture and development, and gets employed in related fields like Huntington & Harrison show. Chakraborty et al. (2015)[45] argue that the answer may lie in the distinction that the citation of Lipsey, Spark, & Steiner (1976) refers to in the beginning of this chap-

---

[44] p.27; unfortunately, Hoff & Stieglitz confound self-efficacy for self-confidence in their Appendix C, p.53f., and treat it accordingly.

[45] One could argue that in their Bayesian learning function (p.3) their prior could be replaced by SE as their posterior contains the interpretation of passing on expertise, which could instead be interpreted as the likely passing on of SE for entrepreneurial expertise or a combination of both as has been found empirically.

ter: *"Clearly,* level *of income and* rate of change *are different things."* Chakraporty et al. model a capitalist culture with entrepreneurs and wage-workers, and find that under certain circumstances – here: external technological shock that boosts productivity – income levels may still depend on cultural bias while growth rates may be independent. The reasoning lies in the cultural transmission of adult preferences to their offspring that would be overcome by a large enough prospective income change from productivity gains.

More distinct answers on a causal correlation between culture, institutions and economy depend on identifiying operational mechanisms as Gennaioli & Richter (2007) did with regard to precolonial institutions and accountability (see below). It would also be helpful in this context to clarify the principal potential of genetic predetermination, epigenetics and culture. I will come back to this in my discussion on SE and genetics, but want to stress here: at the present state of biological research, human traits and behaviour based on these traits must be regarded as not genetically determined; there may be a genetic potential, comparable – if at all - to human potential to learn a language. The new born child has the potential to learn to make any sound and sound combination physically possible, but acquiring the sounds of his mother tongue step by step "switches off" the other possible sounds, which is a major reason for accents in foreign languages learned after the age of ten. Humans have the potential of developing and learning any mix of culture, with f.ex. more or less cooperation, with being very cooperative within a group and very aggressive and uncooperative to outsiders etc.[46] The actual shape of human behaviour seems to depend on the limiting factors of circumstance: whatever seems best – or profitable in a general terms – in the relevant natural and social environment will be done as soon as it has been learned and understood, or copied, what works best. Whatever cir-

---

[46] Cmp. f.ex. the often wrongly as matriarchaic culture misinterpreted culture of the great Mohawk Nations, who were impressively peaceful and cooperative within their community of six first-nation peoples, and most feared in fighting others.

cumstance lasts long enough will find its way into the lasting knowledge and behaviour repertoire of people in that surrounding, and thus form culture. This correlation exists for environment and culture, and institutions as formalized culture respectively.

Avner Greif (1994)[47] suggests the *"organization of a society - its economic, legal, political, social, and moral enforcement institutions, together with its social constructs and information transmission and coordination mechanisms –* " as determining economic performance and growth, this organization (institutions) as a reflection of its culture, and culture in turn composed of cultural beliefs. Greif goes on to research the different development pathways of an individualistic versus a collectivist group of people and the respective economic impact by the example of medieval Genovese and Maghrebini merchants. He shows how both groups solved the problem of trust in trade in different stages of economic development until one of them – the collectivist – failed to develop modern institutional solutions to expand their tiers. Unfortunately for my work, Greif starts his analysis only after the groundwork for the two different strands had already developed, leaving us without information why they developed so differently in the first place.

When researching the causes for the rise of Europe against the until recently relative lagging of other areas of the world, culture and institutions come to mind as manifestation of feelings and mental models and logical continuation of Weber´s concept of the protestant worker who presumably developed a specific work ethic which seemed especially apt for capitalist production. McCloskey (2015) titles: *"It was ideas and ideologies, not institutions, which changed in North Western Europe, 1600-1848.*" What changed according to McCloskey was the respect for individual life. This does make a lot of sense with regard to the central role of the entrepreneurial individual in the economy, her striving for happiness and fulfillment, her search for novelty, fantasy, ingenuity that creates a

[47] p. 913 and 915.

culture of diversity[48], and institutions that support and secure it. Without individual freedom and support to flourish, fail and retry, there is no possibility for entrepreneurial personality to develop.

On the same note writes Mokyr (2007, 2008)[49] on the European Enlightenment, and draws a straight line to today´s economic success. Mokyr identifies two mechanisms that link the change in thinking and attitude to economic activity: the attitude toward technology which opened the door to unknown potential of new products and production methods, which in turn started a whole new cycle of social, economic and political changes; and secondly, subsequent institutional changes that followed the change in attitude towards humans beings and morality of exploitive practices. Scientific research of the role of culture and institutions poses severe problems of definition and isolation. Alesina & Guiliano (2013) have elaborated on this in great detail.

It is important to note that culture is highly persistent as it becomes part of a person´s identity and forms the core of a group´s identity. Culture has nothing to do with folklore and is not necessarily openly observable, rather, it is the social essence of experiences that reflect the history of a specific group of people in a specific set of circumstance, which are determined by, but not limited to, their environment. Culture codes the fundamental knowledge how to survive and strive in that place and that group. It is always well adapted, because if it wasn´t that group would not survive in their place, regardless of how special it might look from the outside or when somebody leaves that habitat. Culture as a set of norms, habits, and traditions including religion and language[50] is cast into institu-

---

[48] Beinhocker (2007) links economic evolution to quantity and diversity of possibilities, pp. 187-198.

[49] Mokyr´s earlier works, f.ex.The Gifts of Athena (2002) on why the enlightenment happened at first in Europe, trace a long "enlightening" path. He does not operationalize individual factors, but spells them out most comprehensibly.

[50] Highly interesting research finds how language determines the way humans think, i.e. different languages promote different methods and ways of thinking. Cmp. f.ex. Athanasopoulos (2015); Gross (2013).

tions when it gets formalized and usually[51] depersonalized. Even though it is not clear yet how different languages and religious beliefs emerge, it is clear that they form feedback loops with the societies that brought them about: Punishing Gods for example fulfil great many limiting and socially unifying functions as much as different languages shape different social outlooks and abilities in their users. These range from more process to more result oriented ways of thinking, to concepts of time, gender, and blame, abilities of geographic orientation or simply exactness in thinking and expression, or the popular example of Indian numeration fostering calculation abilities. Clearly, religion and language as cultural expressions reflect the natural environment they developed in. A surrounding f.ex., that does not require or allow for storage of food and therefore does not promote planning will foster languages with less expressions for time, time discounting, grammatical tenses that make the language and thinking more complex.

Institutions are shaped from a group´s culture, which is shaped by that group´s history in a certain environment, which than react back on the members of that group. Culture and institutions form the social context of individuals – and the groups they build, while circumstance and environment build the natural context. From both, social and natural context does the individual draw her information for building her self- and world constructs that define her active role in the world, her goal setting, her risk taking, her novelty seeking. While culture is found to be highly persistent in groups, it is more malleable in individuals; Voigtlaender & Voth (2012) f.ex. found attitudes in certain regions to be persistent over hundreds of years, so did Alesina & Guiliano (2013); Nunn (2012) found attitudes, beliefs and institutions all to be persistent; Nunn also argues that culture is what brings institutions about and that it is this interaction that keeps both persistent; Tabellini (2010) found the same persistence in the correlation between institutions from the Middle Ages still influencing attitudes today. All of them identify historic influences of culture and

[51] "usually", because there are complex exceptions in mixed forms as in a dictator or absolute monarch.

institutions on today′s economic performance. Wuepper & Sauer (2016) empirically tested the causal correlation between historical experiences and present day attitude, and found this to be a determinant for economic performance. Michalopoulos, Putterman, & Weil (2016) researched the influence of ancestral ways of life on present economic status. They compared descendants of pastoralist versus agriculturalists and found higher educational status and wealth in the former group, possibly caused by different attitudes and beliefs but not only in their own group, but also via being differently treated by others with regard to i.a. participation in political power (see chp. 5.3).

Theodore Schultz`s (1975, 1980) detection of "allocative ability" identifies an outcome of cultural attitudes and beliefs that influence time discounting, risk taking, and value individual learning and education. He writes: *"... the behaviour of human beings is governed by the criterion of optimization under the constraints confronting each person."* In his Nobel Lecture on The Economics of Being Poor, Schultz identifies a culture of poor people that is very rationally adapted to exactly their survival needs though these are different from those of people who are not poor, which motivates his call for cultural eye-opening in economics and social science. This fully resonates with what Banerjee & Duflo found in "Poor Economics", and Ramirez propagates in his work on communication in development: respect "poor" decisions as well-adapted to circumstance, identify the SE behind them and support exactly that. Schultz′ work on allocative ability encompasses SE and agency in prioritizing and decision-making on allovation of scarce resources.

Amartya Sen (2000), in his talk before World Bank conference members in Tokyo, gives the most comprehensible overview of questions concerning the interplay between culture, institutions and development. Sen calls them the means and ends of the development process, and underlines the obvious relevance of cultural conditions for human behaviour and consequently, economic choices and business decisions. Sen warns from generalizations and oversimplifications in superficially classifying cultural traits, and giving the example of Japan, exemplifies that cultures change, adapt and merge over time – which is really what "culture" essentially is: the sum of evolutionary adaptations for survival of any group of people. In his definition of development as expansion of capabilities and freedoms to be and to do (Sen, 1999, 2004, 2012) (see discussion on agency below), institutional conditions constitute essential instruments of any developmental policy to ensure stability in times of cultural and physical change, while culture is seen as the basic human capital condition, the instrument and the outcome of development.

Culture

When Everett Hagen (1961) reviewed David McClelland´s "Achieving Society" (1961) for an issue of *Science*, he questioned: "*Is there an identifiable personality trait that promotes or retards economic progress in societies*?", and called McClelland´s endeavour to prove just that "*a remarkable project for a scholar to attempt"*. Since then, behavioural economics has incorporated the whole field of psychological research and testing because, as Rabin (1998, p.11) puts it: " *...psychology explores human judgment, behaviour, and well-being, it can teach us important facts about how humans differ from the way they are traditionally described by economists"*. In his paper, he subsumes the status quo of behavioural economic research on individual human economic behaviour on preferences, choice making, biases including "*whether and when experience and learning lead people to overcome these biases*" (p.12). Matthew Rabin, Daniel Kahneman, Amos Tversky, Richard Thaler, Colin Camerer, George Akerlof, George Loewenstein, and Ernst Fehr all work on the interface of psychology and economics, enlighting relevance of culture and institutions for social sciences[52].

---

[52] Highly informative though and important for a background understanding of the field, are: f.ex. Thaler (1988) on anomalies, where he examines "the existence of a cognitive illusion, a mental task that induces a substantial majority of subjects to make systematic error" which may cause market outcomes contradicting economic theory; on neuroeconomics in general see the comprehensive overview by Loewenstein, Rick, & Cohen (2008); on the value of neuroscience

McClelland´s work on the "Achieving Society" revived Max Weber´s (1973, 2010) ideas on cultural, in his case religious, values that bring about self-reliant[53], laborious, disciplined, resilient individuals who are perfectly fit for capitalistic endeavours. McClelland identified a related kind of spirit in certain people and in different strength, and connected this to economic performance, especially entrepreneurial activity. He regarded this drive to aim for achievements by doing something more or better than anybody before him as a cultural trait but leaving it unclear how that originally may have developed. In general, this entrepreneurial trait was regarded as one of the main pillars of Western rise.

Göran Hyden (1983), many years later, turned the argument around, and blamed the ignorance of Western development experts to appreciate traditional African cultures, regarding them as annoying hurdle for quicker economic progress, and the resulting failure to integrate them into the development process as a being a major cause for the lagging of development. He stressed that African cultures had grown on African soil under African conditions and this was what economic policies had to reflect and build on to help Africa catch up economically, but also socially and politically.

Engermann´s and Sokoloff´s work (Engermann & Sokoloff, 1997, 2002, 2006, and Sokoloff & Engermann, 2000) on disadvantaged economic development in the Americas took into account a possibly misfortunate natural factor endowment that favored the development of a monocultural plantation agriculture with its related slave labor, giving rise to a

---

for economics: Camerer, Loewenstein, & Prelec (2005); on decision making theory in economics, which is vital for research on economic performance: Kenning & Plassmann (2005).

[53] Please note that here the term "self-reliance" refers to a psychological condition, not to the political progam of self-reliance as dissociative development strategy against Western dependency as in f.ex. Nyerere (1967); Galtung, O´Brian, & Preiswerk (1980).

rent-seeking small (immigrated) elite, hindering the development of participatory institutions necessary for economic development[54].

Nathan Nunn (2007) rejected their line of argument. While he did find severe negative effects from slavery on today´s economies, he could not attribute these effects particularly on large-scale plantation economy with its institutional dysfunctioning and social inequality, but rather surprisingly, that small scale, non-plantation-work slavery had the worst effect on succinct economic performance.[55] I suggest this to be caused by the totally different labor relations: while plantation slaves could easily despise of the plantation owners and lead their own, though marginalized lives, keeping their identity and sense of resistance, house slaves where very much integrated in the "white" lifestyle with often close, sometimes life-long ties with "their families", at least with the white children they raised. House slaves would often identify much more with their superficially privileged lives, which would actually injure their identity and destroy self-efficacy. It must be noted, that house slavery, though turned into normal work relationships with often disgraceful pay, lingered on until today[56]. Testing for slavery causing slagging economic growth via income inequality and land ownership, Nunn could again not find statistical proof for a causal relation (p.31ff.) He concludes: *"...the positive relationship between slavery and inequality is unable to explain the negative relationship between slavery and economic development. Instead, the data suggests slavery and inequality had two distinct impacts. First, slavery resulted in lower long-term economic growth, and second,*

---

[54] Engermann & Sokoloff's theory could be grouped into the next category of endogenous theories as they attribute the utter cause to natural endowment. Their work is discussed here because of the effects of an exogenous colonial elite and world market order, and the reply of Nathan Nunn which falls into this field.

[55] Nunn (2007), p.2, pp 12-16, p.24.

[56] A vivid picture of 1960´s Southern state´s black housekeeping women and their discrimination and endurance between white exploitation and black male violence is painted in: Stockett (2009), The Help, New York; on the same note, cmp. the figure of the black majordomo who fully identified with his master to become the worst enemy of his fellow slaves in the Quentin Tarentino film "Django".

slavery resulted in greater initial inequality, which has persisted until today. These two effects appear to be unrelated." (p.34)
These effects could well be related though when the effect of slavery on a person´s, on groups´, on elites and on leadership´s SE are being taken into account. Slavery is a perfect example how violence and arbitrariness destroy the faith in one´s abilities to influence by own actions the outcome of events. Leaders learn how total control and exploitation are the ways to riches and power; groups, especially elites, learn the same as much as the dangers of not being in control, and everybody enslaved learns helplessness (f.ex. Abramson, Seligmann, & Teasdale, 1978).

The concept of "learned helplessness" was first introduced by Martin Seligmann (1975), confirmed and expanded by many authors since. Seligmann tested extensively how people reacted to adverse situations that they could not exert any influence on, and found passivity and helplessness, enduring in agony at worst: effects that I interpret as conditions of very little or no self-efficacy. Neither of the two seemingly antagonistic groups of exploitors and exploitees learns to develop trust in their own abilities and capabilities. In the chapter on self-efficacy I use Seligmann´s findings to describe especially the problems that arise when weak self-efficacy appears in conjunction with persistence to produce an all-enduring lethargy, or in conjunction with a sense of entitlement f.ex. through religion or belonging to a distinct group of people - this could be a gender, or an elite - which could help produce anything from terrorism to corruption and undemocratic control, depending on circumstance and nature of the group. These leaders and elites are as weak in self-efficacy as their slaves, as they never learned that they could make it by their own virtue, and with power would lose everything without being able to regain on merit. It is worth noticing that this logic is not only valid for the extreme of slave economies, but in differing degree for hierarchical systems in general when power offers privilege and beats merit.

Mbeki (2011), in his book on "*Advocates of Change*" cites the necessity of building capabilities to promote change by good governance: *"Leadership therefore requires at least three capabilities: capacity to innovate;*

ability to implement through mobilizing the required resources; and capability to create followers." (p.6), all three being constituing features of leadership self-efficacy.

An interesting effect of culture and - as I interpret it - lack of SE, and how to use the former to overcome the latter, is given by Abhijit Banerjee and Esther Duflo (2011). They found a cost-intensive program to increase schooling time for girls in Kenya by sexual education as much less effective than giving them a school uniform for free. The latter measure increased years of schooling significantly and was cheaper. How did it work? By employing cultural values to increase the girl´s self-efficacy: being given the highly regarded uniform might have been received as an appraisal of their school work, thereby raised the girls´ believe in their ability to finish their schooling and take up a better qualified profession.

Nathan Nunn in his work on "*Culture and the Historic Process*" (2012) stresses the importance of cultural beliefs, norms and values in analyzing the past economic development of nations. In an answer to Acemoglu, Johnson & Robinson (2001), he underlines that in concert with colonial institutions, those cultural beliefs that brought these institutions about in the home countries of the colonial rulers, where transferred with them, and it is these beliefs that are persistent until today. In identifying that culture functions as heuristics or rules-of-thumb in every day decision-making, he argues that said cultural beliefs were the foundation of European institutions which in turn promoted economic development then, and I would add, hinder it today; it is difficult to develop modern forms of institutions in a surrounding that did not develop the original forms but had them imposed while their own institutions were destroyed.

Nunn´s correlation has been widely established by behavioural economists e.g. Camerer, Loewenstein & Rabin (2011); Gigerenzer & Gaissmaier (2011), Moussavi & Gaissmaier (2014); and Mullainthan (2005). It it also found that these heuristics are culturally inherited through the works of Boyd & Richerson (1985), Boyd, Richerson & Henrich (2011), Richerson & Boyd (2008), Richerson & Henrich (2010). Connecting these two strands of thought - culture and the function of heuristics in economic decision making - and historical circumstances shaping the evolution of economically relevant rules of thumb as an economic culture, could highlight why individuals and whole societies make systematically deviating decisions despite facing the same incentives and constraints as others (Nunn, 2012).

Tabellini (2010) investigates the effect of culture at a regional level in Europe. His selection of cultural traits is based on prior research by others, especially the American political scientist Edward Banfield (1958) who argued that certain cultural traits cause farmers in the South of Italy to be poorer than farmers in North America. He observed resignation and perceived helplessness, a focus on the immediate family instead of the wider community, and interpersonal distrust. Using an econometric framework to control for omitted variables and reverse causalities, Tabelini sought to find whether these aspects of culture have historic roots and matter for current economic development in Europe. He identified historic institutions as their cause and found that social capital and confidence in the individual go a long way in explaining economic differences.

Welzel & Inglehart (2014) find a similar relationship between economic performance and natural environment with regard to Northern Europe. One of the contributions of such research is that by understanding the historic origin of cultural differences and by quantifying their economic impact one might be better able to design more efficient, more specifically targeted development policies (Mullainathan, 2005; Wuepper & Drosten, 2015).

David Landes (1999, 2000) suggests a broad range of influential factors in his theory for the European rise. Like others who ascribe an important role to culture he does so by retreating to Weber´s protestant work ethic, but he also specifically spells out attitude towards women as an important factor in development as well as towards science and religion, both of which have been empirically found much later[57]. Landes cites autocratic suppression causing a lack of political and economic freedom, which may be causal in the lack of entrepreneurship. His view of tropical climates not supporting economic development falls short of a reasoning why that should be so, when the rise of modern civilizations started in Mesopotamia.

Samuel Huntington (1997)[58] also underlines the importance of culture for economic, social and political progress but does so in contrast to Nunn from an evaluating standpoint. In his foreword to "*Culture Matters*" Huntington cites Patrick Moynihan: "*The central conservative truth is that it is culture, not politics, that determine the success of a society. The central liberal truth is that politics can change a culture and save it from itself.*" (2000, p.xiv). Culture is seen as a product of all kinds of possible unspecific influences and factors, ranging from "*geography and climate, politics, the vagaries of history…institutional modifications, often compelled by politics, can influence culture…*"(ibid, p.xxviii). The given evaluation that some cultures could be more "*deserving appreciation*"[59] than others is problematic when the emergence of culture stays obscure, no mechanism being identified by which geography and history, or institutions and politics or any other factors should shape culture, while

---

[57] On the role of religion in economic performance see f.ex. Bénabou, Ticchi, & Vindigni (2015); on religion and innovation: Bénabou (2015); on islam and economy: Chaney (2008); on the general lack of entrepreneurs and the asymmetry between the few tycoons and the poverty of their countries: Freund (2016); on the newly discovered socio-political class-conflict role of the attitude towards women: al-Tahawy (2016).

[58] Huntington´s one dimensional argument and intentional use of mathematical "proofs" to underline his popular theses was questioned by M.I.T. mathematician Serge Lang who successfully fought Huntington´s call to the National Academy of Science twice.

[59] Huntington citing Richard Schweder, in: Harrison & Huntington (2000) p.xxvii.

claiming that culture shapes history and politics[60] and that politics then reacts back on shaping culture. While Huntington describes in his foreword "*Culture Counts*" (2000) the importance of culture for economic performance of a nation, he does not attend to the question what brings culture about in its innumerous varieties all over the globe or by which instrumental ways culture than frames economic performance and could do so in a technologically highly developed world. Clearly, I would expect different skills and traits to be beneficial in different stages of economic development, basic industrialization differing greatly from economy 4.0, an agrarian plantation economy bringing about and demanding different cultural traits and institutions than a silicon valley kind of high-tech industry.

Huntington´s observations cumulate in the remark "*South Koreans valued thrift, investment, hard work, education, organization, and discipline. Ghanaians had different values. In short, culture counts*" (ibid,xiii), in apparent consensus with Lawrence Harrison´s book "*Underdevelopment Is a State of Mind*". Some cultures in this interpretation of being more or less "*deserving appreciation*" apparently make wrong decisions, having wrong values, and therefore they are poor. With Huntington and Harrison, poverty becomes a question of fault and failure, a mistake that deserves correction, if so from the smarter, better outside or be left alone, as Huntington suggests in his "*Clash of Civilizations*" where he claims that Western nations have to protect themselves and their unique culture from misunderstanding and aggressive others, basically rewording his recommendation from 1968, that the West should discourage modernization as it would lead to destabilization, and endanger the West (Huntington, 1968).

This view has earned much criticism from political scientists and economist, including Jeffrey Sachs (2000) and Amartya Sen (2007). One effect of exclusively blaming culture is that, with their influence on American

[60] The occasional mentioning of politics happens without operationalizing by which mechanisms culture and politics interact, here as in Huntington, 1997, cmp. f.ex the whole chpt. 9.

foreign policy, Huntington et al. stereotyping serves to create exactly those conflicts they claim to describe. Another, possibly even more disruptive one, is that the actual causing factors end up being ignored instead of tackled, left to grow and do their damage.

In a comment to Jared Diamond and Jeffrey Sachs, co-editor Harrison in his introduction to "*Why Culture Matters*" declines any substantial correlation of economic performance with other aspects than culture, again without suggesting how culture acts to promote development if not by a putative Weberian ethic: "*Geography cannot adequately explain the striking contrast between the north and the south of Italy; comparable contrasts among Guatemala, Honduras, El Salvador, and Nicaragua on the one hand and Costa Rica on the other..."(Harrison, 2000).* Jared Diamond is misleadingly cited with partly concurring: "*Cultural factors and influences...loom large,...human cultural traits vary greatly...some (of which are) no doubt a product of environmental variation....but...A minor cultural factor may arise for trivial, temporary local reasons, become fixed, and then predispose a society toward more important cultural choices*." (ibid, p.295) When Harrison discusses the undemocratic history of most Latin American countries, he does not pay attention to the role of an exploitive culture and institutions left behind by exploitive Spanish and Portuguese colonial rulers, the interconnection between culture and institutions, and their persistence. Harrison suggests that not only institutions but also culture can be purposefully transmitted from a foreign source, which Nunn explicitly denies (2012). Not only does this concept apparently not take into the account past experiences from colonial rule, it ignores the very American history of being unable to build a common culture or progressive inclusive institutions with their native American or African-American communities, or fully engage the former confederate plantation economy and their cultural beliefs; instead, one may ask, how much reconstruction of confederate institutional thinking has been transmitted into the Northern states[61]. It also underrates the experiences of brake-downs of forced modernization in Yugoslavia and Iran, and the struggling of all North African countries to find a peaceful balance between foreign/French-exported modernity and national/Islamic tradition. Aside of the question of the possibility of a peaceful transmission of culture and institutions, the question of legitimacy of such an endeavour is answered by a stipulated higher production of individual well-being by some cultures. The idea of purposeful culture and institution transmission might also be based on misjudging the experience of Singapore and South Korea, who did not enforce a foreign culture to a traditional community. Singapore was a sparsely inhabited island (except for a small community of fishermen and functioning as a pirate hide-out) until the British built it up as their South Chinese ocean trading center with British institutions right from the start in the late 19th century. South Korea is a unique case altogether with their special relation to the U.S., but the country could build on the existing rice-farming experience[62] and U.S. aid, investment and personal interference (f.ex. via missionaries).

[61] Several socioeconomic parameters show that the U.S. is a divided into first world - predominantaly white – parts with growth promoting culture and institutions and less developed – predominatly colored – parts with growth-impeding culture and institutions: 22% of Americans are factual analphabetics, 40% of afroamerican children are considered poor, 50 % of black fourth graders score below the basic reading level, as do 47% of Hispanics and 49% of American Indian, in: rif.org/pdf/literacy-facts; infant mortality in non-hispanic whites is about 5% while in non-hispanic blacks it is 11,3%, in: kff.org/other /state-indicators on infant mortality rate by race/ethnicity for 2013. As Jeffrey Sachs blames the electoral system for Congress (first-past-the-post), today´s American institutions can appear as oligarchic (Sachs: corporatocratic), and influenced by the example of the extractive plantation economy of the Southern (formerly Confederate) states; cmp. Sachs (2011). In recent years, there has been a growing class of poor whites that has reinvigorated the old race segregation, backlashing on those who instrumentalized the division between poor whites and poor blacks for stabilizing a political system.

[62] There is extensive research on the effect of rice farming on culture, work-ethics, time preferences, f.ex. Thomas et al. (2014); Henrich (2014); on time preferences Galor & Özak (2014).; cmp. here fn.70.

Contrasting the neo-conservative approach to culture and development was the program of Jeffrey Sachs (Gallup, Sachs & Mellinger, 1999) who concurs in identifying culture as the result of an array of influences but stresses the importance of geography and climate. His conclusion was diametrically opposite though, stipulating quick privatization, broad range liberalization measures especially of foreign trade. Applied in former Yugoslavia and Brazil, his theories stood the proof of reality as little as Huntington´s in South Africa and Brazil. In his major work "*The End of Poverty*" (2005)[63] Sachs calls for a – much criticized - increase of development aid money from the industrialized countries to lift the poorest countries out of an alleged poverty trap which they could not do by themselves or with the help of only traditional development aid. Sachs suggests that after reaching the first step on the "ladder" of industrialization, the countries could ascend further with little or no further help. This is a new thought in the debate and resonates with my suggestion (and empirical findings in Ghana) that economic development happens in a kind of swinging movements between environment, individuals, culture, institutions and economy, producing temporary stages of different requirements to pass through to the next stage and interdependencies. Clearly, the dependence on natural environment decreases with industrialization and institutional requirements change. (Agrarian surplus can well be produced with exploitive institutions and undemocratic rule, creative computer apps, rock music or high fashion much less so!)

My argument throughout this work is that countries in environments that do not support natural evolving of high SE can have a hard time to get to that "*bottom rung of the ladder of economic development*" (Sachs). But once they have been helped out if their strong dependency on that non-supportive natural environment, and to build institutions that compensate for lack of SE in some individuals, they can ascend.

Talhelm et al. (2014) and Henrich (2014) finally identify causal correlations between environment, culture, and institutions, finding differences

---

[63] A journalistic interim balance with disenchanting results draws: Munk (2013).

in cooperation, collectivism and individualism between rice and wheat farmers. They test against factors like climate or geography and clearly find what especially Diamond, and Sokoloff & Engermann, have been suggesting: that environmental differences in being better suitable for certain ways of working the land with crops that need different types of planning, investing, and cooperation lead to the strengthening of different human traits, fostering different cultures and succinctly, institutions, all of which get culturally transmitted and thereby form persistent distinctions. Interestingly, in a prior study on the psychological effects of residential mobility, Oishi & Talhelm (2012) found a causal relation between mobility and anxiety and familiarity seeking which have effects on range of economic decisions. Though researched on modern conditions, one could expect similar findings for nomadic lifestyles and descendants thereof.

On correlations of history, culture and environment, Wuepper & Sauer (2016) not only found culture to be an important factor in the successful introduction of new business forms, here contract farming; they also found that it was the ancestral history that explained cultural differences between current farmers and their propensity for successfully adopting this novel way of producing, cooperating and marketing. "*Indeed, we find that culture is a significant predictor of the (thus acquired) income ... We find culture effects of different historical production systems, the trans-Atlantic slave trade, malaria, the experience with colonial cocoa cooperatives, and the impact of Christian missionary schools. The most important cultural traits are self-efficacy (), trust and village social cohesion."*(p.1) Interestingly, they found that positive experience of ancestors with colonial cooperatives is causally correlated with higher self-efficacy in their descendants and better success of working today with contract farming, whereas the effect of missionary schools was dampening on social capital today: positive on self-efficacy, but negative on social cohesion, the latter effect dominating. (pp.35f)

One effect of culture on economic performance has been intensely studied under business and management aspects: effects of group or "herd" behaviour, conformity pressures and naturally developing conformity, as all of these heavily influence decision making in companies, social problems in urban areas and even creativity for economic growth in developed countries. In his Nobel lecture, Daniel McFadden (2000) gave a full outline of the central role of economic choices and how economic theory had come to appreciate psychology and culture as determining factors. Group and herd effects have been researched by Roland Bénabou (2009), who found effects of "individually" rational decision-making in collective reality-denial in groups, organizations and markets, which were f.ex. identified by Richard Feynman in his report on the challenger disaster to NASA. (These effects are discussed in chpt. 4 as they heavily influence the cost of learning and behaviour change.) It can be deduced that a group´s culture is decisive for its propensity of change and development. Abhijit Banerjee (1992) developed a comprehensive model of herd behaviour, formally acknowledging: "*There are innumerable social and economic situations in which we are influenced in our decision making by what others around us are doing*" (p.797). How strong this effect turns out, I may add, depends not only on the strength of the signals we´re are getting, but very much on the ability to inflict costs on deviating opinion and behaviour.

Basically, most of the authors regarding culture as important for progress - except Theodore Schultz with his concept of "*allocative ability*" and Amartya Sen with his concept of "*agency*", both of which are connected with SE - do not operationalize the mechanism by which culture should exercise its effects, except in retreating to Weber´s work ethic that brings about some labourious disciplined worker or entrepreneur. The absence of the latter in a society is a phenomenon that Chakraborty et al. (2015) describe as following from an anti-capitalist cultural bias; I wonder if this cultural bias has a power-stabilizing function: keep self-efficacy low in those people who would otherwise demand their share. After all, it was merchants, not the old noble elite, who brought about change for modernization in Britain, and merchants who pressed for American independence.

Amartya Sen[64](1988, 1999) worked on individual effects of culture: what makes an individual take on the responsibility for their life and actions, what makes him an agent of his own behalf? Sen identified the individual human agent to be the bearer of development, for once not in the Weberian sense, not even in that of just being an entrepreneur, but ideally in the sense of emancipation. As one of the most prominent critics of the theory of rational choice, Sen concentrates on abilities and capabilities of people to do what they chose as a measure for development, rather than their potential to produce a certain outcome. Instead of hoping to produce a social or political trickle-down effect of democracy and individual freedom via economic growth, Sen suggests a different chronological order for development: start with emancipation and empowerment to give people agency to produce economic growth. This quite resembles the chronology of the rise of today´s rich nations. Over long periods of poverty, instability and struggles against monarchic totalitarianism, civil rights and freedoms developed slowly and painfully to conquer ever more parts of civil lives until a class of entrepreneurs and workers could gain enough bargaining powers to demand institutions fostering and securing their economic endeavours. As a stern critic of Huntington and Harrison, Sen rejects their alignment of peoples and cultures into stereotypes. Instead, Sen pledges for a view of culture as a rich variability of identity affiliations, one of the most demanding challenges of the presently supported cultural conflicts. In the next chapter, I will attend to the question of transition of identity, the role of identity and the difference and connection between Sen´s concept of agency and self-efficacy. I suggest that SE developing under favourable environmental, i.e. supportive natural, geographic and climatic conditions, fosters development of culture and institutions that create reinforcing feedback loops in favour of development. Note that the more developed an economy the less influential are

[64] Operationalized were Sen´s ideas by the Oxford Poverty & Human Development Initiative, here: Ibrahim & Alkire (2007. A systemization of identifying collective and individual agency, and the respective fostering circumstance is offered by: Dietz & Burns (1992).

natural conditions for a society´s culture and development of SE. The so developed culture and its resulting heuristics filter access to and interpretation of information, and influence structure and performance of economic, political and social processes.

"Our self-made men are the glory of our institutions." Wendell Philips (1860)

Institutions

Acknowledging the vital role of culture for various economic choices, Alberto Alesina and Paola Guiliano (2013) research the interplay between culture and institutions[65]. They base their study on the findings of Putnam et al. (1993) who found great differences in the institutional history between center-north and the south of Italy, which are indeed economically at different ends of the scale. These findings were in turn tested by Guiso et al.[66], and found that the performance of today´s institutions is actually based on institutional and cultural experiences in the Middle Ages: *"We study whether a positive historical shock can generate long-term persistence in development. We show that Italian cities that achieved self-government in the Middle Ages have higher level of civic capital today than similar cities in the same area that did not. The size of this effect increases with the length of the period of independence and its intensity. This effect persists even after accounting for the fact that cities did not become independent randomly. We conjecture that the Middle-Age experience of self-government fostered* ***self-efficacy beliefs*** (high-

[65] This chp. discusses interaction between individuals, cultural sphere, and environment with institutions without attending to the theoretical contribution of New Institutional Economics, except in chpt. 5.4, referencing Hodgson, Pelikan, North, and Kauffman. There is in addition interesting research on the interplay between ecology and institutions, f.ex. Young et al. (1999); comprehensive: Paalova & Adger (2005).

[66] Guiso, Sapienza, & Zingales, 2008/2013/2014/2015; the citation is from their June 2014 online version.

lighting, bd) - *beliefs in one's own ability to complete tasks and reach goals – and this positive attitude, transmitted across generations, enhances civic capital today. Consistently, we find that fifth-graders in former free city-states exhibit stronger* ***self-efficacy beliefs*** (ditto, bd) *and that these beliefs are correlated with a higher level of civic capital.*"
They found that social capital today was higher in the formerly independent cities than in the suppressed ones, and find high correlations between today´s economic performance with that of 300 years ago, which shows a high degree of persistence for culture, institutions and economic success. Their study may have also found an implicit SE effect of rice farming (see Talhelm, 2014) as the center-north was not only host to early urban centers but also the traditional rice-farming region of Italy.

Hodgson (2003, p.172f) too, discusses how culture and institutions interact as institutions react back on individuals living within the culture that brought them about. He calls it "*moulding*" of individual habits and dispositions in a process of reconstitutive downward causation via institutions to cultures, and thereby rejects Gary Becker´s and George Stiegler´s ideas of fix preferences and neutrality of information, and supports John Kenneth Galbraith and Vance Packard in their view of the possibility of influencing human agency. With reference to Duesenberry (1949), he also questions the assumptions of rational choice for determining (consumer) behaviour and rather suggests habits, circumstance, culture and individual cases as important for decision-making. Hodgson calls for a new acknowledgement of reciprocal causation of upward influence from individual to institutions and downward from institutions to individuals.
Several authors have found determining effects of environmental conditions on institutions, i.a. in a recent study by Mayshar et al. (2015). In a new study and using statistical modeling methods similar to Wüpper & Drosten (2015, 2016), Mayshar et al. show how a certain social hierarchy "*following the Neolothic Revolution was an outcome of the ability of the emergent elite to appropriate cereal crops from farmers and not a result of land productivity...*". They argue that "*cereals are easier to appropria-*

te than roots and tubers, and that regional differences in the suitability of land for different crops explain therefore differences in the formation of hierarchy and states" (p.1). Several, especially agricultural, economists have been finding similar effects: that institutions – and indeed levels of self-efficacy – differ greatly in relation to cultivated crops; f.ex. with regard to gender roles (Alesina, Giuliano, & Nunn, 2013). The differences do not only occur with regard to work intensity, long-term planning and need for cooperation as was shown in rice farming by Talhem et al. (2014). Mayshar et al. show a great difference arising from the storability of the produce on the example of cereals versus roots and tubers, the former giving rise to a non-food producing, protection-from-looting providing elite, and require more planning which changes time discounting. Galor & Özak (2014)[67] found these differences in time preferences depending on the cultivated crops, which clearly lead to a different long-term behaviour with regard to investment, cooperation, and risk taking.

Moeletsi Mbeki (2009) pledges for governance as the key to African progress. In his book "*The Architects of Poverty*" he identifies exploitive institutions and exploitive elites who simply took the place of the Colonial rulers as the factor that inhibits a kind of catch-up development that many former Asian colonies have achieved. As Engermann and Sokoloff (1997) in their study on the Americas had found the negative effects of exploitive institutions on economic growth (and here clearly identified environmental conditions for fostering them), Acemoglu and Robinson (2012) spell out institutions as the key to Europe´s rise against the struggling rest, especially the difference between what they call "*extractive*" institutions versus "*inclusive*" ones, but basically do not account their character to environmental or geographic factors. In their earlier paper on the "*Reversal of Fortune*", Acemoglu, Johnson, & Robinson (2001) had suggested a correlation between environment and institutions, but did not connect this to culture and population. Chanda, Cook, & Putterman

[67] The measured data identified as time preferences may actually show self-efficacy instead; the way time preference is defined is very similar to how Wuepper & Drosten (2016) define self-efficacy.

(2014) however, argue that the reversal of fortune had actually not happened if one took the population movements into account: apparently, when Europeans settled in an out-of-Europe home they took their institutions with them if their number was high enough. Chanda et al. showed that the new rich where the old rich, as the fortune stayed with the European population, in Europe and elsewhere. In his comment on both papers, Jared Diamond showed, that what the Europeans had brought to their new countries was not necessarily just institution, but possibly they imported also naturally not available environmental endowments like certain crops and animals which influenced the profitability of the land.

In their 2012 book *"Why Nations Fail"*, Acemoglu & Robinson ascribe the development of institutions first and foremost to politics and rest their findings on a rich source of political science and sociological theory. What is missing though, even when taking culture, circumstance and events into the account, is where these political processes for building institutions originate if not in culture and environment. The case of Botswana´s good governance f.ex shows, how their inclusive institutions were built on inclusive traditional ones, developed by a traditional inclusive culture. How had that inclusive culture originally developed while all around Botswana it had not? I argue, Botswana was lucky to be blessed with a natural environment that was completely useless for plantation crobs. Neither any early local nor any later colonial agrarian exploitation was possible in a country two thirds of which are covered by the Kalahari Desert. Early colonialism was simply not interested, and the Tswana people were left alone to stabilize and save their inclusive traditions into modern times, inclusive, because that was the only way to survive on that kind of land. In a second lucky strike, their diamond resources were only discovered in 1967, one year *after* independence, to provide good funding for good governance.

Gennaioli & Richter (2007) finally succeeded to operationalize one way in which institutions actually influence economic performance: via creating possibilities for accountability. They researched the impact of precolonial centralization in Africa on colonial and modern African institutions, and found similar to the above example of Botswana, a strong *"association between the provision of public goods such as education, health, and infrastructure in African countries and the centralization of their ethnic groups' precolonial institutions"* (p.185). They ascribe this to increased accountability of local chiefs. Their findings "*stress the importance for developing countries to create mechanisms to monitor local administrators of public projects"*. Their work also demonstrates how much today's institutions are built on historic ones. Robert D. Cooter and Hans-Bernd Schäfer (2012) argue similarly that only institutions are able to solve the dilemma of trust in business: econmic growth relies heavily on innovation and innovation adoption. Innovators have to trust their investors by revealing their ideas, and investors have to trust the innovators with their money. Both sides being strangers, this "double trust dilemma of development" can only be overcome by laws and regulations, and trusted enforcement of both, the question remaining how the political will for creating and enforcing the institutional framework can be supported in the first place.

Policies

Scientists who have chosen a pragmatic way of searching for best actual policies and measures, may have oftentimes coincidentally found ways to promote SE: when Ramirez & Quarry (2009), building on the works of Fuglesang (1982), and the Dag-Hammskjöld Foundation, call for "*Another Development*", they do so based on life-long field experience. They describe projects that aim for empowering local structures and groups – and without calling it so – include measures that promote SE into their conduct: f.ex. incorporating local knowledge (equals recognition and respect increasing SE!) in an aid project added not only to its acceptance, but also led to increased and longer lasting positive effects, which they could not attribute to the informational value alone[68]. When Duflo & Banerjee research the effectiveness and efficiency of development

---

[68] Summarized from a conversation with Ricardo Ramirez, Guelph, Aug. 2008.

measures, they often find well-meaning measures designed according to theoretical convictions being neither effective nor efficient, as the underlying cause-effect logic did not work in the field. They usually retreat to simple measures that do work - as in the example of schoolgirls in Kenya given above – by including SE and self-value enhancements.

Contained in the works of scientists like Kappel (2011, 2015b), or Delgado & Ketels (2014)[69] are potential leads to efficient ways of practically promoting SE and economic growth in one move with sensible industry building measures. If this can synergistically be put to work depends not only on what is done but how it is done: reproducing exploitive structures or building human capital with SE. In their blog on the WEF, Delgado/Ketels show recent data on Botswana as (former?) example of good institutions. They now identify a weakness in microeconomic competitiveness, signaling that the country has reached a stage of development where the macro level of national institutions and policies is not sufficient anymore to keep the economy striving. Apparently, institutions were not enough: Needed now is individual entrepreneurial expertise, initiative, activity, and cooperation, all of which require SE. Pragmatically enforcing sensible policies like building industrial infrastructure where there is none, regardless of why there is none, may build SE as a side effect, very much adding to the attempted goals.

SE works as a self-fulfilling prophecy once that virtuous cycle has been started, which could be one explanation of why it is so difficult to get out of that bottom rung, as Sachs calls it, and so much easier once that hurdle has been taken, and the path of building human capital entered alongside.

In the controversy on how best to help countries and peoples to modernize from outside, two scientists have found two seemingly contradicting answers: Paul Collier (2007) in his analysis of the poor and poorest nations "The Bottom Billion" and William Easterly (2006) writing on the West´s failure with regard to the poverty problems of the world.

---

[69] this blog was based on a nber paper: Delgado, Ketels, Porter, & Stern (2012).

Collier identifies four conditions that trap countries in poverty, with the points one, two and four being closely related:
- dangers of civil war,
- discovery and export of natural resources,
- being a land-locked country with high transportation/trade costs,
- and bad governance.

Collier uses his analysis for a call on rich countries to actively construct right conditions for economic growth in the respective countries, i.e. help to install a modernizing industrial, financial and economic policy.

Easterly, on the other hand, diagnoses a complete failure of Western policies, on trade and aid alike, to provide for catch-up development amongst poor countries. He blames the basically wrong big-goals-big-solutions-theories behind policies. He calls for small–scale, grass-root, targeted initiatives in cooperation with the local people. Easterly argues for a process-oriented approach: instead of setting big goals which are hard to achieve in the dire reality of development work, and putting the implementing agencies under pressure from the funds providing superior organizations, focus should lie on the actual ground work with close interaction with the targeted people at any stage of the process, which entails, if not explicitly in goal, but implicitly in result, an empowering of the people involved via raising their self-efficacy.

Banerjee & Duflo (2011) opened the scientific door to this approach by researching the actual economic decisions of people living in extreme poverty. While these decisions often look irrational and economically wrong to outside observers, Banerjee & Duflo show that quite in the opposite, poor people adapt their economic decision making perfectly well in an optimizing manner to their extreme constraints. Building on their expertise to promote SE for changing into better conditions could offer a powerful instrument for development.

Above discussion of development and modernization theories revealed similarities and differences in explanaining human intervention in environments. Self-efficacy has been found to be of great explanatory value and a decisive policy tool. In the sense of Thomas Kuhn (1962), the concept of self-efficacy does not necessarily offer an explanation for everything, but explains the human role in modernization processes better than anything else we have right now.

"Learning is like rowing against the current, as soon as you stop you drift back again."
Benjamin Britten

4. Modernization as a Process of Individual and Collective Learning

GDP growth rates are not necessarily the result of successful processes of modernization within a society, neither are consumption patterns nor urbanization rates[70]. Societal modernization is a process in which individuals and collectives receive information that induces change in thinking, feeling, attitudes, judgment, self- and world-constructs, and behaviour. Underlying this is a process of learning or imitating. Eventually, effects of individual and collective changes in reciprocal feedback loops are reflected in cultural and institutional adaptations. This process is potentially destabilizing as it questions collective structures and hierarchies as well as individual identities and social roles. Individuals and groups have different utilities of change and learning depending on their SE beliefs which lead to people and communities struggling with this process, sometimes violently amongst each other or with outsiders, depending on who is looking for someone to blame for instigating impulses of change.

If someone learns depends on his expected costs and profits as largely determined by his surrounding, conformity pressures and opportunities.

[70] for anecdotal examples of economic growth with a lack of modernization in Iraq, Kuwait, Libanon, Syria, Egypt and the Emirates cmp. Al-Rawi (2002).

"Countries lead wars in order not to learn"
Karl Otto Hondrich (1992)

4.1 Modernization is Learning for Change

If we learn to identify those who profit from learning and change, and to identify those who profit from not learning and not changing, and those who profit from keeping others from learning and changing, we can help the first group, work on integrating or at least somehow coopting the second, and attempt keeping the third from doing harm. And at best, learn how to encourage the second and third to join the first. Possibly even more acutely, it could help us design integrative measures to smooth the social fallout and destabilization that come with modernization processes. What is modernization and how does it happen? What stimulates modernization of structures in a society? What fosters or hinders the diffusion of innovations coming from outside of a given collective, and stimulates their development within? Can adaptive learning processes and behaviour change be initiated and even be navigated by political measures? If we have a better understanding of what happens in groups and individuals in the course of adaptive processes and why so, we can aim to develop better policies to support these processes, and help to prevent or cushion potentially dangerous and destabilizing effects that harm the common social and cultural web that knits a society together and forms the core of a functioning economy. In the following, I do not attend to learning theories or the cognitive process of learning as such, but focus on social aspects of learning and behaviour change as they influence the respective utilities, and thereby foster or hinder learning and change in modernization.

Mokyr (2002, 1990) discusses problems accompanying the term modernization and retreats to employing it to describe "*the basic and mundane observation, that economic performance, our ability to tease out material comforts from niggardly nature, has improved immensely in the past two centuries.*" (2002, p.2) This helps to avoid getting entangled in the great many social, economic and political symptoms of transition processes which may or may not demonstrate modernization or merely flash-lighting a copycat of modernity. He points out that any type of economic activity is based on knowledge, which as it grows, produces growing utility and more knowledge.

Economic and societal modernization is not simply tied to the visible aspects of modernity, the production or consumption of modern products, nor to industrialization, rationalization or urbanization. One can adhere to very traditional cultural norms like female genital mutilation while enjoying all the amenities of modern lifestyle. Also, the term modernization has often been criticized for being culturally eurocentric/ Western, and politically imperialistic as to assuming there was only one long-term system option of individualism, democracy and liberalism (Lipset, 1960; similarly argue Inglehart & Welzel, 2009). This criticism may stem from a mix-up with the term "development" which more easily implies judgment at least in normative terms. Development implies developing from a stage of lesser development to one of some kind of higher level. How and by which means is this done?

I suggest development is done by learning "new", i.e. more modern ways, which is ergo, by modernizing: modernization, often used in contrast to traditional or old-fashioned, describes the process of adaptive transition over time which every economy has to do at any level of development. The most modern economy needs to modernize continuously in order not to become out of date. Strauss realizes critically: *"...people are more or less developed along certain lines or in regard to certain tasks. The observer, who stands outside the race, possesses tools for measuring crudely or precisely the amount of progress...*(assuming, bd) *fixed goals or norms against which the aspirants' movements can be chartered* (and which may be, bd) *perceived as a series of stages or as steps along a continuum....Like the idea of a ladder,...arrival at the final goal is a resting place beyond which progress is not calculated.*" (Strauss, 1959, p.64f) Indeed, there is no such thing as a final goal, modernization is a never ending necessity.

What we usually call "modernization" is actually the process of individual and collective learning which leads to modernizing updates in interior structures of humans and external structures of their surrounding societies, which is: in culture and institutions. If these changes do not occur, the process in question cannot be regarded as modernization; in this case, it is merely one of economic growth produced by external factors or natural resources exploitation, which could lead to isolated effects. Modernization happens when new information (or old information in a new way) is dealt with in an inclusive, incorporating way: any change in individual knowledge, i.e. the storage and personalizing of information, and behaviour, is preceded by a process of data reconciliation, which is actually a process of learning. Some impulse to reconsider the reservoir of known information and somehow treat the new data is needed to start the cascade of learning. In this process, new data passes through individual and collective filters of culture and institutions, and has to overcome decision-making barriers of partially antagonistic utilities of learning between individuals and different collectives. New data by their very nature questions the status quo, which is a major cause of different utilities of learning. Whoever profits most of the status quo has a lower utility of learning than someone whose present situation would profit from change.

Groups and individuals have to adapt to changes in their environment for survival. The less changes in the environment, the less adaptive processes are necessary or promoted. It has to be noted though that not every adaptation of behaviour can be regarded as an outcome of originary modernization as it is not always a sign of prior learning; analogously, not changing behaviour is not always a sign of not-learning. The reason lies in conformity pressures; these may foster an imitation of behaviour without personal learning, or storage of otherwise change suggesting information for times when greater behavioural diversity is acceptable.

Modernization as a process of change produces insecurity and fear of the unknown future. The two basic ways to obtain assets: redistribute the existing or create new ones, cause anticipative insecurity amongst the privileged of loss and inability to regain; the less privileged can either demand their share of the existing through redistribution or of opportunities to create new ones. The latter demands creating new personal structures and institutions of social organization, demanding of all those involved to leave familiar terrain to go into the insecurities of the unknown, the "*cloud*" as the evolutionary biologist Uri Alon (2013) calls it, and which can naturally not be organized nor planned in a hierarchal, orderly, calculable manner. The grandness and unsettling potential is actually comparable to Thomas Kuhn´s (1962) observations about a paradigm shift in science: individuals and collectives have to change, adapt, modernize their identities, self-construct and future outlook. This suggests modernization happens in stages, demanding different organizational solutions for each stage that produces different outcomes, levels of order and complexity (Beinhocker, 2013).

The process of learning itself can be painful and potentially unsettling: the learning subject has to be able accept at least one of three conditions:
- I don´t know: if you already know the answer, there is nothing to be learned;
- I cannot do it: if you can do it, there is nothing to be learned;
- I´m not quite sure if I do this correctly or thow hink about this, there must or could be a mistake or better way: if you do not allow for alternatives, improvements, doubts and self-questioning, there is nothing to be learned to improve your performance or understanding.

Hence, learning includes admitting not-knowing and the wish to change: if you know it all to start with, there is no room for betterment, you can only do worse which would be against our intuitive understanding of learning as entailing improvement or moving forward, not back[71]. But this admitting of not-knowing takes SE in two regards: in one´s learning abilities, and in one´s abilities to do well in changed conditions caused by learning.

[71] This idea resonates with the old Zen wisdom that the master cannot fill the students cup before it is not completely empty.

The question if somebody profits or loses from change and learning therefore depends significantly on her level of SE and her objective constrains, including the SE-determined behaviour of her reference groups which determines her social costs of learning: Does she believe to have or know what it takes to keep her status or better it under changing circumstance? Does her present status depend decisively on certain conditions, privilege, powers that could be eroded if these conditions changed? Is the SE of important groups, individual members and leaders high enough to see chances for profit in her change or rather a thread to their own profitable status?
The utility of learning at all levels of hierarchy, including leaders, leading elites, and ordinary people, depends on a person´s and her reference groups´ self-efficacy as this is what decides over the costs of change.

Harari (2014) identifies the ability to admit not-knowing as the "*Discovery of Ignorance*" and actual cause for the scientific revolution that started the extraordinary economic rise of European countries:
*"**The willingness to admit ignorance**. Modern science is based on the Latin injunction ignoramus – `we do not know`. It assumes that we don't know everything. Even more critically, it accepts that the things that we think we know could be proven wrong as we gain more knowledge. No concept, no idea or theory is sacred and beyond challenge."* (p.279, highlighting b.d.)

It is by no coincidence that the discovery or rather admittance of ignorance happened in Europe first as it takes self-efficacy to do so. Europe offered the most favorable conditions for the natural evolution of self-efficacy through climate, agriculture, relative absence of tropical dangers, geographic proximity of others to promote exchange and inspiration as well as cooperation and competition. So far unresearched, one might wonder how strong the influence of religion and religious institutions in building self-efficacy may have been in pre-medieval Europe. The individual relationship to a deity and thereby the underlining of the unique value of every human being as taught by the religionthe Neither a king nor a prophet nor any other authority could claim to be in possession of any eternal truth, everything can be right or wrong or proven to be in a certain way at a later date by and increase in knowledge in that matter. This new freedom poses a constant threat to any status quo or privilege as legitimization has to be won by merit, not by position, claim or heritage. The admittance of ignorance actually gave rise to the idea of meritocracy which caries in itself the core of democracy and emancipation: everybody can learn to know better, better than the neighbor, the king or the yesterday-me. Risk taking requires the chance for failing, for trying again, indeed for learning from mistakes. Any development of novelty, of any innovation requires the same: learning and failing are the two sides of the same coin. The higher self-efficacy at all levels of society, the more the culture of knowing which cherishes status, tradition and hierarchy, will move towards a culture of learning which promotes change, modernization and ever more learning. And will analogously create and be created by democratic, emancipated, and self-reliant political, social and economic subjects.

4.2 Different Kinds of Learning: Collective and Individual

Hondrich´s above cited interpretation points to the fact that learning and change are difficult undertakings, facing great obstacles, producing aggression, defense, and avoidance strategies. But he actually continues to say that "after the war, losers as much as the winners have to learn" (Hondrich, p.52)[72].

Behavioural biologists like Eibl-Eibesfeldt (1997) agree that humans do not have an intrinsic impulse for learning but rather, are equipped with an inborn sense of curiosity that leads the way to novelties, to trying out, to discovery. All humans are genetically equipped with it, but the extent to

---

[72] The problems around the potential political and social implications of his remarks are intensely discussed in their book reviews by Gantzel (1992), who titles "war – learning from the consequences or what are the consequences of learning" (transl. b.d.), and Senghaas (1992), who argues "against scholarly bellizism" (tranls., b.d.).

which it is encouraged or hampered depends widely on individual conditions (mainly fears) and environmental and social context (cmp. f.ex. Traulsen et al., 2010)[73]. Learning as such is a human ability that functions as a tool for survival. Learning enables quick adaptation to change, danger, information impulses. Any genetic determination would leave the species unable to adapt to sudden changes as genetic modulation takes several generations, which could have suffered extinction on the way. Genetic predetermination limits the possible habitat, feed, behavioural repertoire. Little genetic programming and large ability to learn and adapt enabled humans to populate the whole planet with the most different conditions and requirements; the same logic speaks against a genetic determination of SE.

Humans developed two different ways of learning: individual and collective. As both methods offer very different advantages they are most profitable in different conditions, for different people who organize their social life in different forms generating different cultures and institutions that produce different results, but always for the same purpose: to increase the chance of survival for individuals and group. Collective and individual learning both represent a form of adaptation as most appropriate for different stages of development and different environments. The transition from one method to the other, from collective to individual learning, poses one of the greatest obstacles to development as both, groups and individuals have to adapt their identity, their self-construct and their future outlook. This requires certain prerequisites to enable the necessary learning as such: it takes self-efficacy, the belief to be able to learn a new way and handle whatever new and unknown will come along.

Richerson, Boyd, & Henrich (2011) call collective learning "social learning" and describe how in the absence of technology for communication and storage of knowledge, survival depends on the ability of humans to

---

[73] cmp. f.ex. the extensive research of the Max-Planck-Institute for Evolutionary Biology on different human traits and behaviour like cooperation, reciprocity, public goods, volunteering, reputation; they find that individual behaviour basically depends on boundary conditions and can be altered accordingly.

learn from each other: not every individual needs to know what the whole group knows and has been learning and optimizing over generations about survival in a specific habitat, nor could any individual actually acquire all the necessary knowledge by herself. Giving the example of Canadian Inuits, Boyd et al. describe all the extensive knowledge any individual needs to apply – and cannot possibly acquire by herself! – to survive above the Arctic Circle, about food, hunting, shelter building, cloths making, hunting weapons making, canoe building, safe ice conditions and routes, weather signs etc., all of which has been developed and optimized since prehistoric times in this group of people. Any individual by herself would certainly have been dead before she could have learned even a minute part of this vast knowledge. Even in much less challenging conditions on the American East coast, would the Pilgrim fathers not have stood a chance to survive had the First Nation people of the Wampanoag not have shared their food, seeds and knowledge with them.

Collective (cultural, social) learning develops under circumstance where individual survival depends on the group, where technology for communicating knowledge over long distances or time is not available, and thereby reduces the for survival relevant groups to the immediate and present surrounding one. This dependency is not one-sided though, as every community is also dependent on the individual´s knowledge and abilities: when in 1642 the first Europeans arrived on Tasmania, the aboriginal population had "forgotten" how to build shelters, make harpoons or other fishing devices, general tools and even cloths from local plants of which archeological findings showed that all of this had existed in their early times of arrival on Tasmania (Eberle, 2013). Similar observations were made with Inuit groups in North-East Canada and resonate with the findings of Hendrich et al. (2014) who show that populations below a certain number of individuals are not only unable to produce progress, but are endangered to lose and forget what they had already achieved.[74] In the immediate lack of survival pressures, the passing on of old knowledge in small communities cannot survive the individual death of knowledge bearers. Social learning communities produce a different kind of individual and group identity, and respective perceptions of self-efficacy: achievements will tend to be ascribed to common efforts rather than individual ones and therefore not increase individual self-efficacy. This constellation will make change less likely: as individuals are the learning subjects their lower individual self-efficacy will decrease their propensity to learn and change, while groups for stability and coherence reasons - as we will see below - have differing utilities of learning.

Equally, individual learning is really only possible under circumstance that enable individual survival without the support of her immediate group, i.e. when the environment does not require complex knowledge and adapted behaviour for immediate survival. This is possible when other groups exist that can be joined or individual survival on her own is possible, for example in a modern surrounding with technological problem solving tools and organized social networks. If this potential for group changing or individual survival exists, it will by itself change the originating group´s treatment of individual learning and possibilities for changing behaviour: either to much more strictly preventing and regulating it or to supportive, tolerant and diverse group norms to remain attractive. Which one it will be depends on the group´s identity and self-efficacy in the face of alternatives which are – as technology increases – the modern form of threads to group coherence. It is again a development in self-enforcing loops: it takes self-efficacy to learn individually and learning individually increases self-efficacy. The problem of change, also

[74] There are indications that the Neanderthalers´extinction was at least partially caused by being too small of a population to survive an external shock. Beinhocker in his book on the Wealth of Nations shows several virtual simulations of how much surplus in people and ideas it takes to produce novelty and solutions for problems, which is practically impossible with shattered and geographically separated small groups of people.

with regard to the form of learning, lies heavily in the antagonistic utilities of individual learning for the individual and her reference group. Interestingly, there are first empirical indications that collective and individual forms of learning are differently supportive for developing individual self-efficacy. Theoretically, individual learning and cultures that support individual development promote higher self-efficacy as the individual ascribes her successes and accomplishments to herself in a self-efficacy fostering feedback loop. This virtuous cycle cannot get equally started if the virtues are ascribed to the group as a whole or some hierarchically higher members of that group. In a forthcoming study on descendants of nomadic herdsmen and pastoralists in Kenya, Wuepper, Lang, & Benjamin (2017) research the importance ascribed to and success in formalized education, and find that the long standing underprivileged situation of this group, which usually reaped less income and less fortunate social indicators, has actually started to be overcome by the new free schooling initiative. This may be partially ascribable to overcoming disproportional lifestyle disadvantages as well as supporting transition of individual and group identity for building self-efficacy – similar to the above given example of the girls′ school uniforms in Kenya (Banerjee & Duflo, 2011).

The differentiation Eric Beinhocker (2013, pp.354-379) makes between learning and adaptation is based on his observations of organizations that tend to have problems adapting: *"Learning is the acquisition of knowledge in pursuit of a goal, while adapting is changing in response to selection pressures from one's environment. Although adaptation requires the acquisition of knowledge, and learning can occur in response to environmental pressures we will find it useful to maintain a distinction...As we will see, while organizations are generally good at learning, they have more trouble at adapting."* (p.355) I think this distinction results from not observing self-efficacy and the different utilities of learning between individuals and groups. Organizations (as groups) need to preserve their status and coherence, and therefore learn what fosters their self-set goals; adapting however, as described here, is giving way to outside-of-group pressures which questions the existing hierarchy and leadership, and easily provokes demonstrations of holding-on to power and status instead of fostering adaptation. This reaction depends greatly on the self-efficacy of the organization and her leadership elite or leader.

4. 3 The Act of Learning

Humans do not have a specific organ or any other way to identify reality or truth as Kleist (1801) wrote about Kant´s epistemology (Erkenntnis-theorie) (1781/1974), giving the example of green pieces of glass instead of spectators´ eyes who then would interpret their world unknowingly in a green haze. The newborn child has neither knowledge nor concept of the world or herself, and learns about herself in the reflection of her own image in the people around her, thus constructing her self based on the filters of her human and environmental surrounding. This self-constructing process is fully depending on environmental impulses as demonstrated in its extremes of animal-raised human children who fully adapted to their non-human hosts – often irreversibly (cmp fotoproject of Fullerton-Batten, 2015). Any information for the rest of her life will be processed through the filters that were first installed by her direct surrounding, and are normally renewed, strengthened, and broadened by new, but matching ones according to her reference groups[75]. The actual reason for this strong tendency towards continuity is thought to be the avoidance of cognitive dissonance which causes stress and anxiety, as well as providing for group stability for survival reasons.

Information and Knowledge

Information is the basic ingredient for a rational decision. If information is incomplete, lied, manipulated, filtered, or in any way more distorted

---

[75] cmp, the concept of different self-constructs in relation to one´s several reference groups, and their bonding and identification rituals, in: Neufeld & Maté, (2013)

than in the “eye of the beholder”, it loses its function in rational choice making. New information represents an extrinsic impulse that induces a reaction from the individual and group at the end of which it is either internalized or discarded. It has to be “sufficiently“ similar to what one already knows in order to be processed via association with a chance to enter her knowledge reservoir. If it is not processable, the new information will get lost. If it is sufficiently associable, the information processing can take several forms:

- it can be ignored, fully or partially, leading to no or little behaviour change;
- it can be imitated without internalizing its informational value, leading to an imitation of behaviour without learning the underlying rational; in this case the information and behaviour will be lost again once the information flow stops; also, it is imaginable that through long-term imitation some kind of implicit learning may take place;
- it can be fought in various degrees of aggression ranging from lying about it to fighting the messenger or representative, leading to a negative behaviour change with increase of intolerance and strutting of the old rational and behaviour;
- it can be memorized and stored for future application without immediate behaviour change – possibly causing cognitive dissonance and stress;
- it can be adapted in the form of learning to become part of one´s own fundus of knowledge in reappraisal of the old and leading immediately or over time to a modernization of behaviour to avoid cognitive dissonance.

Once information has been stored to knowledge it becomes part of an individual´s identity and heuristics, the base of group identity and bonding[76], and is assumed to be inelastic to change, but rather seeks self-assurance[77] to avoid cognitive dissonance. Note that cognitive dissonance

---

[76] How much people build their institutions on the “stories” they believe in was shown by Akerloff & Shiller (2009)

[77] For an extensive discussion of information and knowledge in economics, including Gary Becker´s definitions in: Wessling (1991)

(Festinger, 1962)[78] is a state of stress to be avoided when new information could lead to conflicts between new and old inner images, group bonding, individual identity, behaviour patterns and beliefs.

Information can occur as targeted – at specific groups or individuals – or random. It is caused by and a symptom of an occurred change in one´s environment. Note: globalization of information f.ex. offers information of change that did not necessarily occur in one´s own environment and still reach someone, possibly stimulating adaptive processes alien to his environment, f.ex. with regard to self-image and consumption goals, or gender role and aspirations. New information can also be fed by old knowledge of an individual or group that could not be accessed before, because of group filters (taboos), or was intermittendly forgotten.

Filters

New information has to pass the filters of individuals and collectives, several of which surround each individual. Following interactionist theory, I refer to the relevant groups as "reference groups". It is from the common culture of a reference group that an individual in the process of decision making will draw her own values (Shibutani, 1962), thereby reacting to the group function of social control. *"Deliberately, intuitively, or unconsciously each person performs for some kind of audience..., conduct is oriented toward certain people who are somehow deemed important."*(ibid, p.129)[79] Filters can be implicit or explicit. Explicit filters are primitive in their structure and rely on rules like taboos, censorship or technical hurdles. Poverty filters work explicitly by physically preventing an individual open access to information and information processing like education, but also implicitly by preventing an individual to develop her

[78] The concept has been thoroughly discussed, enlarged, rejected, and replaced by alternative explanatory theories for human behaviour, but a series of tests with brain scans has found the basic principles, including physical arousal, and predictions to be valid: Jarcho et al. (2010).

[79] This is an important reason for bonding to be so vital in learning (Neufeldt), and why self-efficacy raises independence in decision making!

potential and information seeking. Culture with all its aspects like norms, values, roles, beliefs functions as explicit and implicit group filter on information that work like heuristics predetermining an individual´s openness and reaction to new information. Indeed, *" `social control´ refers not so much to deliberate influence or to coercion* (in Western societies, b.d.) *but to the fact that each person generally takes into account the expectations that he imputes to other people"* (ibid, p.129). Though groups can exercise different degrees of tolerance and freedom of individual learning and experimenting, they have an intrinsic interest in ensuring the stability of the group. Stable groups are skilled in well-proven methods of preserving the old knowledge and not endangering the stability of the group or status of its members by experimenting (too much). This objective survival pressure will regularly lead to cultural and institutional developments that discourage deviant behaviour, different degrees of conformity pressures, and critical reception of novelty on parts of the group, all of which lead to developing filters against new information that can range from mythically demonizing to a modern world censorship. Basically, dividing the world in groups of "them" and "us" already filters the information coming from the "non-us" by greater suspicion, scrutiny or downgrading. This group preserving, immanent, collective motivation is flanked by those individual motivations, that profit from group hierarchy, i.e. of the leader and leading elites, and possibly other members, who profit from relations and favors.

Leaders and leading elites have yet another intrinsic interest to control new information and avoid learning: Their status and position is often based on real or pretended "knowledge". The act of learning itself, however, depends on the ability to acknowledge and admit not knowing. (cmp. "discovery of ignorance" as the origin of Europe´s rise (Harari, 2013, p.275, 94). A leader who admits not to know though, endangers his position to whoever claims to know better instead of him, and risks to lose the trust of his followers, which clearly lowers his incentives to admit insecurity or doubt, for learning, and for encouraging learning around him.

To formalize an example of cognitive processing of new information, Feola & Binder (2010) developed the following map showing the interplay between an individual (agent 1) and the filters of his reference group (agent n). They developed this schema after researching use or not-use of protecting devices against pesticides during application amongst Colombian smallholders. They find that the most important single factor for use of protective equipment was neither schooling nor information about potential health dangers; rather, the decision depended mainly on the actual or assumed behaviour of neighboring farmers, hence conformity. All other potential explanatory factors (age, gender, education, income) were equally ignorable as cultural context, cognitive problems, discomfort or culturally determined risk perception. Their Integrative Agent-Centered IAC framework sums up the presently discussed influential factors on individual reaction to innovation in interaction with others:

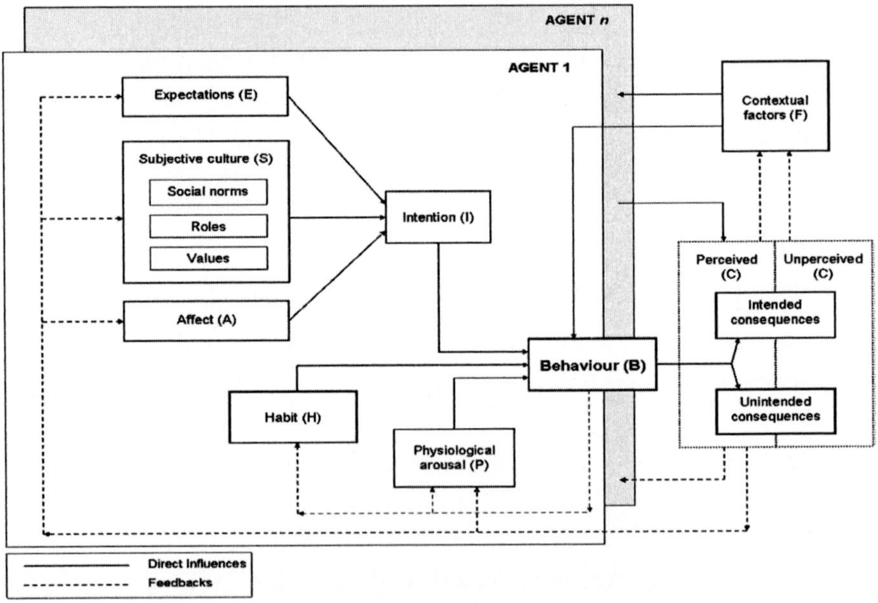

Above IAC framework was developed by Feola & Binder (2010b) and cited from Ecological Economics, 69 (12).What the IAC framework lists as „subjective culture", I regard as those group-determined filters that function as blockage or group-conform heuristics for the individual in dealing with new information. Similarly, authority-as-filter-effect or group-conformity-as-filter-effect have been thoroughly researched, and findings are analogue to those of biologists who research conformity and learning in animals[80]. Banerjee (1992) developed a model on herd behaviour and reasons it produces valuable heuristics; he offers an explanatory bridge between individual and collective learning. Roland Bénabou (2009) identifies conformity in organi-zations as "group think" and describes how this filtering of information can lead to denial of information and reality in groups, markets and oganizations. He develops a model that shows how conformity pressures make this denial individually rational, but collectively detrimental. Mostly, when looking at the effects of this "conformity bias" which goes back to the cultural evolution theory of Boyd & Richerson (1985) we look at its harmful effects of distorting information [81]. But this seemingly obvious notion has been questioned in business writing about the "wisdom of the crowds" (Surowiecky, 2004). Research by the ETH Zurich seemed to find that while swarm intelligence tested positively in many animal groups, it did not so in humans: humans in crowds behaved less rational than individuals (Eng et al., 2006/updated 2014). But other studies show that it seems to work both ways, depending in some cases on content of information and circumstance: studying signal processing in networks Golub & Jackson (2010) find *"(the signal recipients) naïvely update beliefs by repeatedly taking weighted averages of neighbors' opinions. We show that all opinions in a large society converge to the truth if and only if the influence of the most influential agent vanishes as the society grows. We also identify obstructions to this, including prominent groups, and provide structural*

---

[80] Aplin et al. (2014) f.ex. found that "experimentally induced innovations lead to persistent culture via conformity in wild birds".

[81] Padalia (2014) titles: "Conformity Bias: A Fact or an Experimental Artefact?" and questions not so much the whole concept, but its widespread use as an over-simplification, and calls for greater scrutiny in identifying other social causes for the observed behaviour.

conditions on the network ensuring efficient learning. Whether agents converge to the truth is unrelated to how quickly consensus is approached." (p.112)

They clearly identify leadership and hierarchy to impede proper information processing in groups by their mere existence. Inversely, one can deduce that the higher SE amongst members of the group, the less the conforming pressures in favour of the leading elite, and the higher SE amongst leaders, the smaller their incentive to actively obstruct information flow. In the analysis of data from smallholders in Ghana, Wuepper & Drosten did find links between openness to novelty amongst farmers and supportive rather than disinterested chiefs who promote insecurity instead. Aulinger (2008) clarifies that human collective intelligence relies on the organization of the group: if individuals in a group – as in the example by Golub/Jackson – act independently from each other they will, as a collective, reach better results than each of them could by herself, while individuals acting collectively fall prey to group pressures and biases and produce lesser results as a group than as individuals.

Reference groups facilitate perspective taking, which shapes identity and outcome expectancy for different behaviours. Shibutani (1962, p.130) notes: *"A perspective is an organized view of one's world, what is taken for granted about the attributes of objects, of events, and of human nature. The environment in which men live is an order of things remembered and expected as well as of things actually perceived. It includes assumptions of what is plausible and what is possible. Without such an order life would be chaotic; even doubts become possible only within an unquestioned frame of reference. Having such perspectives enables men to conceive of their ever changing world as being relatively stable, orderly, and predictable."*

Note the dilemma for people changing their reference groups or worse, their surrounding culture through emigration, with regard to their identity which is essential to build SE, and to their personal bonds which are important for learning. People take "perspective" by knowing what to anticipate from others.

The following graphic shows filters of information, knowledge and behaviour changes all of which depend on degrees, generality and domains of SE of individuals, groups and leaders[82]. Filters protect the self, constructed self, individual identity, group coherence, all of which form the mental core of an individual and group. Due to the inability of humans to "know" reality or truth, the inner core is unobservable. Outside of psychoanalysis, the self-construct in toto is also not observable as it is revealed only as targeted "to an audience" (Strauss): more or less consciously and intentionally in differing aspects, "roles" or "identities", and according to the impression the revealer wants to evoke in the respective observer.

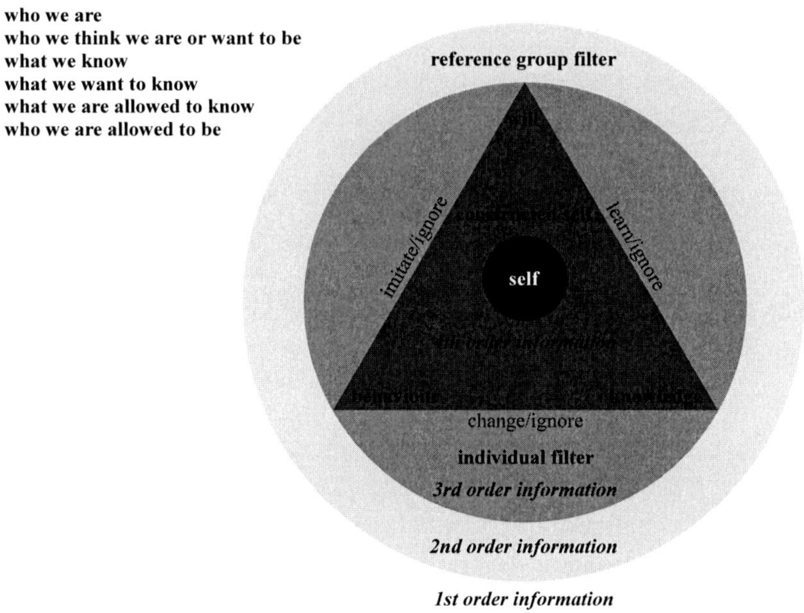

[82] This chapter is a revised and extended version of a presentation by the author at a 2011 seminar meeting on Behavioural, Social and Neuroeconomics, courtesy of Prof. Dennis Snower, Institut für Weltwirtschaft Kiel – Kiel Earth Institute.

Filters of information are a major instrument of stabilizing a collective that is based on extrinsic or secondary bonding (Neufeld, 2013)[83]. They function as change prevention and status quo protection, and can come under external pressure as for example internet and social media influence have shown during the Arab Spring. They stabilize individual reality constructs about oneself and all others, and are not just limiting individual freedom of choice and development, but fulfill an important role in stabilizing individual life.

In their function as heuristics, information filters reduce complexity, which makes them an important help for individuals and groups to function and reduce transaction costs in the sense of Coase[84]. These filters may be the reason for the aforementioned persistence of culture in groups. Their effect on stabilizing existing hierarchies and profiting from the status quo in turn, makes their adaptation to change a sensitive matter for targeted policies. Adapting of information filters basically has to develop locally and within the group. Cases of externally induced or exploited breakdowns of these group filters have proven to be uncontrollable and destabilizing and may have f.ex. added to the fall of the Shah regime in Iran as much as to the breakdown of Yugoslavia after Tito, when in both cases new and new-old reference groups could extend their bonding stories by utilizing older "stories" (Akerloff) and their respective filters.

4.4 Behaviour Change

The decision and process to change one´s behaviour puts an individual in a situation of reappraisal of not only her relationship to her self-construct, but also to her surrounding world. She has to reposition herself towards

---

[83] Neufeld describes extrinsic bonding is based on symbols, superficial external identification like uniform cloths, hairdo, specific behaviour or language etc. while intrinsic bonding is based on emotional connection.

[84] Coase theorem, as part of allocation theory, describes how market participants reduce their transaction costs by directly communicating within a given framework of institutionalized property rights.

herself and towards everybody else, and that is done in public: learning cannot be "seen" before it is publicly demonstrated through behaviour change. She makes herself observable and exposes herself to a reactio of either applause or critique and sanction.
Depending on the extent to which behaviour change deviates from group conformity, which usually depends on the extent of group diversity, individual behaviour change entails the possibilities and dangers, i.e. benefits and cost, of:

- loss of group approval, and
- loss of position in group hierarchy,
- through leaving the group consensus, possibly the group identity,
- all of which possibly leading to expulsion – which in the human evolution would have meant almost certain death as survival was hardly possible for a lone individual for many habitats for large periods of human history, and
- risking group retaliation;
- loss of factors of identity,
- altogether loss of several reality defining parameters.

Furthermore, behaviour change is the publicly observable demonstration to have been wrong in the past and to not have known (better), and publicly extending this evalaution to the group and its leaders: they too were wrong in the past and I stray from their lead as I know better now. The price of this social and identity risk has to be clearly lower than the uncertain future gains of the change which include even successive uncertainties of one´s own capabilities to learn and master the new. The old has to be given up before the new is fully known and mastered. Behaviour change can, but does not necessarily happen after new information has been made available to an individual. It is not only induced by actual learning, but can occur as imitation. The former may lead to in-group conflict, the latter is usually done to avoid it for conformity reasons and can go both ways, change or persistence. In any case, change will occur more frequently under approval or tolerance of the reference group as that lowers individual costs. Conversely is behaviour change less likely or to a lesser extent so, if it is expected to be sanctioned by the group, i.e. the expected costs are prohibitively high. Because of social costs and gains lying in an uncertain future, behaviour change induced by new information may actually occur in steps and with a time lag, thereby reducing uncertainty.

The accessibility of an alternative reference group and the possibility to change over to it, heavily alters extent to which the old group can sanction undesired behaviour and levy social costs on its members. This is one channel how f.ex. the Arab Spring movement was spurred: social media create a global public which offer the possibility to identify with people outside of one´s usual range. A girl living in a traditional family in Cairo or Jeddah can identify with blogging, rap-music loving New York youths, actively communicate with groups of hipsters via facebook, instagram or twitter all around the globe, sign Avaaz and Sum-of-Us petitions in direct political participation, and actually feel part of a group of people which totally differs from those around her, and still not feel alone or left out. This fundamentally changes costs and benefits of behaviour change, and in the short term, increases immediate group incentives to use repressive power to limit access to an out-of-group-public that undermines their tolls of power.

4.5 Utilities

Every individual with his specific SE beliefs belongs to a variety of reference groups (Sherif & Sherif, 1964; Kemper, 1968) with their self- and group-efficacy beliefs; these reference groups are of different size and make-up reaching from family, peers, clan, tribe, religious group, to nation or race etc. Depending on their level and generality of SE, these reference groups each have their own calculation of costs and benefits for the group, their leaders, leading "elite" and ordinary members, and in interaction or competition with all other groups. Though "group" and "leader" are differnet entities with different properties, here I limit the discussion to the former as if it was an organism. Any group aims to determine and enforce social costs and benefits for the desired behaviour of their members accordingly. This group rational can be represented by a "production function" of learning, wherein the group "produces"/facilitates a level of learning (via her members) and behaviour change that it considers favourable, f.ex. increase number of members, identification, stability, power, privilege, influence. This group rational constitutes a large part of the group "culture" and is reflected in institutions.

Individuals who can be group members, elite members or leaders, and at the same time have a different status in different groups as well, according to their role and status and SE beliefs, have utilities of learning and behaviour change that can not only vary but also be antagonistic from those of their reference group, which is influential in the process and outcome of modernization. Individual utility functions represent the result of the group´s "production function" of learning.

Learning and behaviour change are both difficult and scary. The unknown by itself increases anxiety and stress[85]. The question if individuals or groups profit from learning and will therefore foster learning for themselves and others, depends on their self-efficacy beliefs: weak groups tend to fear change when their present status offers privilege that they don´t trust to hold in the future and which may not be regainable, while strong groups tend to foster learning and change when they trust to be successful in keeping group identification stable and profiting as a group or in favour for their leader/leading elite. The anticipated (feared) social costs of learning can be expected to be more decisive for dealing with

[85] Eibl-Eibesfeldt (1997) identifies four human reactions to perceived danger, be it virtual or real I add:.since the brain does not differentiate between the two, perceived danger encompasses movies, computer games, virtual reality; sudden new information pose a thread or risk until proven otherwise and induce mammal brains to produce the chemical, mostly hormonal reaction fit for any of these four pairs of emotions and actions: fear and flight (insecurity and avoidance!); anger and fight (physical, verbal, virtual, imagined – dominating, impressing, threatening or downgrading behaviour to actual physically fighting; negating of information); resignation and submission; self-confidence and cooperation; cmp. also Schwarzer (2000).

new information than the anticipated (hoped for) benefits due to biases like the well tested endowment bias, risk adversity and socially developed heuristics that hamper change amongst individual group members[86]. Furthermore, the ease and possibility to change one´s reference group is likely decisive for the incurrence of costs as well as their evolution as being decisive for the enforcement possibilities of sanctions in the first place. While individual benefits from learning can range from increasing self-esteem to income, they lie in the future and are merely expected or hoped for and uncertain. Social costs, however, for leaving the common grounds of one´s reference groups have usually been observable in the past and are part of the group narrative.

Tetzlaff's "historic learning subject" is hence neither reference group nor elite as collective entity, but rather the individual human being in her social roles as member of various collectives, holding differing positions of hierarchy and self-efficacy. Leaders and members of a leading elite act as individuals and group members on their own account in their own interest. In the course of growing up in different groups, individuals construct their "self" in constant discourse with their environment. The constructed self yearns for coherence, efficacy, and protection or safety (survival) for which it will usually seek integration in groups that offer some or all of the above. The individual is such in a latent conflict between her own interests and those of her reference groups in every change of behaviour she may seek. Groups, as an amalgamation of individuals, develop a common "culture" of roles, traditions, symbols etc. that offer the experience of coherence, efficacy and protection to their members, but in turn discipline them through the same instruments to stabilize the group. Groups may actually have an interest not only not to "learn" (collective learning consists of adapting the group culture to changes in the environment as well as amongst their membership) as a

[86] Cmp. Kahneman & Tversky (1979) and Tversky & Kahneman (1992) on biases and risk adversity for their work on prospect theory; Thaler, Tversky, & Kahneman (1997) on Myopia and Loss Aversion in Risk Taking; Kahnemann, Knetsch, & Thaler (1991) on endowment, status quo bias, and loss aversion.

collective, but also to sanction individual learning of its members when learning could destabilize group identity or endanger privilege and status. Also, organizational hierarchy offers the possibility for individual members to gain power over other members, individual non-members or other groups. In this case, the group effect of supporting their members is being reversed, and the need to discipline and raise costs for deviating behaviour may rise up to the point of possibly life threatening consequences - which is the exact antipode of why groups developed in the first place. Analyzing the situation of individuals and their reference groups in a given situation under the aspect of who profits from learning or from preventing people from learning offers insight in the chances for development and for empowering the learners, develop strategies for incorporating the non-learners and those, who may lose a privileged status. It may even lend itself for developing a better understanding of learning stages in a society, i.e. at which point of group organization basic rights and freedom granted to the group members like physical immunity, right to exercise a religion, sexual preferences, gender rights etc. can be granted to non-members as well and become universal rights.

Utility of Individual Learning[87] and Prospect Theory

The idea that people still have an incentive for learning and changing their behaviour in situations where environment does not require it for survival reasons, builds on the economic logic of rational choice (Simon, 1955)[88]: People rationally decide on their behaviour after evaluating the pros and cons of alternatives, taking heuristics as short cuts (with the scientists′ difficulty to differentiate between habit and heuristic (Clark,

---

[87] Analogue to suggestions of Ackerloff & Kranton (2010) formulating a utility function on identity and other biases, these simple schematic descriptions in the form of general utility schemata are aimed to help visualize the relationship between influential factors. This section profited greatly from discussions with Steffen Ahrens and David Wuepper; any flaws are those of this author.

[88] Despite controversy about the actual contribution of rational choice theory to understanding human behaviour, its basic concept is still very present and influential.

2010)). As this assumed rational choice often seems to lead to decisions that look suboptimal not only to others, but also to the decision maker herself, economist have been looking for explanations and found some in calculating mistakes, biases, and imperfect or "framed" information, which the field of behavioural economics is researching. Sociologists look at evaluating different information on the ground of "perspective" which refers to the values shared amongst members of a reference group.

Analogue to Banerjee & Duflo´s findings on rational economic decision making under the constraints of extreme poverty, I find it helpful to assume that human behaviour is perfectly rational, but subjectively so, and regularly unobservable from the outside. While any human behaviour may be perfectly rational by her very own, individual cost-benefit calculation, it cannot be observed from the outside as her personal utility not only depends on her own preferences and conditions, but on those imposed on her from her complex net of social interaction, her reaction to this, and the filters of information from her surrounding and her own, self-construct protecting, tools[89].

Becker & Murphy (2000) suggest a utility approach to social interaction in total freedom of choice, including changing the reference groups. I consider this approach as not commonly applicable and ascribe a large aspect of the social costs to the fact that this change will normally be as difficult as costly or even impossible in large parts of the world still[90] and certainly in the greater part of human history.

---

[89] One the greatest stress factors for humans is when their self-construct is endangered. This will usually be avoided or fought off; learning of information that endangers self-construct and constructed identity is one of the greatest challenges in the modernizing process; ple see chpt on identity, and f.ex. the present European discussion on refugees and fear of identity loss on both sides. Cmp. Lehmann (2012) on: Die Bedrohung des Selbst als Ursache von Stress – eine experimentelle Operationalisierung des SOS-Konzeptes (stress as offence to self due to failure or downgrading by others, b.d.).

[90] for discussion on rational choice and framing of decisions Tversky & Kahneman (1986).

However much rationality or social influence one will ascribe to human decision-making, it is commonly assumed that an individual´s decision to act in a certain way depends on that person´s subjective assessment of her benefits and costs incurred in conjunction with that behaviour. While Adam Smith had discovered self-interest as “the motivating force that drove the economy” (Beinhocker, 2007, p.28) without explaining the actual process of translating it into economic action, Jeremy Bentham identified “the pursuit of self-interest (as, bd.) a rational activity based on the calculus of pleasure and pain” which could be quantified by “utility” (ibid, p.28). This correlation was first identified by Daniel Bemoulli in 1738, and again by Jeremy Bentham in 1744 (ibid, p. 461).

It can be expressed as simple general relation where utility equals benefits minus costs: U = B – C

Keep in mind that both benefits and costs lie in the future, and are therefore as risky as uncertain. The decision maker i aims to maximize her utility U which equals the benefits B minus her costs C with regard to specific alternatives of behaviour j: $U_{ij} = B_{ij} - C_{ij}$

McFadden (1974, 2000) shows that the probability that a decision maker decides for one specific alternative of behaviour can be expressed as:

$$P_{ij} = \frac{e^{Uij}}{\sum ee^{Uih}}$$

where U_{ij} and U_{ih} is the utility of the alternatives which are here:

- learning with change of behaviour

- learning without change of behaviour

- no (intrinsic) learning, but behaviour change due to imitation

- no learning, no behaviour change

Following the suggestion of Akerloff & Kranton (2010) to construct a utility function to include behavioural aspects, a general function of utility could be adapted to include different factors of influence on an individual´s decision to learn:

$$U = \propto + I(se)(\beta_1 B + \beta_2 S + \beta_3 R) - \beta_4 \left(\frac{C}{\Delta G + X}\right) + e$$

where

- U represents individual utility of path-dependent, long-term factors as well as context-dependent, short-term influencable factors.

Utility here equals total expected outcome of the behaviour "learning" depending on the qualities of self-efficacy.

– $\propto$ is a constant that picks up a fundamental individual utility of learning that is assumed to be $\alpha > 0$

It corresponds to the long term individual utility structure that is assumed to be a life-long stable function created by early life experiences, taken over from important bonds (like parents) and is part of the constructed self. It also reflects those costs of learning that the self-construct suffers from having to adopt to exogenous impulses.

In cases where $\alpha < 0$, we have a case of "pathological learning", i.e. only forcibly by failure.

- *I* is the influence on changing one´s learning behaviour as a function of the believe in one´s self-efficacy. (This compares to Akerloff & Shiller´s (2009) concept of "story": individual perception is the measured factor, not how realistic it is.)

- *B* subsumes any expected benefit which includes material, emotional, financial benefits as well as greater coherence to one´s self-construct or to actual or desired relationships.

– *S* represents the factor of state dependancy, i.e. if an individual is presently learning or not.

- *R* is the factor that shows how strong and important the individual bonding is to her self-construct and to her reference group.

- *C* are the total expected costs , divided by the possibility to change the reference group plus the potential for externalizing costs of learning and behaviour change. These costs are another pragmatic lever for policy measures: by designing policies that directly lower the costs of learning for different groups of people, f.ex. women, their utility of learning rises directly.

- *e* is the unobserved part of the utility function.

Note that due to risk adversity, benefits have to be considerably greater than costs, before a change in learning behaviour can be expected. Also, endowment effects, i.e. effects that have an individual ascribe a higher value to the status quo than to an only future potential can be assumed to add to the upward pressure on the benefit/cost ratio (Kahnemann, Knetsch, & Thaler, 1991).

There has been fierce discussion and critique about the question of if and how behaviour, expected outcome and self-efficacy are related. When in his later works, Bandura included "outcome expectancy" with self-efficacy as both determining behaviour (here it would be $l = se + u$), he was heavily criticized for it. His critics insisted that expected outcomes had been proven in experimental settings to influence self-efficacy perception and thereby invalidating the whole se theory. Bandura rebutted critics with the argument that the perception of self-efficacy was not invalidated by it being influenced by expected outcomes. This dispute may have resulted from another misunderstanding about the concept as a whole that I have found even amongst experts and followers of Bandura´s theory: the question of what self-efficacy really refers to: tasks or goals or domains or processes or else? (And from the lack of a comprehensible demarcation from all other concepts like self-esteem or self-confidence, agency and locus of control, to name a few.)

I suggest: SE for a certain behaviour (here: learning l) that is supposed to produce a certain expected outcome u (modernizing and promotional benefits of learning) influences outcome expectancy, but not the actual outcome directly (as in $se(u)$), but via reinforcing the effort in exercising the procedural behaviour (here: *I*, learning) that is meant to produce that outcome. If someone beliefs she has the ability to play soccer really well, she will put in extra effort to win the tournament. This will indeed increase her chances to win that tournament, but: her belief to be a great soccer player will not win the game, her extra effort produced through self-efficacy will.

A positive expected result will not increase self-efficacy towards the process that brings the expected or attempted result about, but may lead to greater effort and yet better results in a self-fulfilling prophecy and following this, increase self-efficacy in the next period.

A negative expected outcome may lower the incentives to take on the task of working towards this outcome with great effort – *but* it will not decrease the agent´s SE for conducting the process that would have brought that outcome about. If SE for the process was high beforehand it will not decrease through an expected low outcome, ceteris paribus.

Once the process has been performed and the actual outcome produced, learning-from-experience may set in and influence future expectations as SE for the respective process has increased. This, however, is something else than a priori outcome expectations. As a result of a posteriori experienced positive outcome, the increase of SE is a learned trust in one´s own abilities to do well in this kind of process and for similar actions in the future.

In the case of negative outcome experience, SE may not sink but remain stable or even increase as the cause for less than optimal results can be projected onto others or circumstance. Also, one may be dissatisfied with the result and still be proud of one´s effort, work, persistence and may undergo the satisfaction of having learned a valuable lesson to be better prepared for the next time, and thus increase one´s SE perception.

SE is neither goal- nor task-specific but process- and domain- specific, and thereby not directly correlated with results or expected results. SE and outcomes are correlated only via the belief in being able to do well in the process that may eventually lead to that specific aspired outcome (Bandura, 1986; for critics: Williams, 2010). There are objective constraints to reaching certain outcomes that cannot be influenced by more effort or any other purposeful action but are determined by third parties and circumstance; locus of control and the respective SE refer only to those aspects of the process that can be influenced by the agent. In all other cases or aspects, self-efficacy is irrelevant for the outcome.

There are cases where the expected outcome is highly attractive, but the agent does not have SE belief in the necessary capabilities and will therefore not attempt to act. In yet other cases, higher self-efficacy can lead to greater efforts and longer time of attempt so that initial constraints can be overcome and positive results achieved nevertheless.

Kahneman & Tversky (1979) took the probability of an event under risk into account, and found inter alia a "certainty effect" which leads individuals to underweight outcomes that are merely probable in comparison to those that are certain. They interpret this effect to add to risk aversion, an endowment effect and other biases that lead people to value what they have more than what they can possibly get. But this effect may actually be causing risk aversion in the first place in all those cases where a lack of SE leads the individual to doubt her abilities to reach the uncertain result. When people make choices over behavioural benefits that lie in the future, they can only speculate about their probability based on
- their experiences from the past about circumstance and
- the behaviour of relevant others, and
- their belief in their own abilities to attain what they desire.

Kahneman & Tversky expanded traditional expected utility theory by assigning values not to the final outcomes, but to the gains and losses incurred, and replace probabilities with decisions weights. I sugges to take self-efficacy as a function of the expected costs and benefits into account. In their "Advances in Prospect Theory", Kahneman & Tversky (1992), and Heath & Tversky (1991, in their work on preferences, beliefs, ambiguity, and competence) already found self-efficacy effects: "*More recent evidence indicates that people often prefer a bet on an event in their area of competence over a bet on a matched chance event, although the former probability is vague and the latter is clear*" (1992, p.298), but Heath & Kahneman call it "competence", and find several proofs that perception of competence (which is the perception of one´s abilities equalling the definition of self-efficacy) changes behaviour and decision making with regard to classical predictions .

Group "Production" of Learning in Strong and Weak Groups

Any given collective represents a reference group for those individuals who are or want to be a member or associate of the group. As mentioned before, every individual is at the same time and successively member of several more or less formalized groups, which may have contradicting rules, norms, demands regarding the desired roles to take on. The group shares common identification marks based on a common self-construct and the according "stories" that may be channeled into behaviour, language, looks, values, norms, rules, etc. which all serve as bonding factors according to Neufeldt (2013). Individual learning potentially endangers this "social glue" if it puts the individual in deviation from the group, and will therefore be sanctioned with costs to discourage it. Groups have incentives to filter information getting to its group members ranging from actual censorship to discrediting message or messenger, the more so the less stable is the group, the more endangered it feels by change, the more it fears to lose out as a group or as leaders and leading elites who doubt to be able to regain privilege. The less the leader or leading elite are inclined to learn for themselves, the greater their incentive to keep others from learning as so they themselves can acquire more status-quo preserving, ruling knowledge. The weaker group efficacy, and self-efficacy of its members and leaders, the higher the inclination to prevent or sanction change. Strong groups profit from learning, weak groups are threatened by it.

In a strict sense, a production function shows the amount of yield produced from different amounts of inputs. The "group utility function" of learning looks basically the same as the former utility function of individual learning but with one important distinction: assuming that the costs C of individual learning in the above function are determined by the reference group, one can argue that the group´s utility function of individual members´ learning equals the group production function of individual learning. The yield equals the utility of the group because it shows the best mix between offering the group members the possibility to learn while keeping a maximum of group coherence and status:

$$Y = Ug = \propto + \lg(se)\,(\beta_1 B + \beta_2 S + \beta_3 R) - \beta_4 \left(\frac{C}{\Delta G + X}\right) + e$$

Here, we can assume that:
the group´s yield will be the utility *U* of the group *g* for the behaviour learning *I* in the form of granting to its members different degrees of learning and behaviour change, depending on the self-efficacy of the group and according to its expected benefits *b* in the form of group stability, status, influence, power, privilege and access to resources, with *S* representing the present state of learning and *R* the stability of group coherence.

Group behaviour is super-imposed by individual member interests, individual leader interests, and interests of individuals, who belong to different hierarchical layers including the leading elite. I find it helpful to look at the different utilities in this schematic way to demonstrate the possibly antagonistic state they can take. It becomes obvious that learning individuals endanger the stability of the group and thereby its status, and all of the above listed factors of benefits for its non-learning members including those in the higher ranks. This correlation applies to formal and informal groups and demonstrates why individuals are the bearers of progress – when they profit - and why groups have a natural interest in preserving the status quo. The same is true for leaders and leading elites: as long as they profit from the status quo they profit not only from not learning but also from keeping others from doing so.

Acemoglu & Robinson (2012) identify this "stabilizer-in-slump" (pp76-95) as preventor of evolutionary appropriate adaptation to change in their discussion of extractive and inclusive institutions. They describe the incentives for leading elites to institutionalize their fears of Schumpeter´s creative destruction, as their extractive privileges are at stake. Any attempts to modernize will be more successful if those who profit from non-learning and keeping others from learning, are identified and espe-

cially targeted in a coopting, SE building[91] way. The higher their SE, the higher their trust in their own ability to still do well under changed circumstance, the less reason to fear the ascend of others, and the higher their own incentive to learn and trust they can profit from the newly appearing opportunities.
The respective SE forms an important part of the self-construct and identity of the potential learner and his prerequisites of learning: aside of the circumstantial conditions, it is the perception of one´s ability to learn and make the best of the new possibilities that determine whether change and novelty will be regarded as chance or as thread.

> *"A sense of identity `is never gained or maintained once and for all. Like a good conscience, it is constantly lost and regained'." Erik Erikson (1954)*

4.6 Learning and Identity

The difference between self-construct and identity lies in its origin and purpose: identity is the self-construct in differentiation from others, i.e. identity splits the world in me and not-me, while the self-construct defines me from inside. Identity includes different roles and functions the self takes on. Identity defines what someone thinks she is in the eyes of the world, what she wants to do, be and have in conjunction with and differentiation from others. Positive identity therefore is very much built on the experience of respect for her mere existence.

---

[91] In a personal discussion with Jens Weidner as an expert for especially difficult non-learners in aggressive youths, Weidner said that different cooptation measures like giving people extra tasks or extra status had been found successful amongst violently destructive, criminal youths up to the point, when only complete separation from the more cooperative individuals was possible for least-learners, who defied any attempt of winning them over into cooperation, or even tried to violate the efforts of others; also Kilb & Weidner, 2013.

The German Basic Law starts with asserting "Human Dignity is Inviolable", for it is the experience of deserving respect simply for being human that lays the groundwork for having an independent life: there is no self-respect without the experience of being respected, there is no positive identity to function as natural anchor for building SE. Without it, SE cannot develop, compensatory and supplementary traits take its place: entitlement, resignation, stiffling enduring instead of activating resilience.
If somebody f.ex., has less SE than she needs for satisfying her identity about status or consumption she can compensate this lack through a sense of entitlement. Instead of fully using her learning potential according with the however low or high SE, this asymmetric entitlement may keep her from learning, thus staying below her potential and in turn preventing her SE to increase. In the case of high SE, entitlement works as a supplement, and increase aspiration and learning ambition.
Resilience, in turn, can work both ways: supplementing the perseverance aspect of SE, resilience would increase SE for the process of enduring hardship and adversity, and enable restarts from longer and more severe draw-backs. It could also compensate or substitute SE, and thereby prevent its development by helping to endure negative circumstance without believing to be able to escape them by one´s own virtue. In these cases, the necessary prerequisite for building SE is missing: the locus of control.

In social science, psychology and philosophy different aspects of identity and identity building are researched. The common ground is that individuals and groups have their own general identity as well as partial and overlapping ones: individual, gender, national, cultural etc. Identity is the result of a process of self-identification in which a person or group associate themselves with specific characteristics in contrast to or association with others that do not or do share the same ones. Identity and a positive transition of identities throught a lifetime are important for mental health and social functioning. Identity endangering occurrences are major external shocks causing severe reactions of denial, submission, flight or fight comparable to Eibl-Eibesfeldt´s earlier discussed identification of human/mammal reaction patterns to danger. Positive identity transition is vital for modernization and its underlying learning processes on the part of the individual in her different functions and hierarchical status as well as her reference groups. Individual and group identity come under pressure when new information emerges, and the old identity is not sufficiently in tune with the new data. Every human being undergoes conflicts when passing though the different stages of life: when the old child identity does not fit the adolescent, or the adolescent does not fit the adult life requirements, transition from young to old person, single to parent etc. Most cultures have developed rituals of some kind for these transitions to help cushion the destabilizing effect, and offer some kind of mold for the new identity, clearly defined do´s and don´ts, roles and behaviours to take up, even ways to dress.

Modernization is destabilizing as I argued above, but even more so when people are forced - unprepared and unsupported - from traditional into modern life in the case of migration, flight and foreign/top-down-installed modernization. Huntington´s conclusion to better discourage modernization altogether is neither sustainable nor ethical. Equally, economic modernization is neither, unless it is carried out by self-efficacious agents who shape it in their very own form: support in identity transition has to accompany it for people to redefine their place in a changing world, to not be left behind in fear, anger or resignation, but to embrace and develop their potential to keep pace with her changing surrounding. Promoting SE thus takes out the notion of paternalism or imperialism as it does not present a ready-made program, but supports people to come up with their own. That is respectful, empathetic and pragmatic.

Anselm Strauss (1959), in his essay on "Transformation of Identity" describes stages of natural transformation during an individual´s lifetime, those caused by external shock, by group demands to fitting into differing roles, and those caused as an unexpected and possibly unwanted result from decisions made about something else, like migrating to a better life and finding out that your identity does not fit your new role. He does not answer the disputed question to which extent people´s core identity actually does change or whether changes after adolescence are merely variations around that core, but treats the observed problems as "revealed" identity conflicts. He describes f.ex. the conflict of people who feel betrayed by their group or group-induced role when it does not hold up to the test of reality, which though first written in 1959, sounds prophetical for the late 20th century follow-up generations of migrants who cannot keep their family conformity duties while trying to find a new positive identity in their new home countries and develop the respective SE for it. Equally problematic is the situation for those who do adapt their individual identity and risk to lose their group bond. Groups often provide for their members more structured passages of transformation, offering security in change but little room for individual variations and development. Steps and phases of change are susceptible for crisis. If the level of SE is not sufficient to counter "acute strain" of (group) conflict and change, the protagonist may "(abandon, bd) *the regular or institutionalized sequence of steps…and break away in desperation or with defiance, leaving their occupations, families, social classes, and other such organizing frameworks of commitment and loyalty.*" (p.77)

This describes the present, 2016, situation of well-established second-generation, middle-class immigrants who leave their well-paid jobs f.ex. in the UK to join a terrorist group in a far-away country they have never even lived in, speak the language or are used to the hygienic conditions, which may be an indicator for the long ignored pressures people suffered. Their personal utility calculation is higher for leaving everything and being able to keep their "inherited" parents′ identity than staying, learning and transitioning. Strauss decribes turning points of realizing the change of identity being related to feelings of "*surprise, shock, chagrin, anxiety, tension, bafflement, self-questioning.*"(p.67) Note that a major part of the process of change happens first nonconsciously in the psyche, and is then realized as a need to change consciously, putting practical questions of observable behaviour and relations under the stress of a new definition. It is then when the decision to go through with the change or to fight it off becomes a question of self-efficacy being strong enough to support it; if not, the "*sense of personal continuity*"(p.82) becomes an

"*imagined persistence*" deducted from symbolic acts (as the person has already started to change inside but adheres to the old identity for reasons of insecurity). This can result in unbearable stress for the individual caught in the middle between two sets of demands from family and (host) society, and personal wishes. Western societies have not developed support mechanisms to empower agentic identity transition but will have to, or spent the money saved on suppressing the consequences forcefully.
Shibutani (1962) states that it is not the whole surrounding of an individual or all the groups she belongs to that are important for identity building and potential for learning and behaviour change, but only her reference groups of "*significant others*" (p.138): those whose judgment is of identity-building relevance. This relevance is a result of bonding and the reason why we can have different cultural systems side-by-side without reciprocal influencing for a long period of time: the roles, expectations, values, perspectives of one are not relevant for the respective other group. Reference groups are an important source of social control (p.128) and build the groundwork on which institutions have to function. Modernization and economic progress against major reference groups´ interest and profit seems difficult. Emancipatory and empowering policies to support individual learning via SE building, coopting major reference groups or limit group influence altogether are major policy aspects on the pathway to a learning society. It does, however, carry a great risk of destabilizing individuals and the social network.

4.7 Prerequisites of Learning

Learning requires moving from a stagnant stage of knowing to a time, energy and effort consuming process of change with uncertain results and benefits, and certain risks. This has to be sufficiently beneficial with regard to gains and costs, meaning: given endowment bias and risk aversion, the anticipated gains have to be over-proportionally higher than the anticipated costs. Expressing it in a physical image: It takes a lot more impulse energy to get the ball rolling again after it has lost its potential energy than to keep it going while it´s still rolling.

The individual needs self-efficacy for learning
- to develop a stable identity that is strong enough for transition and
- to develop a positive anticipation of the reaction to change of the members of her reference groups, or,
- in cases of negative reactions or unstable group bonding, have self-efficacy and actual possibility to enlarge or change her reference group.

Collectives need group-efficacy for learning and to have a leader or leading elite who have leadership efficacy for learning
- to foster stable group and leadership identity strong enough to not feel threatened by learning-induced changes;
- to allowing for new information entering the group and reaching the group members without knowing the effects;
- for tolerating or fostering learning and behaviour change of its members and non-members.

I regard all of the above necessary for the single most important prerequisite of learning: the acknowledgement of not-knowing without weak egos or greed having to fight Harari´s "Discovery of Ignorance". This is what I interpret as the actual reasoning of Hondrich´s suggestion that countries lead wars in order not to learn - for a short time, the aggression of war can cover up the pain and insescurities of having to learn.

Daniel McFadden (2001, his homepage) identifies that choice of behaviour is the result of an individual decision making process which aims to maximize utility based on one´s preferences and according to data from memory, information and situational constraints, similar to "statistical information processing"; in accordance with classsical economic theory, he assumes utility of outcomes to be predetermined and stable. McFadden shows how past experience creates the base of memorized knowledge on which to build the perceptions and beliefs including self-efficacy, and preferences which then under the given constraints of individual life produce a certain choice of behaviour.

In the following, I have adapted McFadden´s suggested scheme to include feedback loops and interconnectedness of preferences and variable utilities of outcomes that flow into the information feed for the next period and are influenced by information from the last period (including through worldwide marketing expenses multiplied via the worldwide web, social media and personalized advertising algorithms).

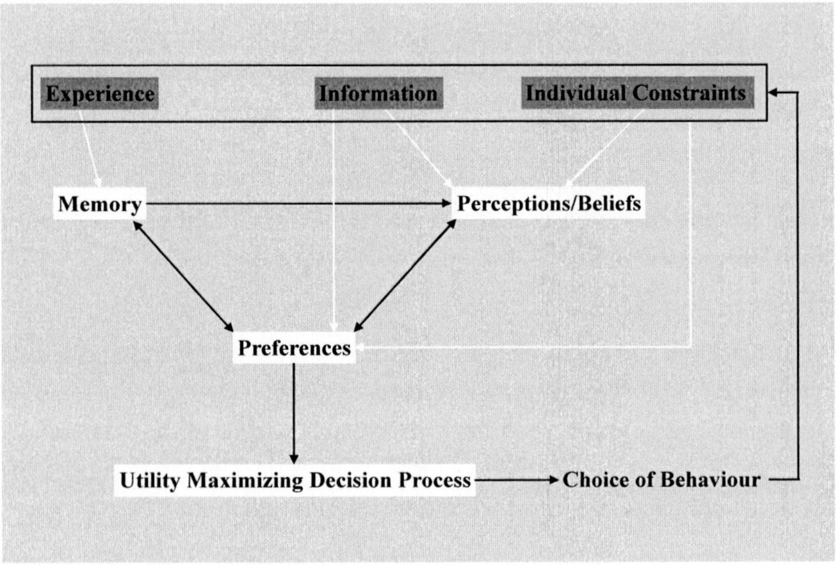

Drosten (2018) based on McFadden (2001)

In contrast to Gary Becker and classic theory, I assume preferences more realistically not to be fix or predetermined, and stable only up to a point, reflecting their probable link to people´s identity which changes throughout a life time. There has been debate over the classic assumptions as a multi-billion dollar advertising, marketing and lobbying industry seems to suggest otherwise. It still needs to be examined if the noted - and by those industries targeted – diversifications of preferences are mere variations rather than originary changes of preference. Neurosciences find that our memories are continuously reshaped ; my chart therefore shows feedback loops that influence this reshaping of memory, perceptions, preferences, utility and the external information flow in the next period.

"Hero in War but a Coward in Peace"[92]

4. 8 Negative Ways of Learning

Martin Meredith (2005/2011) in his book on Africa since independence, describes the path several African countries and explicitly, the new African leaders have taken since the 1960s. Titling "The Great Plunderer", he decribes the former president of Kongo/Zaire as perfect example of all three ways of negative learning. Mobutu developed from a quite effective modernizer in the 1960s to a worldwide symbol of African despotism and corruption, assumingly having looted over U.S. $ 5 bn from his impoverished country´s natural assets and foreign investors. Within short, Mobutu started to copy King Leopold, "*an ambitious, greedy and devious monarch*" (p.94) who treated the country as "*his personal property*" in his "*lust for territory and wealth*" which he seeked to satisfy with a system of brutal subjugation, and with international approval, obtained "after much manoeuvring" in 1885. After starting out with an economic modernization program in 1965, Mobutu quickly employed what he seems to have wrongly learned from his colonial teacher about rule: a mix of cooptation, nepotism, bribe and brutality to exploit and stabilize a country in despair, and play the international community. While Leopold´s rule had not lastet, Mobutu held on to his recipe when the economic and social situation deteriorated dramatically and international support plummeted. Having once learned a wrong lesson on power, he despised to learn new information and adapt to changing conditions that his wrong- and non-

[92] Lyrics from: Malaya, 1998, Rock in the Tide.

learning had created, with only short glimpses of compromise through pathological learning when things had become so bad as to have no choice, like in 1976 when he had to reopen the country to foreign investors, too late and with little success[93]. Mobuto is just one, though glaring example of someone exhibiting all forms of negative learning which lead to collaps, paid for, usual when socializing of costs is possible, by others much more than by himself.

Wrong-Learning

Learning for the pleasure of self-enhancement is a luxury of fully secured living conditions. Most people live in conditions where learning has to be part of their survival strategy. Most lessons are learned under some kind of social strain, risk of unknown consequences, uncertainty of eventually required identity adaptation, and group conflict. Imagine a foreign aid worker to suggest changing centuries-old cultivation traditions: The old woman who as the first and only one in her village changes her methods while all other farmers decline his advise, takes onto herself a number of risks by denying group-loyality and conformity: others may treat her as a traitor, if she succeeds she may reap envy, if she fails she may reap gloating and loss of solidaric help. She has no way to decice up front which of the information is right: that of the foreigner or that of villagers. People will normally decide on right or wrong by experience and how much the informant is trusted. This makes new information coming from outside a group less trusted and is also true for learning false or manipulated information, interpreting things wrongly, making mistakes in the application. As we usually learn from our surrounding reference group, wrong-learning may put us in conflict with our reference group, either when we learn the wrong information or when we want or need to "unlearn" it unlike the others.

---

[93] Meredith, p.300; pp.293-308 describe all three ways of Mobutu´s negative learning.

Studies show that believing in "fake news" increases group cohesion the bigger and more absurd the lies. This has to do with the "cost", i.e. the effort and distance to others that are bigger the bigger the lie. Equally, the sunk-cost logic of leaving behind a bad investment, makes it difficult for people to give up wrong "knowledge"

Wrong information is double difficult to "unlearn" or cover up with yet new information as it carries the burden of a doube not-knowing: One has to admit to not have known in the first place to learn whatever, and then, to admit to have made a mistake in learning the wrong thing. If the new "wrong" has already led to behaviour change and reaped publicly observable action it is a triple incentive to hold on to the "wrong".
It is important here who evaluates what is wrong and what is right: if it is someone from outside of one´s reference groups, one may rather fight them off and hold on to the "wrong" despite of any information suggesting otherwise. If the evaluator is part of the group, holding on to a non-conforming belief may cause group retaliation in different degrees of severity, up to the point of expulsion.

Coming back from wrong-learning takes more effort, more strength, more support, and ever more so the longer and deeper the wrong-learning had been internalized, and the more actual behaviour was involved, than it takes to support initial learning. When the wrong-learning and possible wrong-doing has happened in concert with others from the same reference group, the effects are rooted yet deeper. Experiences of rehabilitation of people who fell prey to religious, political, criminal groups demonstrate the concentrated essence of a painful modernizing process[94]: inner and outer structure may get lost or shaken up. Modernizing is al-

---

[94] Drug addicts, or girls suffering from anorexia f.ex., seem more endangered to suffer from relapse, possibly because of the social aspect of their addiction. When people feel alienated from their surrounding majority, they often form strong bonds amongst other addicts. Rehabilitation and getting "clean" mean losing their peers. Similar effects may apply to veterans or migrants; common convictions (and deads) and habits separate them from their new surrounding, when new learning is passed by.

ways a difficult, insecurity causing endeavour; but when the past can be honored as having been good and right at its time, it can be left behind as just outdated. In this case, one can still keep most inner and outer structure-giving factors, especially one´s beliefs and constructs. But when the modernizing process happens or should happen after the past is identified as wrong in the sense of undeserving respect, all structures, inside and outside of a person, come under stress. One may identify with the undeserving old, and cling to it for misinterpreted loyalty and lack of self-efficacy in one´s learning and modernizing abilities.

If learning has to be grounded on a perceived need to separate oneself from a reference group that suffered a moral wrong, possibly by the only available new reference group, the conflict becomes dilemma as the normal loosening of structures in modernization cannot be counterbalanced by new structure-giving bonds. African Americans having to decide for the identity of the former slave owners, less developed countries ahving to decide for the identity of their old colonial powers, the State of Israel having to trust an international order to provide for their security after six million of their fellows were murdered in the presence of that order with little help or protest, are extreme examples of identity, loyality and learning conflicts. Problems with second-generation immigrants may entail some of these aspects[95].

All of above the factors of identity and utility foster persevearance in a distructive way. By all we know to this point of the effects of self-efficacy on all the factors listed here and discussed below, I suggest that the most effective single policy are self-efficacy building measures. The

[95] Cmp. Geiger (2015), Warum Ärzte und Ingenieure in den Dschihad ziehen (why doctors and engineers go to jihad, bd); by the title "The Roots of Radicalization. It´s Identity, Stupid" Shiraz Maher (2015) asks: *"What links a white Englishman from Buckinghamshire with a second-generation British-Asian man born in Dewsbury and a missing family of 12 from Bradford?"*, and with regard to their common journey to jihad answers: *"...strip away all the grievances and myriad individual triggers that might drive an individual to join an extremist group and you find underlying issues of identity and belonging."*

Saudi Arabian government has designed a program for the rehabilitation of Al Qaida fighters that seems to build exactly on these principles; long-term effects remain to be seen.

"Many of history's worst authoritarians started out as losers" Elizabeth Warren (2016)

Pathological Learning

Given the ego costs of learning, one may chose to avoid voluntary or pro-active learning, and reconsider the known and acknowledge the new with some kind of learning process only if forced so by circumstance. The pathological learner is one who will react only to the stick of failure, not to the carrot of incentives. It is a costly behaviour as it causes time loss in adaptation, wastes resources in inefficient set-ups, alienates modernizing elements and thereby loses out for a future even long after he himself may have given in to learning and the "normative power of facts". The pathological learner is whom Hondrich described in his remarks in "Lehrmeister Krieg" (transl: "War, the Great Teacher", bd) as needing the utmost pressure or suffering to move position.

With regard to countries, pathological learning is a typical case of group and leadership efficacy being too low for the usually falsely high sense of entitlement to power, privilege and profits to expect to still be satisfied under modernizing conditions. And it is also an example how easily low and weak self-efficacy can be destroyed and instrumentalized by negative rhetoric: when in times of change parts of a population are haunted by the insecurity of not being able to cope with the anticipated future, these fears can easily be mobilized by an elite or populist leader who fears the same and in their favour. Holding on to a status quo or often successful attempts of reconstruction are examples of this phenomenon. Monarchs, clergy, nobility, all ranks that enjoy profits on the grounds of status rather than merit suffer the same pressure to avoid modernization unless they find ways to modernize their function in their society too. Constitutional monarchies have found a compromise and could possibly be an example for the pragmatic incorporation and cooptation of formerly anti-modern groups on the way to modernization.

"When the Gods wish to punish us,
they answer our prayers"
Oscar Wilde (1895)

Non-Learning

Non-learning does not refer to who cannot learn or to limited personal capacities. This whole work assumes that the potential results of people´s learning efforts will differ in quality and quantity for natural differences and circumstance. But I assume that learning as an evolutionary behaviour is part of human nature, and having the chance to do so as important and satisfying for individuals and their social collectives. But there are individuals and groups who will neither learn, nor change nor adapt in toto or with regard to aspects of their life that offer privilege unrelated to merit. These non-learners insist on and cling to a given status quo, usually because they profit from it with regard to power, social status, financial profit, unjustified greater rights. Their fate is to go down with the ship they built if they succeed to fight all learning pressures from social or natural environment.

Non-learners find ways to externalize the costs for their not-learning to either other members of their group or to outsiders if individuals do not stop them or if institutions do not hinder them. War is the most dramatic way of externalizing costs of non-learning as Hondrich noticed, every shout-out in human interaction being its miniature version.

This behaviour is not limited to a ruling class or leader, it could be a whole gender, race, religion, political movement which at some point in history provided their members profits from undeserved - based on merit - inequality and thereby prompting incentives for non-learning.

In a natural environment, this rigidity, even if it was only being too slow to keep the pace, would be punished by long-term extinction of that trait. Humans though have been able to gain some independence from natural laws. While outside of the human race, reciprocal limitation governs the space everyone can occupy, humans have found ways to fight being limited or determined by others and thereby rid themselves of evolutionary pressures to learn and adapt to environmental and other exogenous pressures.

In the short term and until the negative effects of stagnation fall back unto its originators, this behaviour poses more of an immediate risk for others than for the non-learners themselves. The non-learner has a vital interest in keeping others from learning and modernizing as otherwise the pressure to also start learning would rise. Non-learners will tend to gather others like themselves, justify this behaviour, defending it by creating feelings of supremacy and superior tradition, inventing stories of loyalty, denouncing learners as traitors to the common cause, nation, team, village, religion. Because the causation for the unwillingness to learn and change lies in the fear to not be able to gain, keep or regain the privileged position on behalf of one´s own virtue and merit of work, it is actually a lack of self-efficacy in occupations connected with knowledge or ability that has to be substituted with a some kind of Weberian charisma or talent to succeed in a hierarchy. This changes the algorithm for chosing leaders from competence to pretence: to who can win over an audience instead of solving problems and organizing constructive measures.

At the core of this phenomenon is an asymmetry between self-efficacy and the sense of entitlement. I assume that leadership self-efficacy may have a crowding-out effect on a leader´s other domain-specific efficacies, and possibly even on those of the people around him: a great leader may actually discourage learning by his mere example of being great by pretense, offering an easy way how to get a lot without being able to do a lot.[96] This crowding-out effect is an important field for future research as it may be a complicating factor in integration efforts in migration, and in cooptation efforts of "old" elites in modernization.

[96] An example could be found in American "gangsta idols", rap musicians who often have a criminal record and are still, with their demonstrated riches, popular role models for adolescents, which Obama has deplored as especially African American youths lacking idols of lawyers, doctors, scientists, or architects.

5. Questions around Self-Efficacy

5.1 Asymmetries

Beliefs about oneself, actual abilities and capability for future potential do not always correctly coincide, and may lead to too much or too little confidence and effort. But does it also lead to too much or too little SE beliefs? Overconfidence f.ex. can lead to inappropriately adapted behaviour and has been found to cause distortions in decision making[97]. Too much SE would mean someone´s trust in her abilities to act successfully in a certain situation was higher than her actual skills. As SE opposite to confidence, does not refer to an aspired result of action but to the process of action itself, the asymmetry between belief and ability leads to greater exercise of effort to compensate for the lack of competence. This increased effort could then enhance the outcome of a process and/or increase competence through learning. People with high SE have been found to blame their failure not to circumstance or somebody else, but to their own failure to employ enough effort (Bandura, pp.83ff). If a process turns out to overstretch someone´s abilities, she would tend to blame it on her lack of effort and thereafter, try to do more and thereby learn, increase her abilities, and in a self-fulfilling prophecy learn to have what it takes to do better next time. Should this not be possible or still lead to a negative result, the respective SE would undergo a corrective movement downwards, like addressing an asymmetry between supply and demand for a certain good via the price mechanism in a functioning market. If the remedy of more effort still does not help, SE beliefs will be lowered and aspired goals recalibrated to produce success on the next occasion. Too much SE is possible, but only for a short period of time to then either produce higher competency or effort or realistically downsized. Too little SE is much more difficult to tackle as its self-enforcing mechanism leads to avoidance of exactly those mastery experiences that could enhance it.

[97] Cmp. Dunning-Kruger-Effect; overconfidence thas been linked to outcome over-optimism, representativeness, framing etc.

People with low SE tend to shy away from challenge, set lower goals, give up earlier, invest less. Without external support from a third party who provides for verbal encouragement, vicarious or own mastery experience, or situations that stimulate affective arousal, low self-efficacy is usually persistent.

SE for processes that produce an aspired result is a prerequisite for a political and economic system that links profit to merit. If people lack a sufficient sense of SE to receive what they desire, they may still develop a sense of entitlement to these gratifications. At all times groups of people have invented common myths to justify their entitlement to more rewards than their merits would have earned them, based on religion, color, race, gender, lineage, nation and else. In modern times, advertisement and marketing have inflated a social problem by creating consumption wishes that the economic situation of many does not support. It is the same economic situation that at the same times undermines SE beliefs in growing parts of the population through increased competition, rationalization, unemployment, precarious jobs, uncertainty through time contracts. Having low or weak SE and high sense of entitlement is a socially dangerous product often enough of modernization as technology spreads information on the possibilities of consumption long before the economic base for acquiring them is build. Interesting in this context is the American dream that for generations propagated that great personal effort was able to get everyone what they desired. This promise of merit is not being kept anymore as social vertical transperence has decreased with the reconstructive tendencies of the late 1970s. The new idols are now still very rich and demonstrating it, but ascended to (short-term) fame and riches not by merit and effort, but as rappers, fraudster and trash tv celebrities. The effect on average SE can be expected to be detrimental, and in conjungtion with asymmetrically high entitlement socially dangerous.

Resilience at the other end of the social disturbances scale, is often regarded as part of SE. I do not agree: persistence is an integral part of SE and leads to longer and more effort investment. The ability to spring back after failure - which is the definition of resilience – is not an indispensable part of SE, as a person with high efficacy can ascribe her failure to not having tried hard enough or to factors so out of her control that it does not touch upon her SE belief. That having been said, people with high and possibly general SE often do feature resilience as well. I ascribe this to their belief to be able to cope, which gives them a more optimistic outlook on future endeavours even if things went badly wrong. People with low efficacy beliefs usually have neither a great portion of persistence in effort nor resilience as the ability to spring back after drawbacks, but suffer from an unfortunate endurance in adversity without the impetus to go about changing it, producing the opposite effects of SE. The learning and adaptation effect of experience is important for SE beliefs to be realistic in a given situation for a given activity. It is therefore vital that resilience after failure is not dominant to keep someone from reevaluating her efficacy beliefs. I regard resilience as an independent trait that can and often does appear in concert and adapted strength with self-efficacy to possibly make an extra strong or extra stubborn agent.

5.2 Proxies

I have argued that SE develops naturally according to the evolutionary pressures and responsiveness of one´s environment, and that by creating self-enforcing feedback loops, SE is important for a country´s economic performance and social, political and institutional organization and modernization. Through several described behavioural effects SE fosters economic success, cooperation, risk taking, effort, opportunity recognition, political participation, human empowerment, emancipation, and other normative outcomes. But not every individual can, needs or wants to undertake the efforts to develop high and generalized levels of SE. In these cases, individuals profit from proxies that mimic or substitute individual and even group SE, but can come at a high price for both individual and society if tipping points are ignored.

Remember that high SE means that an individual believes in her abilities to - under the necessary material conditions - execute her activities well and successfully. By believing to be able to satify her existential needs she is able to ease her existential fears. Institutions can compensate for a lack of individual SE through relieving the individual from having to develop agentic abilities in and by herself. Defined rules, regulations, norms, common myths to believe in, roles to fit into, enable agentic behaviour by following instructions, rules and patterns, without the otherwise necessary SE. If an individual is in a de-individualized position with de-personalized responsibilities that endow her through office, hierarchy, position, title, position, uniform or other symbols of status with authority, she can follow a set of rules and procedures of how to act; she neither has to develop great capabilities nor much SE: her symbols are about fulfilling tasks, not mastering processes! People can take on efficacious roles of *representing* a "self-efficacious" authority.

A similar effect can be observed in cases of having money or position that was *not* generated in the comfort of self-efficacy-reaping merit and trusted ability. Having gained through circumstance a lot of money or a favourable job position enables people to play the role of success and abilities; it opens access to social status, opportunities and privilege, and enables the individual to get what they want and again, feel safer from existential threads. The problem is that this was not attained by own work and genius, but rather through factors that do not lie in the control of the privileged individual: one can only exert control over one´s own effort and work (disregarding questions of health here), but not over factors that lie in the discretion of others. Consequently, one can only claim responsibility and take credit for factors within one´s own control both of which is necessary to develop the respective self-efficacy beliefs. The lurking risk of losing it all without believing in one´s ability to regain it (through factors within one´s control: work and effort), will dictate reconstructing or adhering behaviours, like attempts to exert some kind of force or manipulation for preserving or securing the status quo – behaviours that can be observed in some societal and economic elites as well as criminal clans. Incidently, the same rational of perceived security goes for people with small amounts money, influence, and skills. If someone has low SE beliefs about his capability to keep or regain what he once attained, they will feel threatened by change just as those on the other end of the social hierarchy – which explains the unfortunate coalition of these two seemingly antagonistic groups in times of change, and the possibilty to employ populistic preying on these fears for manipulation– and why it is first and foremost the merit-based middle class that carries the burden and potential of stabilizing a liberal-democratic system.

Reputation if not based on merit but on self-marketing, works in the same way as money or institutional self-levitation. The individual steps into a position, follows the norms and expectations of conduct or attire to reap power, profit and privilege by virtue of the role she is filling in. This gives her all she needs to perform as if she had the competence and respective SE as her position and appearance can cover up her deficiencies.

SE proxies include benefits and dangers, which have to be considered carefully to avoid unintended effects and be able to tackle problems because of knowing why they arise. On the upside, proxies are an important factor in explaining why the process of modernization can continue over generations in an accumulative way without having to start from scratch with every new-born baby. The next generation can partially just step into efficacious roles even if their own up-bringing did not lead to the development of SE in strength or area as needed in their life and surrounding. This incidently also explains why individuals f.ex. in migration, integrate much easier into a new surrounding then a whole group of people, for which such a "common role" does not exist; they have to develop their individual *and* group SE anewly if their efficacy beliefs that developed in completely different environments turn out to be maladapted and outdated under new conditions. SE proxies can stabilize societies and modernization processes in societies with a general high level of SE; they can be cost efficient by reducing collective costs for individual learning and are a short-cut to profits – but only up to a tipping point! Proxy effects counterproductively dampen evolutionary pressures on individual

SE and thus the average level of SE in a society, which eventually causes an overall decrease of SE; some individuals stay weaker in a state of low SE and dependent on their crutch-like proxies.
Over time, this has two negative effects:
- it deepens the segregation between those with high SE and growing numbers of those with lower SE fostering income and wealth inequalities;
- without intervention, this process continues until a tipping point of affluence, high culture and social cohesion is by-passed, when the number of individuals with lower-than-average SE reaches a critical value and total SE in that society falls below the point necessary to keep up the level of economic performance and democratic functioning.

Interestingly, the opposite can happen where proxies are used by an exploitive low-SE elite: when general SE in that society grows through development measures and global internet information streams, it can reach the tipping point when general SE or that of a large enough number of people exceeds that of the low SE elite.
In the first scenario, reaching the tipping point of too little SE in too many people in a society can lead to economic and cultural downturn of a society, while in the second case, reaching the tipping point of enough people raising their SE above that of their low SE elite will lead to the downfall of that elite for having lost their falsly claimed competitive edge and justification for their position.

Lack of SE causes several undesired behaviours: Individuals feel the insecurity of low self-efficacy with negative consequences as described herein: less opportunity recognition, risk taking, effort investment, less trust and cooperation, and in general less adaptability to circumstance and change. Proxies do not raise SE, they just enable low-SE people to lead a life as if they had more of it. Profiteers of proxies tend to overstress the compensational instruments and cling to the status quo; groups suffer from change-fearing individuals who despise novelty with different degrees of intolerance, aggression and emphasizing status quo preserving mechanisms – often these are the individuals who aim for leadership positions in groups with faulty leadership algorithms: chosing a leader for his ability to win the position instead of being able to do fulfill the tasks. The anti-modernization effect clearly undermines the well-being of a society and economy, and it threatens the political and institutional framework as it fosters populism, intolerance, isolationism, xenophobia and racism (to fight off potential competion) or aggressive expansionism for the same reasons.

By cushioning or compensating evolutionary pressures, proxies distort evolutionary signals and lift the incentives to develop SE from the individual. Modern societies have used competitive sports and other high-performance pressures – like competitive school admissions, early-age educational paths commitment - to set-off this dooming effect that may have added to the downfall of former societies and empires. But these artificially created "evolutionary" pressures do not reach all members of society alike and are not well-adapted to the totally different needs of fostering SE in migrants or poorer residents; they may therefore add to societal segregation, keeping some strong and some weak.

5.3 Fostering Self-Efficacy

The concept of purposefully boosting self-efficacy has been extensively studied and tested in many fields of human behaviour in psychology, pedagogy, education, sports, and medicine. The mechanisms of targeted intervention are well understood as is how SE beliefs can be injured and weakened, namely by verbal devaluation, devaluating treatment from others, and de-engaging individuals from making mastery experiences. Raising children without destroying their natural SE is probably the most cost efficient way of increasing a population´s general SE level.

Policies to reinforce financial, industrial, infrastructure, political, educational and social measures, potentially build SE implicitly as they may lead to jobs, a more valuable and appreciated surrounding, and efficacy building experiences. The efficiency and effectiveness of conservative economic measures will in turn profit from more self-efficacious people in the economy to receive them and put them to use.

Explicit measures aim for empowerment of those people who must carry out or tolerate (from the latin tolerare, meaning to be able to endure!) the actual modernization process, and best at young age. Though it can be developed at any point throughout a lifetime, SE works like a self-fulfilling prophecy and thus builds up over time from observed and one´s own success experiences and growing abilties that in turn reap more success. It simply accumulates and reaps more results if it starts early, and when all possible life paths to choose from are still open.

Müller, Sievert, & Klingholz (2016)[98] show what can go wrong when well-intended policies do not observe SE as a limiting condition. The authors identify what seems counterintuitive at first glance: the high educational status of the young population in the MENA (Middle East/ North Africa) region as causing political and social unrest, high migration pressures, and very little economic growth, when for a long time education and higher education were propagated as the first instrument of choice for catch-up economic development and societal modernization. Stéphane Hessel (2011, p.205ff, 235ff) had prophesied just that when he criticized that the educational systems of former French colonies were formed exactly after the French haute ecôle system instead of according to the needs of developing countries. Müller et al. find high degrees of formal education without much practical abilitiy, little culture of (or self-efficacy for, bd) entrepreneurship to offer employment opportunities, little inclination for self-employment (SE), and due to the lagging economy little financial clearance for state financed government jobs. Also, they attribute the small number of well-educated women in official employment and the high rate of reproduction as a result thereof as further factors of deterioration. The message is clearly, that education by itself does not create jobs and economic growth, but education that conveys skills and

[98] See also here chpt. 2.4, p.41.

self-efficacy to take initiative, identify opportunities, taking risks, overcome difficulties, and to tolerate – female - competition could.

Supportive programmes should mimic the conditions of how SE develops naturally in an environment that rewards effort and investment, hard enough to be challenging, and responsive enough for the challenges to be overcome by effort and persistence:
- Create mastery experiences: f.ex. offer trainees a goal to reach or task to fulfill which takes effort, persistence, planning, possibly resilience after failures, so that a positive experience from affording these features is made. The learning effect should be that effort, openness to new experiences/methods/ideas, overcoming frustration, cooperation, exercising persistence, and possibly resilience reap profit, success and, very importantly, personal emotional gratification.
- Enable trainees to observe role models and peers master a difficult and ambitious activity: training could be carried out by people from the community who were trained by experts separately and beforehand, so that the target group experiences one of their own ranks to be the expert teacher to have a deeper vicarious experience.
- Keeping in mind that SE is easier destroyed than build-up, everybody involved should exercise positive verbal enforcement and encouragement, rather than critique as teaching method; verbal persuasion, lectures or videos are best followed directly by a mastery experience for it to be of long-lasting effect, building robust SE.
- Physiological arousal can foster or harm SE. Situations that cause stress or anxiety lower efficacy beliefs while positive emotions like excitement or joy increase it; in both cases does emotion make the belief more robust! Design lectures, videos, trainings and exercises such that participants a) experience positive emotions for the conveyed content and b) can imagine themselves positively in similar situations.
- Overtraining should be avoided: there is suggestive evidence (chpt. 6) that formal training from foreign experts can have a tipping point, when participants at first profit from formal training by developing higher levels of SE; this may drop again and make way to a feeling of dependency

and inability if participants keep on coming back for ever more training. In the Ghana study, we saw such cases occurring after the 3rd training course; if the sheer number of completed courses caused this, the experience of never ending inferiority to foreign experts or other factors, needs further investigation.
Current research shows that SE fostering interventions can bring individuals in contact with the "right" role models, i.e. successful, content, fulfilled persons who are similar to the respective individual. Once SE is increased, success breeds success. As individuals update their SE when they achieve an ambitious goal, and when they observe role models or peers to be successful the social multiplier effect sets in so that they themselves become role models for others.

5.4 Self-Efficacy is Not Genetic

From an evolutionary standpoint, human behaviour has to be able to adapt in pace with natural changes in the environment or with exchanging one´s environment (not at the speed of a jet plane, but on foot). To assume the presence of certain genes could by itself determine something as complex as human traits is undercomplex; attempts of scientifically linking one to the other is prone for misinterpretation as I will show on a popular example below. Evolutionary biologists find indicators that strongly suggest human behaviour to depend predominantly on circumstantial/environmental limiting factors, with a genetic predisposition and epigenetic triggers, and the ratios of which to vary in every instance.[99] Many twin studies, which have traditionally been used to try and differentiate between nature and nurtue, genes and environment, exhibit

[99] cmp. f.ex. research by Max-Planck-Institute, Ploen; on cooperation see fn 73. Discussion-worthy examples of twin studies to simplify causation by omitting or simple correlating: on criminal or aggressive behaviour the famous study of Mednick, Gabrielli, and Hutchings (1984), on self-efficacy: Waaktal et al. (2013). The study by Mednick et al. correlates f.ex. criminal behaviour of the adopted son to his biological father thus being genetic, without checking for alternative factors like the role of f.ex. trauma of being separated from him.

methodological problems like omitting potential, but often unobservable influences or flawed statistics.

The story of the dopamine receptor gene variant DRD4 (D4 indicating the suppressing of dopamine) and its imputed effects on human traits may serve as a negative example of how genetic findings can get misinterpreted even in renowned journals (Williams, 2014), and with regard to human behaviour; the interpretations of genetic conditions for SE as for intelligence are equally sensitive as they suggest a fateful genetic determination, unchangeable by policies and prone for false categorizing, including racism. It is very important to note that

- the influence of hereditary factors change when environmental factors change (only the rate of variation in the population stays fix),
- the present state of genetic research and knowledge does not allow for any science-based conclusions,
- the *malleable* effects of epigenetics on the expression of genes are thought to be greater and more likely to influence traits than the mere existence of certain gene alleles
- possibly most influential could be the conditions of mother and child during pregnancy (and in the case of girls: during the pregnancy of the mother´s mother) on what we call character or traits; this research is only starting now to detect f.ex. effects on hormones and brain metabolism over three generations of women through smoking, hunger or war trauma.

Several study results that claim genetic causality for intelligence could not be repeated; Chabris et al. (2012) find that "Most Reported Genetic Associations with General Intelligence Are Probably False Positives", some were proven wrong or found much more complex both of which I will show below with regard to DPR4, which was alleged to cause SE.

Intelligence for example - without discussing the important question what it is and how it can be tested - has been found to be determined in children by 20 to 45% genetic influence depending on age and study (Chabris et al., 2012), the remainder depending on synapsis building (Neisser et al.

1996) which in turn depends on nutrition of mother and child during pregnancy and after, and emotional and intellectual stimuli pre and post partum. This is the reason why socially deprived children in North America exhibit considerably lower scores in IQ tests (Brooks-Gunn et al., 1996). Taking into account that poor families have a higher incidence of nutritional deficencies, substance abuse and socio-economic stress, it is realistic to assume that these conditions influence epigenetic triggers for brains to become less sensitive to environmental information. The Flint-effect explains that environmental feedback loops have caused an 15% increase in IQ in Western populations over the past 50 years. Whatever link between genes and intelligence may exist, it is apparently neither decisive nor unchangeable.

Analogue, the linking of self-efficacy to a certain genetic polymorphism is not purposeful. Human traits must be changeable and influenceable in the short-term to enable quick adaptation to uncontrollable change in environment and circumstance; this is an important factor for the survival and success of the human species.

Several studies have nevertheless argued that entrepreneurial behaviour – as vital for economic growth - can be linked to novelty seeking which was then thought to be genetically conditioned and inherited (Galor & Michalopoulos, 2012; on genetic inheritance of self-efficacy Waaktal & Torgersen, 2013). It was assumed that the genetic polymorphism DRD4 was correlated to novelty seeking (Benjamin et al. 1996; Ebstein et al. 1996). Extensive research could not verify this. In a comparative study between different populations, different incidences of this specific polymorphism - in the American (high) versus Asian (low) - Chen et al., 1999 could not sufficiently link them with any specific effect. While Chen did find higher frequencies (specifically of DRD4-7R) of certain genetic make-ups in nomadic in comparison to sedentary populations (implying the former to be more novelty seeking than the latter group of humans), other studies tried to link novelty seeking to exploratory and excitable brains more ascribed to another gene (the DRD4 48bp VNTR), which again could not be verified. The only presently assumed association between novelty seeking and one specific polymorphism of a certain gene - -52 1C/T – could not be sufficiently connected to its implications for human behaviour. In several meta-analyses (Faraone et al., 2001; Munafò et al., 2008; Wu et al., 2012), the link between novelty seeking and these genes was found to have been a mislead interpretation. Interestingly, later research on DPR4-7R showed that the incidence of this gene in children can lead to two completely contrary behaviours depending on the social conditions: either prone for hyperactivity, substance abuse, and other social dysfunctions, or extraordinary levels of empathy and positive social behaviour[100], which is another indicator that the mere incidence of a gene does not necessarily determine a specific effect, least behaviour.

Finding it would have carried the danger of falsely regarding it as a historically determined genetic heritage and fate, unchangeable by policy measures and supporting modern revivals of ascribing differences in economic development to – constructed - genetic differences analogue to discussions on intelligence: self-efficacy is shown here to have developed in response to natural conditions and these were different on continents, in climate and geographic zones. For example, those groups of humans who stayed on in Africa where they knew how to survive had little pressure to develop new methods for survival, while those who left for Asia and Europe had to constantly adapt to new existential challenges. What this created over thousands of years was the experience of having to cope and being able to do so in new, often harsh and changing circumstances, while often finding more responsive environments with greater need and rewards for human intervention and planning as colder, harsher conditions or more fertile soils were encountered. The result was self-efficacy to act and influence one´s environment.

---

[100] The explanation is highly exitable brains are more sensitive to environmental information: Belsky & Pluess (2009) on brain plasticity. On the same note argue Marinus von Ijzendoorn, Tom Boyce, and Bruce Ellis.

Entrepreneurship is in any case much more than novelty seeking. Though it does take interest and openness for novelty to be a successful entrepreneur, it also takes less adventurous, but pragmatic and complex qualities like planning, persistence, high frustration tolerance, hard work, learning, cooperation, decision making, initiative, opportunity seeking and recognizing. Complex human behaviour like entrepreneureship can be assumed to be the result of interaction and feedback loops of genetic disposition, epigenetic triggers, education, example, and personal and environmental circumstance (Chakraborty et al., 2015). Merely the disposition for a brain´s reactiveness to certain stimuli in its complex electro-chemical interaction can be linked to genes. If and how this disposition translates into actual complex human, including entrepreneurial, behaviour or can be altered throughout a life-time depends on opportunities, experiences, rewards and restrictions of personal life conditions. In general, the level of sensitivity of brain metabolism does not differentiate between the triggers that cause chemical rewards in the brain: substance abuse, aggression kicks, entrepreneurial risk taking or novelty in any shape or form can set off similar chemical rewarding effects in the brain. The question if more or less dopamine sensitive brains cause people to act more entrepreneurial, or more aggressive-kicks seeking, or self-indulgently hedonistic. If an environment neither requests nor rewards a certain behaviour it will usually not persist or spread (except of those odd cases where a special feature developed as useful in certain conditions and was not given up as useless after these conditions changed when it was not harmful). Regularly, only what is needed and pays off the effort will be repeated in acts of individual and collective learning, and respective genetic changes passed on and spread if the gained advantage is also one in reproduction. Phenomena like the absence of wide-spread entrepreneurial traits within the ranks of 19th century nobility as suggested by Galor & Michalopoulos (2012) could for example not be explained except by environmental triggers: especially the existence of wealth inheritance and status-quo conservative culture made entrepreneurial behaviour neither necessary nor desirable, and left the system of rewards for hard, risky and environmentally adapted entrepreneurial work to those who needed it. More so, noble life style would have been supportive for building a sense of entitlement, not SE for entrepreneurship.

The generational correlation Wuepper & Drosten (2015, 2016) identify in Ghana, was one of merely better reproductive success of those who developed higher SE through better livelihood (cmp.f.ex. also Chakraborty et al., 2015). And this effect works two-fold: People with higher SE will likely be more affluent and thereby healthier, making for more attractive reproductive partners. Their better livelihood can be expected to raise more and healthier offspring. This effect of increased reproduction of people with higher SE causes more children to grow up under more promoting conditions with individual and possibly collective cultural learning in a community of more adults with greater SE. Children learn from their parents and other important adults to form their self-images not only by conscious association through speech, education, stories, but also unconsciously and thereby highly resistant to change as a meme , by habituation and sensitivation (Kandel, 2006). As parenting has been found to have a significant influence (Bandura, 1993; Whitbeck et al. link socioeconomic conditions to parent behaviour and children´s SE) another line of generational influence via greater SE may also positively influence the development of entrepreneurial traits: parents tend to actively teach their children to follow their survival strategies, and pass on especially their entrepreneurial knowledge which tends to accumulate over generations (Chakraborty, 2015). Note that it is difficult to differentiate between actual technical knowledge that constitutes an exclusive advantage, and the accumulated SE of generations: we can do this, we have been experts on this for generations. The grandson of a medical doctor whose father was also a doctor, choses the profession not by virtue of having learned specific skills over the supper table but because he had the vicarious mastery experience by which he deduces his self-image with respective SE. With regard to entrepreneurial skills, I argue the bequest is the self-efficacious belief: if they can do it, I too can succeed in business, rather than exact technical skills, which outdate too quickly anyways. By the same token, a sense of entitlement passed on by generations of pro-

fessionals of any trade as well as a higher level of resilience of generations who were able to cope well in their environment, in summary, traits of an empowered person well-prepared for successful economic behaviour in her habitat, can be expected to be culturally bequest but biologically made possible through family bonds and enhanced by epigenetic triggers of neurotransmitter driven arousal.
Building on the work of Douglas North (1993)[101] and Stuart Kauffman (1993) on the origin of order in evolution, development and human society, Hodgson & Knudsen (2006), and Pelikan (2013) suggest a combined model of instruction-based genetic and social operations for evolutionary and developmental processes. In comparison to insufficient, racialistically exploytable exclusive genetic explanations, it offers the incorporation of human traits like SE which facilitate adaptive and innovative advantages.

Here, a basic genetic hard-wiring in conjunction with environ-mental triggers and stimuli constitute individually limiting factors of potential which will be optimized by social, i.e. institutional, software. The models provide for emerging self-organization and including individual-instruction-group dynamisms. Richerson et al. (2010), and Richer-son & Boyd (2005) suggest genetic-cultural coevolution of cooperation, which describes a very likely process of self-domestication. Their excellent world-wide data implicitly show outcomes of SE resulting from the process described herein. SE fosters cooperation and self-referential responsibilities instead of cooperation-undermining scape-goating. In the absence of specific genes for cooperation or other changed genes, we presently have to assume that the apparent differences in behavioural preferences amongst societies are cultural and possibly epigenetic, enlarged or weakened by institutional effects.

---

[101] North defines institutions as "*humanly devised rules-constraints, such as formal law and informal social norms*", offering insecurity-reducing definitions and limitation of choice, p. 4; citation from: Pelikan (2003) on institutions and evolution.

5.5 Empirical Testing of Self-Efficacy

Empirical research entails the difficulty of knowing that the found cause of action is actually self-efficacy, and how to distinguish the gathered information from related concepts. One needs to avoid "noise", concentrate on asking for processes instead of outcomes, be aware of the ordinary interviewer traps of influencing the interviewees even ever so subtle, and delimit SE in the data which I am describing below:

Compare SE to the Big Bang and it causing today´s cosmic background radiation: we cannot measure it directly but we can measure its short- and long-term effects. I suggest that we can measure the effect of SE, but testing it directly through self-evaluation seems prone for "noise": the mere interview setting obscures possible answers on top of people themselves confounding self-efficacy with other self-evaluations. In asking directly for SE, it is impossible to delimit the answers from influences produced through the interview context. In their 2016 and 2015 WPs, Wuepper & Drosten treated a range of questions that reveal several related, but not identical constructs. According to our theoretical considerations, it is self-efficacy that has a significant effect on the economic success of individuals, because it increases the motivation to act by increasing the belief in one´s ability to act appropriately. Consistent with this expectation, we found questions that measure self-efficacy have the suggested, significant effect on economic outcomes via changing people's investment behaviour including learning, effort, openness to novelty, opportunity perception etc

The revealing pattern we detect is that process-oriented questions identify self-efficacy, whereas result-oriented questions do not.

Questions on:

- whether nature provides what the farmer needs or if it is the task of the farmer to make nature productive;
- most important income determinants, i.e. whether external factors were named (e.g. weather), or internal factors like learning (while controlling

for peoples' observable environment like weather, training, market prices etc)
- how far ahead the farmer plans (periods ranging from one day to the lifetime of his children)

as well as the principal components of the above three (to reduce the measurement error), measure self-efficacy well.

It is important for the individual to believe to be able to do what is necessary to reach a certain goal, which is interestingly enough not much related to peoples' external context but relies on the goal-achieving process about which the individual feels confident. Every question for SE must therefore solely refer to the process and the personal role in the process, and avoid concerning the goal or circumstance.

Simple rephrasing can shift the focus from the process to the result. We found that questions only slightly differently worded did not find SE.

Asking questions on whether:
- the farmer´s current income had been mostly determined by his decisions and abilities or rather not (focus: current income=result, not ability to invest or manage properly);
- the farmer felt to "make his life" or whether "life happens to him" (focus: life responsibility=result, not ability to take on responsibility);
- the farmer feels responsible for the success of his farm or whether the success was mostly determined by factors he could not influence (focus: measured success=result, not responsibly acting to manage or work well)
- the basis of economic success is hard work and creativity or rather connections and/or luck (focus: economic result of hard work/creativity etc, not the ability to work hard/be creative etc.)

do NOT measure self-efficacy!

These latter answers may contain implicit information on agency and locus of control. Further research must be aware about what aspect of the economic process the wording of a question is aiming at as much as the suggestive identity of the one asking. Skin color, gender, age and personality of the interviewer as well as cirumstance and location of the interview affect the self-evaluation of the interviewee. Current quantitative studies of culture (e.g. the World Value Survey), in their current wording, are unlikely to capture SE precisely. Asking directly for self-assessment of SE is commonly used, but likely to measure self-confidence, and self-image biased by the relationship between interviewer and interviewee, and include aspects alien to SE.

In the statistical analysis on the effect of SE amongst pineapple smallholders in Ghana, a specific instrumental variable (historic farming systems) was used to find out, if the empirically observed correlations between SE and household income had a causal link. One looks for a variable that generates exogenous variation (changes caused by non-controllable influences) of the endogenous variable (here: SE). In other words, the variable is used to predict what the variation in the endogenous variable (SE) would be, if it was not endogenous. This approach, however, works only if an important assumption is valid: The variable used as exogenous predictor can only affect the outcome of interest through the endogenous variable and not otherwise. If there are any additional causal channels, this will cause omitted variable bias, because some of the other effects will be attributed to the endogenous variable itself. The researched southern part of the country was traditionally host to different crops that yielded distinct returns on investment, thereby fostering differently high and strong SE beliefs regarding agricultural investments. We had to make sure that the observed correlation between historical farming systems and SE were not caused by other causal channels like inherited wealth, bigger farms, family size, higher profits etc.. Econometrical testing against a wide range of possible other influences finds a statistical relationship only between the historical farming systems and SE but not between the historical farming systems and other productive assets or circumstances. For other fields of study, self-efficacy scales (Luszcynska, Scholz, & Schwarzer, 2005; Luszcynska, Gutiérrez-Doña, & Schwarzer, 2005; Chesnay et al., 2010) have been developed and widely tested. It is possibly a helpful tool for testing questions around individual SE keeping above limitations in mind. It must be noted though, that Bandura himself has been very critical of these scales as a one-size-fits-all mistake which by definition cannot measure self-efficacy as *"a differentiated set of self-beliefs linked to distinct realms of functioning"* (Bandura 1997, p.36). Additionally, these scales work with self-evaluations the limitation of which has been stated above. If one choses to work with them, the questions must carefully concern a process only, not the outcome, and the wording must target capability: like "can do", not intention: "will do". The potential to deter the results in using scales is so plentiful that Bandura (2005) wrote up a guide of probably practical use prohibiting complexity.

6. Pineapple Farmers in Ghana: Historically Evolved Investment Self-Efficacy and Current Economic Outcomes[102]

To empirically research the evolution of self-efficacy and its correlation to economic outcomes, pineapple smallholders in Southern Ghana were surveyed, and extensive current and historical data analyzed for an arrey of factors influencing farm investment and household income. Ghana is presently an especially suitable country for this kind of research. Her pineapple farmers are right on the interface between traditional and modern agriculture (Conley & Udry, 2010), exhibiting trajectories of development and cultural change. On the one hand, farmers have the financial incentives to grow high quality pineapple for export to the European market, on the other hand, many structures are still rather adapted to subsistence farming than global value chain participation.
As in most parts of Africa, intensification of agriculture is a major policy challenge for Ghana (Government of Ghana, 2010; World Bank, 2011). It is not well understood, why farmers are not investing more into making their operations more productive. Explanations include dynamic learning processes (Conley & Udry, 2010), tenure rights (Udry, 2011), and uninsured risks (Karlan et al., 2012), all of which, however, are unlikely to fully explain it (Udry & Anagol, 2006; Foster & Rosenzweig, 2010).

We investigate investment and income differences amongst smallholder pineapple farmers in Ghana, and find that farmers in regions that historically depended on cereals invest significantly more, and thus achieve significantly higher incomes than farmers in regions that historically depended on other crops, such as roots, tubers, or tree crops. We argue that cultural evolution explains this finding. Cultural Evolution Theory suggests that a lot of important information gets largely unquestioned verti-

---

[102] This chapter is based on a WP reflecting the field work and econometric analysis conducted by David Wuepper in Ghana in 2013; Wuepper & Drosten (2016)

cally transmitted from parents to children, which generally improves decision making but which can also make individuals better adapted to past than to current contexts. We consider the culturally transmitted belief in one´s ability to make profitable investments decisions and carry them out successfully. This so called Perceived Investment Self-Efficacy (Bandura 2012) is reinforcing, because individuals with high SE (PISE here abbr. SE) tend to set themselves ambitious goals, invest a lot of effort, and persist in doing so, even in the face of adversity. In case of failure or setbacks, high SE individuals tend to ascribe the causes to their own range of responsibility and hence, increase learning and effort instead of scapegoating them to uncontrollable factors or others. Individuals with low SE, in contrast, tend to regard their skills as insufficient to reach more ambitious goals, therefore setting themselves unam-bitious goals, invest low effort, blame external causes for arising problems, and give up more easily, which means their reluctance to try prevents their learning about their possibly true and greater potential.

We show that this belief has historical origins and a persistent large effect on investment behaviour and incomes. As a domain or activity specific belief about one´s own ability to carry out an activity or skill well, SE can reach a certain grade of generality in similar, domain overarching activities; it´s self-fulfilling prophecy effect will strengthen the initial SE beliefs. The perfectly rational homo economicus assumed in classic economic models has high SE: Whatever his initial beliefs might be (irrationally high or low SE), he quickly learns about the truth (Gilboa et al., 2012). Actual humans, however, start with culturally inherited and biased prior beliefs that affect what is subsequently learned (Guiso et al., 2010: Dalton et al., 2016; Wuepper et al., 2016). Irrationally high SE is commonly corrected in a Bayesian fashion – unless proxies take out the evolutionary correcting information and pressures (see chpt. 5.2). It is possible, however, to be "trapped" in a low SE equilibrium as described above, if low SE leads individuals to minimize risk, effort and ambitious goals (Bandura, 1997; Pajares, 2002; Bandura, 2012), thereby avoiding to be corrected, here: to receive encouraging signals about their skills and potential which could have raised their SE.

According to Bandura (1997), general SE affects preferences including time discounting, goal setting, risk taking, openness to novelty and thereby recognition of opportunities. It also affects capabilities by changing aspirations, effort, and persistence via motivating agency, and resilience, as failure and setbacks are interpreted as being surmountable via increasing effort. SE affects all intentional behaviour and thereby, agency.

Here, we research the effect of historically different investment experiences on the SE of currently living farmers in Ghana and how this in turn affects investment choices and income.
Low SE can reduce the expected profitability of investments because it reduces the amount of complementary investments, and increases the probability of premature resigning (Maddux, 1995; Bandura, 2012). Economists have just begun to appreciate the importance of subjective beliefs for economic outcomes (Greif, 1994; Hoff & Stiglitz, 2016; Wuepper & Sauer, 2016). Especially, the evolutionary roots of peoples' beliefs are not well understood yet. A partial discussion of this young literature is provided by Nunn (2012, 2014). Especially close to our research is the theoretical model of Doepke & Zilibotti (2014), which is an endogenous growth model that includes cultural evolution, where innovation is driven by the share of entrepreneurs in a society. Recent empirical studies include Talhelm et al. (2014), who present empirical evidence from China that historical dependency on rice and wheat created either more holistic or more individual thinking patterns, and Galor & Özak (2014), who argue that in addition to cultural evolution, also genetic evolution could have shaped cultural differences; they present empirical evidence that historical returns on investment shaped distinct rates of time preference.

In the following, we show that different historical farming systems and historical returns on investment shaped current SE, i.e. how much individuals believe in their ability to make the right investment decision given their skills, and to achieve the necessary performance to maximize the profit. As an example, a subsistence farmer pondering about whether or not to adopt fertilizer does not only evaluate whether fertilizer is generally profitable but he evaluates the perceived probability that it is profitable for him. The challenge is greater than it appears at first, because he needs to adjust other farming practices, and learn how much, when, and how to apply the fertilizer. The ability to deal with this disequilibrium has been coined adaptive capacity by Schultz (1975, 1980). Whether a farmer believes in his adaptive capacity can be understood as his Perceived Investment Self-Efficacy. In the case of Ghana, Wuepper, Zilverman, & Sauer (2017) analyzed if farming skills or SE where more decisive for the adaptive capacity of a cohort pineapple farmers and found that it was indeed self-efficacy that made the greater difference.

We take for granted that historically, everybody had low investment SE (Bandura 1997). The reason for this is that in early human history, humans were mostly adapting to their environment. In a process of reciprocal determinism, economic development and SE accelerated, but not equally distributed, neither across nor within countries. In the following, we show that an important factor that shaped the distinct cultural evolution for different communities could be the environmental feedback to human interventions. People learned how big their capacity was to purposefully intervene in their environment to make a better living of it and taught their children not only the techniques, but passed on this belief. We present a simple agent based model (ABM), which shows how historically individuals might have interacted with their environment. The ABM framework is optimal to simulate how this interaction may lead to feedbacks and emergent phenomena (Berger, 2001; Janssen, 2005; Farmer & Foley, 2009). Our model is general, but because we use empirical data from Ghana to test the model's predictions, we had Ghana in mind when we created it. In historical Ghana, some regions were most suitable to grow roots and tubers, other regions were more suitable to grow cereals, and other were optimal for trees. Important for our research, cereals are different from other crops, in that they historically requested comparatively more investments and rewarded them greatly

(Heisey & Mwangi, 1996; Rees et al., 2012; Galor & Özak, 2014). This is important because societies with low levels of general SE would only have invested in crops with very large benefit-to-cost-ratios and not persisted much against adversity. In our ABM, the historical farmers randomly differ in their initial propensity to invest into their fields. In some regions, the investing farmers gain an evolutionary advantage, whereas in others, the non-investing farmers are better off. Over time, the farmers learn which behaviour is better and converge to it. This creates two distinct development paths: In one region, farmers invest and benefit, learn that they have, and can increase with effort, the ability to raise their yields, and pass high SE on to their children. In the other region, farmers do not invest and thus never have the chance to learn about their ability to increase their yields –not even when the introduction of new crops and technology changes the return on agricultural investments, when globalization creates profitable export markets, nor when extension services and development agencies support agricultural intensification. It is an empirical question how fast individuals adapt their cultural beliefs to their context. With self-reinforcing beliefs such as trust in others (Guiso et al., 2008) or trust in one's competencies (Wuepper & Sauer 2016) this can be very slow or settle in slump.

In psychological literature, SE is developed as a function of one´s own mastery experiences (pursuing and reaching an ambitious goal), observed mastery experiences by social models (observing peers succeeding in an ambitious task), verbal persuasion (encouragement has to be followed by mastery experiences to be robust though), and physiological arousal (situations causing stress or anxiety lower efficacy beliefs while positive emotions like excitement or joy increase it). The first contribution of this research is the proposition of cultural evolution as an omitted, but important source of SE. This cultural endowment of SE is a fundamental building block of agency in all living people who targeted supporting measures should acknowledge. The second contribution is that we test our model's predictions with empirical data from smallholder farmers in

Ghana. We find that the descendants of cereal farmers have currently higher SE, invest more, and achieve higher incomes.

According to our model, evolutionary developed cultural differences between farmers are an important factor in explaining why some seem to have higher incentives and lower constraints (consistent with Schultz 1975's adaptive capacity). Our model predicts that these cultural differences will eventually disappear, while the pace will depend on market and institutional dynamics, but especially on implemented policies.

Other research that investigates how cultural evolution increases average adaptability to environmental demands and suggests why humans sometimes behave more adapted to their ancestors' environment than their own is extensively discussed in Henrich (2015), Bisin & Verdier (2010), Richerson & Boyd (2008), and Boyd & Richerson (1985). Other research on SE and farmer behaviour in Sub-Saharan Africa includes Gebrehiwot & van der Veen (2015), who investigate the relationship between SE and technology adoption amongst Ethiopian smallholder farmers. As a caveat, they ignore where SE differences come from and simply compare farmers with higher and lower self-reported SE, which makes it difficult to understand how much SE is a cognitive bias and how much it reflects unobserved, economic incentives and constraints. When Bernard et al. (2014) conducted their randomized control trial (RCT) in Ethopia, they found that increased SE increases investments. In Ghana, Wuepper & Sauer (2016) investigate the performance of contract farming and find that culturally inherited SE is an important factor, as well as social capital which is in turn increased by high SE (due to lower risk adversity).

In the following, we use agent based modelling to theoretically explore the cultural evolutionary origin of SE differences in response to historically distinct farming systems and environments (2). We then test the model's predictions using empirical data from 400 Ghanaian pineapple farmers; we also investigate whether higher SE actually leads to significantly higher incomes. We explain our empirical framework in section (3), and present our empirical results in section (4). We explore how plausible it is that we quantified the true causal effect of SE in section (5), and discuss and conclude the study on section (6). Our analysis shows that higher historical return on investment is associated with higher SE, and higher SE with more investments and higher income. We do not find any evidence against a causal interpretation of our findings.

We identify as a crucial aspect that farmers, who culturally inherited beliefs from low-return-on-investment environments, would benefit from policies that help them update their SE beliefs to their new context of a potentially high-return-on-investment environment, keeping in mind that raising SE is different from raising aspirations, confidence, or expectations, and it is complementary to mitigating other constraints (all of which will be discussed below).

6.1 A Simple Agent Based Model

We develop our idea in a simple agent based model (ABM) in Netlogo, adapted from Centola et al. (2000). ABM is an alternative to equation based modeling (EBM), such as presented by Bisin & Verdier (2001), or Doepke & Zilibotti (2014). The main difference between the two approaches is that ABM are programmed and simulated, while EBM are written and solved (Berger 2001, Janssen 2005, Farmer & Foley 2009). In many contexts, both approaches can be expected to give the same result, but ABM can have advantages when it comes to complex interactions and emergent phenomena. The basic argument is that historical environmental circumstances have favoured the development of SE in some regions and hampered it in others. In regions where agricultural investments had a higher benefit-to-cost ratio, individuals had more opportunities to learn about their abilities to benefit from agricultural investments than individuals in less rewarding regions.

Our model begins with a population of historical subsistence farmers who can choose between two competing survival strategies: They can either try to minimize costs and live of their natural endowments (endowment strategy), or they can try to increase production and invest in their fields (investment strategy). Initially, all farmers have low SE but there is variation at this low level, such that some farmers start with slightly higher SE than others, which makes them experiment a little more with investments.

If for those farmers who start out with higher SE investments pay off, their SE increases more, leading their investments in the next period to increase further. If the initial investment does not pay off, those with higher SE will ascribe the setback to their own insufficient effort and increase investment in the next period with a good chance of producing higher yield which increases their SE even more, while those with lower SE will ascribe it to their lack of ability or uncontrollable factors, and react with less investment and further decreasing SE. Those farmers who start out with low SE will chose to invest less in the first place. They exclusively choose the endowment strategy, without much consideration of investment opportunities. Their low SE tends to remain low as by avoiding the risk of failure they also forgo the chance to succeed in mastering challenges, which could increase and strengthen their SE.

The differences in strength and level of original SE result from individual factors like personality etc. and prior mastery experience. Farmers with success experiences have higher and robust SE whereas those without prior mastery experiences or family success stories only have lower, and with regard to positive change, weak SE (cmp. Bandura, 1997).

In our model, it is the environment that either rewards or punishes investments and thus determines whether the farmers develop higher or lower investment SE. Exogenous variables are costs and benefits of investing, probability of a random shock that negatively affects return on investment (risk probability), and its severity (risk impact). Furthermore, we include institutions as a second source of feedback in addition to natural environment. For simplicity, these institutions only affect the strength of environmental feedback, which thus may be weaker than before. We only present three exemplary cases for the cultural evolution of investment SE.

Below, the X-axis shows time, the Y-axis the frequency of high and low SE in the population.

Figure 1. The Evolution of SE (Context A)

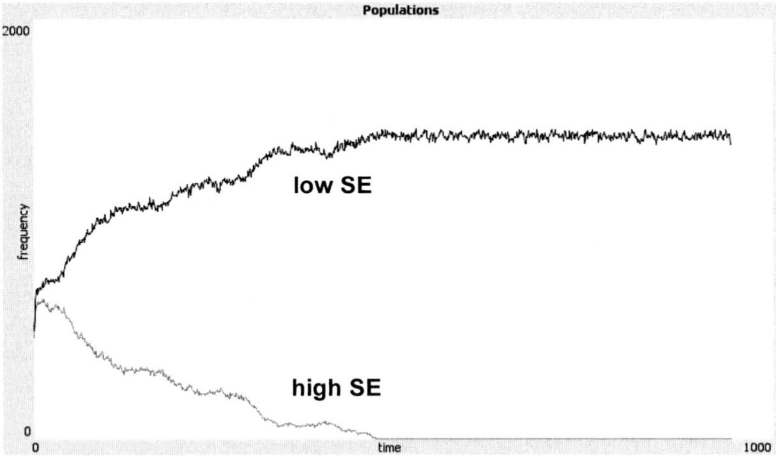

Cost=0.3 Benefit=0.4 Risk probability=0.1 Risk impact=0.5 Institutional persistence=0.5

Figure 2. The Evolution of SE (Context B)

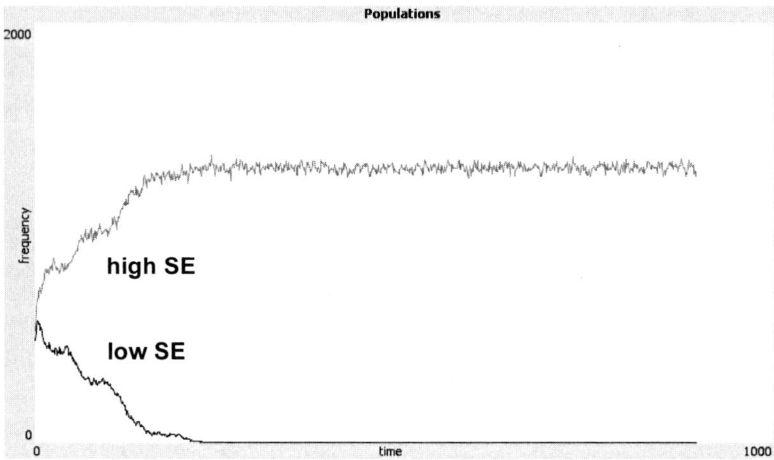

Cost=0.44 Benefit=0.66 Risk probability=0.2 Risk impact=0.4 Institutional persistence=0.2

Figure 3. The Evolution of SE (Context C)

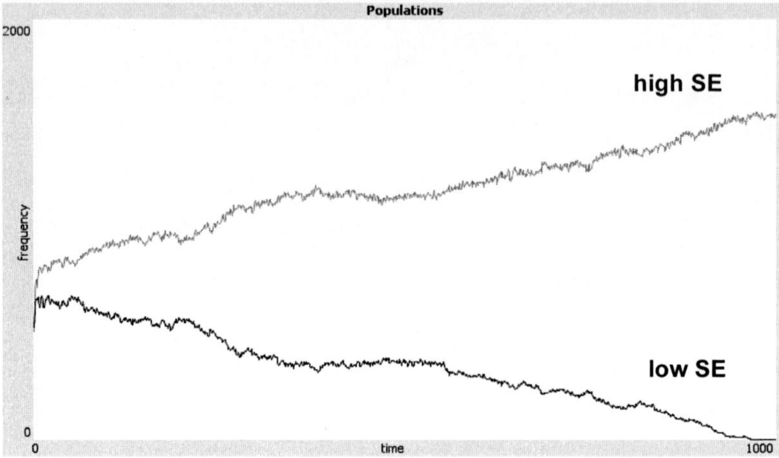

Cost=0.44 Benefit=0.66 Risk probability=0.2 Risk impact=0.4 Institutional persistence=0.8

The situation depicted in **figure 1** is an example for a region in which investments are not sufficiently beneficial for the farmers. Thus, over time, the number of farmers with higher SE dwindles, because their SE is not yet sufficiently high to sustain investments through repeated setbacks. In other words, investments in this region would require very high SE to be profitable. Another interpretation is that there are binding, external constraints that always make investments unprofitable, independent of SE. The important point is that this region has a return-on-investment that is low, so that over time, the population is comprised exclusively of low SE individuals.

In contrast, **figure 2** shows a region in which the return-on-investment is sufficiently large to lead the population into a high-SE equilibrium. Individuals with initially slightly higher propensity to invest demonstrate to their social peers that they all have the ability to benefit from investments. In time, more and more farmers invest, learn that they have the necessary competency to do so, and continuously build higher and stronger SE.

The influence of institutions can be seen in **figure 3**. By assumption, institutions can slow down the cultural evolution of SE, if they are such that environmental feedbacks are dampened. Figure 3 shows a region in which high SE develops but the process is slower than before, because institutional persistence limits the rate of cultural change. (Note that one could also think of institutions that compensate for low SE, which we ignore; see discussionon proxies, p.139f.).

In conclusion, the model makes 3 testable predictions:
H1: Farmers from high-return-on-investment regions have higher SE than farmers from other regions.
H2: Higher SE leads farmers to invest more.
H3: Distinct investment behaviours create culturally induced income differences.

The reason why historical environments affect current beliefs are learning costs. As discussed by Boyd et al. (2011) in general, and Nunn (2014) for economics, learning is usually costly, making it profitable for individuals to simply imitate others in those cases (free-ride on their knowledge). Thus, instead of "re-inventing the wheel", individuals might decide to copy existing ones, without necessarily understanding all the details, and without constant reappraisal of alternatives. Fundamental beliefs such as SE are therefore usually found to be highly hereditary (Bandura, 1997), but more culturally than genetically (Richerson & Boyd, 2008).

It should be noted that cultural learning saves learning costs but at the cost of risking that beliefs are outdated. Technological progress, environmental change, market developments, and migration are some of the factors that can make the knowledge of past generations ill-adapted to current circumstances. **Figures 1** and **2** show that despite the environment clearly favouring one mental model, for some periods both co-exist. With the introduction of institutional persistence, this can last for many periods.

Today, most contexts offer profitable investment opportunities but require SE to be used. It continues to be one of the most puzzling economic phenomena that farmers in developing countries are hesitant to adopt apparently profitable innovations (Feder et al., 1985; Foster & Rosenzweig, 2010). We propose a simple explanation: It takes time for culture to adapt to new opportunities. For farmers from high-return-on-investment environments this can be quick, but for others, it can take very long. Thus, in many contexts, we expect to find that investment differences amongst farmers can be explained with differences in culturally inherited SE and these differences have significant income implications. In the following, we test our three hypotheses with empirical data from Ghana's pineapple farmers.

6.2 Empirical Framework

We divide our empirical analysis into two parts. In the first part, we explore the relationship between SE and investments as well as SE and income. We begin with OLS regression and then use 2SLS to explore the causality of the estimated relationships. In the second part, we extensively investigate the reliability of our analysis.

We begin our analysis with a naïve comparison of farmers in different income categories, to see whether they differ in SE. To test the statistical significance of the observed relationship, we then proceed with OLS regressions of the form

(1) $$Y_{ij} = \alpha_j + \beta_1 SE_{ij} + \beta_2 X_{ij} + \varepsilon_{ij}$$

where Y_{ij} is the income of farmer i in district j; SE_{ij} are alternative measures of SE ; X_{ij} is a vector of control variables, and α_j are district fixed effects.

We also regress different measures of agricultural investments on SE and controls:

(2) $$I_{ij} = \alpha_j + \beta_1 SE_{ij} + \beta_2 X_{ij} + \varepsilon_{ij}$$

where I_{ij} are different investment measures (per hectare input costs, reported success of innovation adoption, adoption of technology); SE_{ij} is a

factor variable capturing the farmers' SE ; X_{ij} is a vector of control variables, and α_j are district fixed effects.
Using observational data, we are concerned whether measured SE is a culturally evolved cognitive bias (as in our ABM) or whether it reflects the objective constraints of the farmers (in which case measured SE would simply be a proxy for a range of unobserved variables).
We attempt to exogenize SE using a 2SLS framework:

$$\text{(3)} \quad \begin{aligned} Y_{ij} &= \alpha_j + \beta_1 \widehat{SE}_{ij} + \beta_2 X_{ij} + \varepsilon_{ij} \\ SE_{ij} &= \alpha_j + \beta_1 H_{ij} + \beta_2 X_{ij} + \varepsilon_{ij} \end{aligned}$$

where H_{ij} is our source of exogenous variation in SE_{ij} and Y_{ij} is the income of farmer i in district j. For H_{ij} we use whether the ancestors of our surveyed farmers were cereal farmers or not. The idea is that the descendants of cereal farmers have culturally inherited higher SE than others. As always, the exclusion restriction must hold, namely that historically different farming systems only affect current farm incomes through their effect on SE and subsequent investment behaviour, and not through any other channel. We extensively explore the plausibility of our assumptions in a separate section.

To conclude the first part of the empirical section, we use mediation analysis to estimate how much of the estimated income effect of SE is explained by differences in investment behaviour.
We proceed with several tests of our previous analysis. First, we repeat the 2SLS regression with alternative measures of SE, to compare and evaluate them. Then, we investigate what explains differences in SE, using another OLS regression:

$$\text{(4)} \quad SE_{ij} = \alpha_j + \beta_1 H_{ij} + \beta_2 X_{ij} + \varepsilon_{ij}$$

To probe the credibility of our instrumental variable, we graphically investigate whether the descendants of cereal farmers might simply have inherited more practical knowledge from their parents, so that human capital differences could be a confounding factor in our analyses. We then use OLS regressions to investigate whether regional suitability for cereals, roots, tubers, or tree crops leads to differences in inherited land or local market prices. This addresses the concern that descendants of cereal farmers inherited more land or live in regions with higher investment incentives.

Finally, we use 2SLS to explore whether our instrumental variable would also work for alternative causal channels, namely social capital, off-farm income, or contract farming:

$$\begin{aligned} Y_{ij} &= \alpha_j + \beta_1 A_{ij} + \beta_2 X_{ij} + \varepsilon_{ij} \\ A_{ij} &= \alpha_j + \beta_1 H_{ij} + \beta_2 X_{ij} + \varepsilon_{ij} \end{aligned} \quad (5)$$

where A_{ij} are alternative channels through which H_{ij} could affect income (farm-size, social capital, local prices).

It is clearly impossible to test every potential confounding variable. However, as Altonji et al. (2005) demonstrate, estimating the same effect despite of varying control variables should at least increase our confidence that other variables will plausibly not change the results either.

6.3 Empirical Analysis

We begin this section with a description of our sampling strategy and data. We then present the results of OLS regressions, followed by the results of 2 stages least squares regressions (2SLS), and finish with mediation analyses.

We representatively surveyed-400 pineapple farmers in the south of Ghana in 2013 (pineapple farming is only feasible in the south of Ghana as the north is too dry). If farmers want to participate in exporting of fresh pineapples to the European Union, they need to have an export certification, which guarantees that certain production and quality standards are met (Kleemann & Abdulai 2013). Such certifications can be obtained from specialized organizations and usually given to recorded farm groups; these certifications can be used for stratified random sampling.

Table 1. Variable Descriptions

SE	Factor variable from the variables below
nature	Whether the farmer perceives nature to be a provider versus a potential (1-4)
planning	How long the farmer usually plans (from only for today to lifetime of children)
investing	How much the farmer believes that her income is determined by her investments
ability	How much the farmer beliefs her income to be determined by her abilities
determinant	Whether farmers report income determinants that are under their control (3), outside of their control (1), or ambiguous (2), from an open ended question.
social capital	Factor variable from the reported frequency of social event attendance, generalized trust, and number of people the farmer could borrow money from
off-farm income	Whether the farmer has off-farm income (1/0)
education	No. of years of formal schooling completed
age	Age of the farmer in years
household	Number of household members
gender	Whether the farmer is male (=1) or female (=0)
training	Whether the farmer received training from an international development agency
amount training	How often the farmer received the above trainings
Investments	Whether the farmer has *successfully* adopted an innovation in the last years
costs	all production related costs, excluding the opportunity costs of family labor

revenues	Quantity of sold pineapples times their price, on the local market and to companies
rain q	Reported, farm specific rainfall quantity
rain t	Reported, farm specific rainfall timing
soils	Reported, farm specific soil problems, defined as how much soils limit productivity
elevation	Calculated in GIS, in meters
topography	Calculated in GIS, as standard deviation of the elevation in meters
farm size	Area where pineapple is grown in hectares, including plots not currently used
prices	Average, local pineapple price
md2 variety	Whether the modern MD2 variety is grown
sc variety	Whether the Smooth Cayenne variety is grown
contract farming	Whether the farmer has a formal farming contract with a processor
tenure security	Reported safety of the plots
company distance	Calculated in GIS, as distance between farms and nearest company, in km
capital distance	Calculated in GIS, as distance between farms and Accra, in km
advantage cereals	Calculated in GIS , whether the biogeography is comparatively best for growing cereals

We sampled as follows: We identified the major pineapple growing areas to obtain lists of groups of export-certified pineapple farmers from which some groups were randomly selected. Of each of these selected groups, we interviewed a number of farmers according to the size of their group. To also include non-certified farmers we asked extension agents and development agencies to identify a representative sample for interviews. These non-certified farmers were sometimes from the same communities as the certified farmers and sometimes from adjacent ones. The share of export-certified farmers in our sample is roughly 50%. It should be noted, that many certified farmers do not make use of their certification and sell their products at local markets instead, whereas some non-certified farmers do not sell there but rather to companies for non-export usage.

We present descriptive statistics about the farmers in table 3, but at first explain our variables (**table 1**) and especially, how we operationalize our SE measures (**tables 1** and **2**). In **table 1**, the upper panel shows our SE measures that focus on slightly different aspects of SE, and it will later be of interest to compare which are most relevant to the investment behaviour of the farmers and their subsequent income. For example, the variable "nature" captures how much a farmer perceives nature to be providing for her, in contrast to being a potential that must be actively used. A farmer with high investment SE would see nature as a potential. After a bad harvest, this farmer would increase her investments to increase it in the future. After a good harvest, she would increase her investment to further increase it (Bandura, 2012). Such a farmer would also have a longer planning horizon. First, because this gives her additional opportunities to achieve more ambitious goals, and secondly, because a farmer with higher SE feels the responsibility to perform well as a result of the perceived ability to perform well (Fernandez et al. 2015). How much the farmer beliefs that her income is impacted by her abilities and choices are very direct measures for a farmer's SE (Bandura 2012). In contrast to the previous questions, an alternative measurement strategy is to openly ask the farmers what determined their incomes in the last two years. This has the disadvantage, that answers must be coded into low, medium, and high SE by the researcher, which raises subjectivity concerns. However, it offers the important advantage that farmers do not get influenced by the researcher´s suggestions, but report what comes to their minds first. Furthermore, from the question, the farmers cannot interpret what the researcher is trying to find out; this helps to avoid associated biases. In table 2, we present a selection of typical answers and how they were coded.

Table 2. Categorization of Mentioned Income Determinants

Under Control (3)	Ambiguous (2)	Outside Control (1)
agricultural practices	training	rainfall
seriousness	productivity	prices
regular weeding	yields	costs
learning		disease

Notes: The table shows exemplary answers to the open question about main income determinants in the last two years. The answers were translated into an index according to whether the mentioned determinants were under the control of the farmer (1), out of control (3), or whether the answer was not clearly within either category (2).

The vast majority of answers were farming related and quite clearly either under the control of the farmers or outside. If an answer describes a variable that is a choice of the farmer (such as agricultural practices, increased knowledge, improved attitudes and behaviours), then the variable "determinant" (for reported income determinant) was coded as a 3 (high SE). If the answer describes a purely exogenous variable (bad rainfall, low prices, high costs, etc.), the variable "determinant" was coded as "1" (low SE); if the answer was ambiguous or intermediate, it was coded as "2". Examples for this last category are training (has the farmer chosen to participate in a training or does she attribute her low productivity to the fact that she is not provided with enough training), and yields (it is not clear which causes the farmer has in mind).

The main explanatory variable in the following analysis **(table 3)** is the factor variable SE, which reflects the commonality of all individual SE measures: "determinant", "nature", "planning", "investing", and "ability". We begin our analysis with descriptive statistics. As we argue that

SE is a kind of capital, we expect that farmers with higher income report higher SE. Other differences between income categories include the amount of training received from development organizations (positive), which pineapple varieties are grown (MD2 Smooth Cayenne being the most valuable), participation in contract farming, distance to the capital city (negative), off-farm income (positive), farm size (positive) and others. The observed differences amongst farmers make clear that we cannot naively compare farmers with different SE

Table 3. Comparing farmers in the lower, intermediate, and upper third of the farm-income range

income	low		medium		high	
statistic	mean	sd	mean	sd	mean	sd
SE	-.313	.940	.194	.832	.548	1.005
determinant	-.155	.961	.017	1.019	.454	.953
nature	-.238	.855	.087	1.051	.552	1.073
planning	-.268	.892	.156	.991	.551	1.057
investing	-.188	1.126	.159	.755	.296	.848
ability	-.157	1.102	.188	.778	.148	.950
social capital	-.004	1.017	-.030	1.087	.068	.761
off-farm income	.186	.390	.196	.399	.343	.478
education	2.641	1.205	2.663	1.103	2.955	1.307
age	44.698	11.987	43.975	9.330	43.761	9.055
household	5.842	2.766	5.819	2.571	6.432	3.129
training	.473	.500	.573	.496	.656	.478
amount training	1.363	.785	1.295	.849	1.298	.778
investment	3.24	2.71	4.09	2.50	5.02	1.93
costs	396.53	517.29	556.25	506.08	1200.6	984.2
revenue	380.59	351.44	1884.5	518.97	8280.6	5370.8

rain q	4.427	1.439	4.483	1.241	4.641	1.054
rain t	3.937	1.533	3.983	1.460	4.462	1.222
soils	1.674	.746	1.655	.820	1.567	.820
elevation	88.825	66.451	86.013	62.311	72.117	39.887
topography	45.811	42.636	40.541	38.004	33.729	17.619
farm size	2.971	3.756	3.389	4.277	7.731	8.246
prices	.431	.187	.373	.134	.404	.096
md2 variety	.200	.401	.368	.484	.552	.501
sc variety	.220	.415	.426	.496	.462	.502
contract farming	.349	.477	.344	.477	.641	.483
tenure security	5.322	1.237	5.765	.728	5.723	1.059
company distance	58615.14	35786.4	34021.4	30641.3	29376.5	31430
capital distance	65191.95	39899.9	40740.6	32765.1	37682.3	27895
advantage cereal	.23	.10	.32	.10	.32	.08

Notes: Variables in the upper panel are standardized (mean of zero and standard deviation of 1). The variables in the lower panel are unstandardized, except for social capital. In the analysis below, all variables are standardized.

Table 4 shows the estimates of 6 OLS regressions, in which we control for education, age, rainfall quantity and timing, elevation and topography, distance to the capital and gender (set 1). In table 5 we vary the control variables, but in table 4, we keep the control variables constant and vary our measure of SE. The included controls are clearly exogenous and theoretically important income determinants. Other variables such as participation in contract farming or which variety is grown, are also likely income determinants but plausibly endogenous to SE. We always control for district fixed effects (FE), and cluster the standard errors at the level of farm groups and communities. As table 4 shows, we regress income of farmers on various proxies for SE (specs 1 to 5), and on a factor variable from all of them (spec 6). Across the specifications, there is a statistically significant and positive relationship between SE and income. The clearest result is achieved when using the factor variable SE, which explains 5% more of the observed income variation than does the variable used in specification 5. A one standard deviation increase in SE is associated with a third of a standard deviation increase in income.

Table 4. OLS Results Income A

	(1)	(2)	(3)	(4)	(5)	(6)
model	ols	ols	ols	ols	ols	ols
dep.var	income	income	income	income	income	in-come
determinant	0.227*** (0.0735)					
nature		0.184** (0.0825)				
planning			0.216** (0.0990)			
investing				0.132*** (0.0407)		
ability					0.106* (0.0614)	
SE						286*** (0.0902)
controls	Set 1	Set 1	Set 1	Set 1	Set 1	Set1
district FE	yes	yes	yes	yes	yes	yes
R-sq	0.19	0.17	0.18	0.16	0.15	0.20
N	398	376	398	398	398	398

Notes: Table shows estimated coefficients and standard errors (in brackets). Standard errors are multi-dimensionally clustered at farmer groups and communities. Significance levels are 0.1 (*), 0.05 (**), and 0.01 (***).

Table 5 shows the results from regressing income on the factor variable SE and controlling for different potential confounding variables. To see how robust the relationship between SE and income actually is, we begin with no controls (spec.1), and add more and more controls from specification to specification. In specification 2, we use the same controls as in the previous table (for easy comparison), in specification 3, we also control for farm size and local prices, and in specification 4, we additionally control for the grown pineapple variety, participation in contract farming, tenure security, and off-farm income. Clearly, especially the last specification is at high risk of over-controlling. Nevertheless, the estimated statistical relationship between SE and income only varies between 0.27 and 0.23, mitigating our concerns about selection on unobservables (Altonji et al., 2005).

Table 5. OLS Results Income B

	(1)	(2)	(3)	(4)
model	ols	ols	ols	ols
dep.var	income	income	income	income
SE	0.269***	0.268***	0.231***	0.231***
	(0.0744)	(0.0825)	(0.0771)	(0.0698)
controls	none	Set 1	Set 2	Set 3
district FE	yes	yes	yes	yes
R-sq	0.17	0.20	0.27	0.29
N	398	398	398	398

Notes: Table shows estimated coefficients and standard errors (in brackets). Standard errors are multi-dimensionally clustered at farmer groups and communities. Significance levels are 0.1 (*), 0.05 (**), and 0.01 (***).

Table 6. OLS Results Investments

	(1)	(2)	(3)	(4)	(5)	(6)
model	ols	ols	ols	ols	ols	ols
dep.var.	invest-ment	invest-ment	costs/ area	costs/ area	fertili-zer	fertili-zer
SE	0.523***	0.481***	0.184***	0.199***	0.122***	0.125**
	(0.0837)	(0.0824)	(0.0347)	(0.0461)	(0.0448)	(0.0568)
training		0.110***		0.0957**		0.0356**
		(0.0380)		(0.0406)		(0.0178)
credit		0.109**		0.249***		0.0265
		(0.0428)		(0.0810)		(0.0396)
risk per-ception		0.185***		-0.0596**		0.00567
		(0.0413)		(0.0253)		(0.0343)
controls	set 1	set 1	set 1	set 1	set 1	set 1
district FE	yes	yes	yes	yes	yes	yes
R-sq	0.30	0.36	0.22	0.28	0.71	0.71
N	398	398	398	398	398	398

Notes: Table shows estimated coefficients and standard errors (in brackets). Standard errors are multi-dimensionally clustered at farmer groups and communities. Significance levels are 0.1 (*), 0.05 (**), and 0.01 (***).

So far, the empirical results are in line with our model; we have yet to show that it is investments that drive the income differences. In table 6 we regress three different measures for investments on SE and controls. We begin with whether a farmer has successfully adopted an innovation in the last years, with baseline controls (spec. 1) and also agricultural training, credit, and risk perception (spec. 2). We also tested risk attitudes, but these are insignificant when controlling for risk perception. It can be seen that SE is statistically significant and positively correlated with this first measure of investment. Our second measure is the expenditure per hectare of the farmers. An obvious difference between the first and second measure is that the first is discrete and the second continuous. Another difference is that the first is targeting innovations and the second is targeting general input intensity. As specification 3 and 4 of **table 6** show, there is a robust, positive, and significant relationship between SE and expenditure per area. To address concerns that our first two measures are relatively vague, we also analyze the discrete choice of using fertilizer or not (specifications 5 and 6). The results mirror the previous ones.

In our ABM we saw that historical returns-on-investment could be the historical source of current SE differences. In Ghana, historical environmental suitability to grow different crops could be a source of such differences. Data on the regional suitability to grow different kinds of crops is publicly available in FAO's GAEZ database (http://www.fao.org/nr/gaez/en/). In **figure 4,** we graphically depict the relationship between SE and the environmental suitability to grow cereals. As expected, it is positive.

Figure 4. Cereal Suitability and Perceived Investment Self-Efficacy

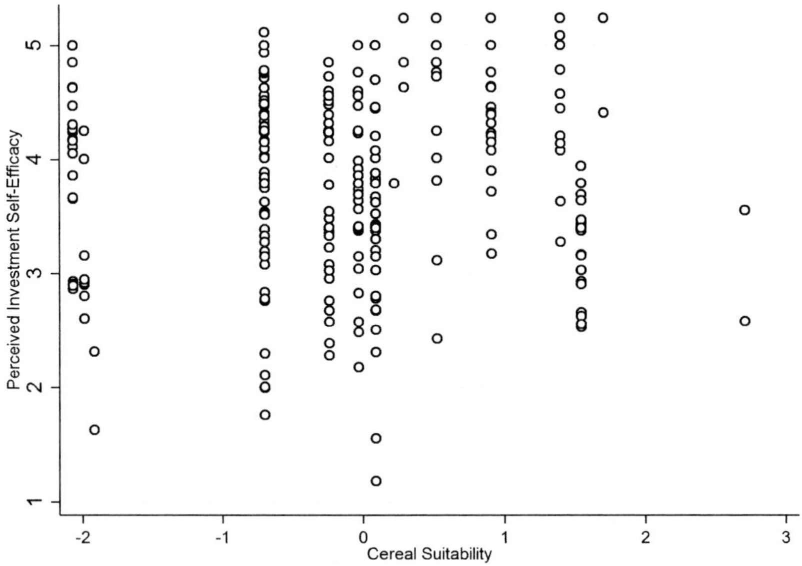

Most farmers in our sample have ancestors who relied on roots and tubers (few also have ancestors who relied on tree crops). The reason is that most of southern Ghana has a comparative advantage in growing roots and tubers. Along the coast of the Central Region, e.g., the farmer found good conditions to grow these crops, which have several advantages. Amongst others, they can be grown and harvested all year long, so they require less planning than other crops, and they are robust and flexible for mistakes and production constraints to be less severe. Their most prominent characteristic is their very low requirement for external inputs (Rees et al., 2012). Trees are similar. A very different kind of crop are cereals. Cereals are less robust and flexible, and require far more investments. On the other hand, they respond strongly to investments and their productivity can be greatly increased with the right agricultural practices at the right time (Heisey & Mwangi, 1996). The region in the south of Ghana that had a comparative advantage to grow cereals is located in the Savanna zone north of Accra. Even further north, biogeographic circumstances favored tree crops, the production of which is more similar to that of roots and tubers than to that of cereal crops. The explanation why such a historic variable can persist to affect current farmer behaviour is cultural evolution. The basic idea is that individuals can save learning costs by imitating their parents and peers. Even without understanding why, a farmer might behave well adapted in her environment if she chooses similar investment levels as others in her community have always done. This strategy, however, works better in environments that do not change too much, as past behaviour of one's ancestors has evolved to fit to their context and not to the current one. Thus, migration and technical change are two classic examples why cultural beliefs can become "outdated" (Richerson & Boyd 2008; Henrich 2015) and lose their heuristic value .

Below, we test how likely it is that historical suitability for cereals affects current income only through shaping the evolution of SE and not through other channels (section 5). In this section, we investigate whether SE retains its significant and positive relationship with income when we instrument it with a dummy variable, indicating whether it was optimal in a region to grow cereals. Whereas this variable is strongly correlated with the actual historical dependency to grow cereals, it avoids a historical selection bias (i.e. that farmers with already higher propensity to invest chose to grow cereals).

Table 7 shows the results of 2SLS estimation. In the first stage, a regional advantage to grow cereals is indicated to be a strong instrument for SE across all specifications 1 to 4. The F test for the excluded instrument is always above 20. In the second stage, the relationship between SE and income becomes even stronger than before. As before, specification 1 includes no controls except district fixed effects, whereas specification 2 includes plausibly exogenous controls, and specifications 3 and 4 also include increasingly endogenous controls. An increase in the estimated effect of SE between specifications 1 to 4 seems counterintuitive, but data suggest that this could be driven by trainings provided by development organizations. Farmers who receive several trainings might develop a feeling of incompetence and dependency; in the data they have lower SE than others. Taking a conservative stand, specification 2 seems most reliable, perhaps showing the true, causal effect. This would mean that a one standard deviation in our SE measure leads to almost half a standard deviation increase in income.

Table 7. 2SLS Results Income

	(1)	(2)	(3)	(4)
model	2sls	2sls	2sls	2sls
2ND STAGE	income	income	income	income
SE	0.397***	0.369*	0.796***	0.833**
	(0.126)	(0.210)	(0.303)	(0.347)
1ST STAGE	SE	SE	SE	SE
adv. Cereals	0.841***	0.619***	0.658***	0.593***
	(0.158)	(0.114)	(0.147)	(0.127)
controls	none	set 1	set 2	set 3
district FE	yes	yes	yes	yes
F excluded	28.38	29.64	20.10	21.67
N	398	398	398	398

Notes: Table shows estimated coefficients and standard errors (in brackets). Standard errors are multi-dimensionally clustered at farmer groups and communities. Significance levels are 0.1 (*), 0.05 (**), and 0.01 (***).

We conclude this section with a mediation analysis on how much of the income effect of SE is mediated by differences in investment behaviour (**table 8** and **9**). In specifications 1 and 2 of **table 8**, we use a dummy mediation variable for whether the farmers report to have successfully adopted an innovation recently. This mediates the investment SE effect by 21-24%; the mediation variable in specifications 3 and 4 is average costs of investments over the last 2 growing periods. This mediates between 32-36% of the investment SE effect. These figures are clearly below 100% but are consistent with SE theory, because much of the investment is unobserved as individual effort, working time and intensity, so we would not expect that our partial proxies mediate the full effect.

Table 8. Mediation Analysis for the SE Effect

spec.	(1)	(2)	(3)	(4)
model	mediation	mediation	mediation	mediation
dep.var.	income	income	income	income
SE	0.212*** (0.0567)	0.185*** (0.0632)	0.184*** (0.0478)	0.155*** (0.0533)
investments	0.116** (0.0540)	0.113** (0.0555)		
costs			0.370*** (0.0457)	0.376*** (0.0464)
ACME	.056***	.060***	.085***	.089***
Direct Effect	.211***	.185***	.183***	.155***
Total Effect	.267***	.246***	.268***	.245***
% of Tot Eff mediated	21%	24%	32%	36%
controls	none	Set 1	none	Set 1
district FE	yes	yes	yes	yes
R-sq	0.18	0.20	0.29	0.31
N	393	393	393	393

Notes: Table shows estimated coefficients and standard errors (in brackets). Standard errors are clustered at farmer groups. Significance levels are 0.1 (*), 0.05 (**), and 0.01 (***).

Table 9. Mediation Analysis Including the Effect of Risk

spec.	(1)	(2)	(3)	(4)
model	mediation	mediation	mediation	mediation
dep.var.	income	income	income	income
SE	0.225***	0.202***	0.175***	0.149**
	(0.0666)	(0.0729)	(0.0590)	(0.0641)
investment	0.117**	0.112*		
	(0.0569)	(0.0585)		
costs			0.379***	0.384***
			(0.0465)	(0.0472)
ACME	.048***	.050***	.098***	.104***
Direct Effect	.223***	.201***	.173***	.148***
Total Effect	.271***	.252***	.272***	.253***
% of Tot Eff mediated	18%	20%	36%	41%
controls	set 4	set 5	set 4	set 5
risk controls	yes	yes	yes	yes
district FE	yes	yes	yes	yes
R-sq	0.19	0.21	0.30	0.32
N	393	393	393	393

Notes: Table shows estimated coefficients; standard errors (in brackets) are clustered at farmer groups. Significance levels are 0.1 (*), 0.05 (**), and 0.01 (***).

For robustness check, we include measures of risk perception, attitudes and preferences in the mediation analysis (**table 9**). Results remain qualitatively the same with a few percentage points change between **tables 8** and **9**. Our empirical evidence does not reject any of our hypotheses. The data is consistent with our ABM, predicting that historical differences in return-on-investment caused differences in SE, which persist over generations, and help high SE farmers to be successful entrepreneurs, whereas low SE farmers would underinvest and achieve significantly lower incomes. As we are using observational data, we now probe the causal interpretation of our estimations.

6.4 Robustness Analysis and Falsification Tests

Figure 4 depicted a clear, positive relationship between our instrument variable: historical suitability to grow cereals in a given region and current farmers′ SE. This may simply reflect that descendants of cereal farmers learned practical farming skills from their ancestors, increasing profitability of their current investments. Cereals required more investments than other crops, and those with more bequest knowledge about how to invest, would be more likely to report high SE, invest more and better and achieve higher income.

Figure 5. Cereal Suitability and Source of Farming Know-How

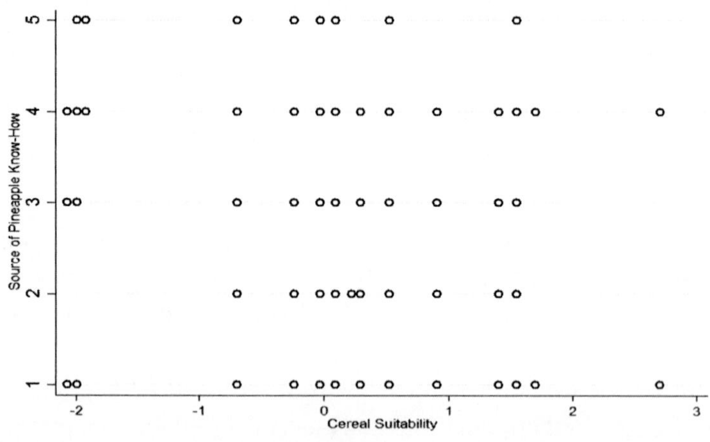

We cannot rule out this concern on theoretical grounds but this alternative explanation is not consistent with our data. **Figure 5** graphically depicts the empirical relationship between historical regional suitability to grow cereals and from whom the farmers report to have mostly learned how to grow pineapples. In figure 5, learning from family members is coded as 1, as a laborer as 2, from friends as 3, from extension service as 4, and learning by doing as 5. If descendants from cereal farmers would have learned more from their parents than others, then we should see a clear clustering of source 2 at the right of the figure. Instead, we see a clear absence of any correlation between cereal suitability and from whom the farmers have learned how to grow pineapples.

A second concern is that historic cereal farmers might have achieved a higher income, and their descendants would have simply inherited more capital than other farmers. On a theoretical basis, this is unlikely because if the cereal farmer really achieved higher incomes than other farmers, a Malthusian dynamic would rather have increased their family size than the wealth of individual offspring (Austin, 2005; Galor & Özak, 2014). It is not even clear that cereal farmers actually did achieve higher incomes before they started to grow pineapples, which is a rather recent phenomenon (Conley & Udry, 2010). Nevertheless, we can also test this concern empirically by regressing the farmers' land endowment (as a measure for their capital inheritance) and the local pineapple price (as a measure for the regional income level) on the regional suitability to grow cereals, roots and tubers (with tree crops as the omitted category).

Table 10 suggests that both the descendants of cereal farmers and the descendants of roots and tubers farmers have larger farms, which is apparent, because the descendants of tree farmers live in a rugged, mountainous region (Kwahu South), which explains their smaller farms. There is no significant difference in land endowment between the farmers in the lowlands (spec.1). Specification 2 of **table 10** shows that there is no significant difference between local pineapple prices and other crops. It thus seems rather unlikely that the descendants of cereal farmers differ significantly from other farmers in how much capital they inherited, except SE.

Table 10. Falsification Test A: Direct Effect of Crop Suitability

.	(1)	(2)
	OLS	OLS
dep.var.	land endowment	pineapple price
advantage cereals	0.142***	0.105
	(0.0349)	(0.189)
advantage tubers	0.110***	0.0471
	(0.0369)	(0.107)
controls	yes	yes
district FE	yes	yes
R-sq	0.13	0.92
N	398	398

Notes: Table shows estimated coefficients; standard errors (in brackets) are multi-dimensionally clustered at farmer groups and communities. Significance levels are 0.1 (*), 0.05 (**), and 0.01 (***).

Our final concern is correlation between cultural heritage from cereals and other outcomes than agricultural investments also correlating with income. One could hypothesize that different crops incentivized different degrees of cooperation leading to persistent differences in social capital; that descendants of cereal farmers are more likely to have access to off-farm income; or that they are simply lucky to live closer to pineapple processing companies providing lower transaction costs that increase participation rate in contract farming. In **table 11** we report the results of three 2SLS regression, where we substitute SE with social capital (spec 1), off-farm income (spec 2), and contract farming (spec 3), and explore whether we could use the historical regional advantage to grow cereals as an instrument. Note that the second stage only has meaning if the F test for the excluded instrument is sufficiently large (we would like to see a double digit value, at best larger than 12).

Table 11 shows that an advantage to grow cereals neither explains social capital differences, nor off-farm income, nor participation in contract farming (with F values of 0.1, 2.7, and 0.1, respectively). In conclusion, we are unable to find alternative causal mechanisms that could explain our findings.

Table 11. Falsification Test B: Instrumenting Confounding Variables

	(1) 2SLS	(2) 2SLS	(3) 2SLS
2ND STAGE	income	income	income
social capital	-15.08 (45.34)		
off-farm income		2.717** (1.332)	
contract farming			-27.85 (97.65)
1ST STAGE	social capital	off-farm income	contract farming
adv. cereals	-0.0417 (0.130)	0.231 (0.140)	-0.0226 (0.0797)
controls	set 1	set 1	set 1
district FE	yes	yes	yes
F excluded	0.10	2.74	0.08
N	398	398	398

Notes: Table shows estimated coefficients and standard errors (in brackets). Standard errors are multi-dimensionally clustered at farmer groups and communities. Significance levels are 0.1 (*), 0.05 (**), and 0.01 (***).

6.5 Discussion and Conclusion

Since the seminal work of Schumpeter (1934), economists see a strong link between entrepreneurship and economic development (Acemoglu 2009; Galor & Michalopoulos 2012). The important role of entrepreneurs is the recognition and exploitation of economic opportunities, which others either do not see or do not dare to take on. Why some individuals are more innovative than others is not fully understood yet, despite intense research efforts (Feder et al., 1985; Foster & Rosenzweig, 2010). More general than only the discrete choice to adopt an innovation or not, we investigate why some individuals generally invest more than others. This is motivated by the literature showing that many poor farmers do not only hesitate to adopt innovations but also seem to underinvest in highly profitable inputs, such as fertilizer or seeds (Banerjee & Duflo, 2011; Benin et al., 2011; Duflo et al., 2011; Collier & Dercon, 2014).

We offer the following explanation for this empirical puzzle: In information scarce environments, individuals rely heavily on culturally inherited heuristics ("rules-of-thumb") to guide behaviour (Richerson & Boyd, 2008). These time-proven rules of thumb have developed over generations in response to environmental demands and often follow a safety first principle (Boyd et al., 2011; Henrich, 2015). Especially important for survival is basic information about how much to trust whom, how ambitiously to behave, how much effort to invest into reaching which goals, and how much to try before giving up. Humans have the amazing capability to basically survive in every habitat on the planet, but this requires, amongst other things, to not waste resources on unlikely goals (in marginal environments especially) or miss opportunities to produce a surplus (in regions with seasonal restrictions especially).

In many developing regions, the return-on-investment (ROI) was historically much lower than it is today. In the example of southern Ghana, access to the European market to export pineapples in the 1990s dramatically changed the economic incentive to invest (Udry & Anagol, 2006, Conley & Udry 2010). Investments did increase in response, but significantly lower and heterogeneous than optimal, so that Ghana currently struggles to be internationally competitive (World Bank 2011; Barrett et al., 2012; Gatune et al., 2013).

Above we define perceived investment self-efficacy (SE) as how much a person believes in her ability to make profitable investments. In an Agent Based Model (ABM) we first simulate how SE differences might have arisen in response to the historical ROI and how these could have culturally developed over the generations. The basic idea is that some environments encouraged experimentation with agricultural investments and others did not, and that successful investments created a belief of being able to profitably invest (SE), which was passed down the generations and continues to explain investment differences amongst the current generation of farmers, who make their living now mostly with pineapples.

In Ethiopia, Bernard et al. (2014) conducted a randomized control trial, where they varied the SE of smallholder farmers by showing the treatment group a documentary about business-success-stories of social peers (vicarious mastery experience: they are like me; if they can do it I can do it too). An experimental design can hardly identify the effect of a long-term cultural evolution of SE but it gives a very clean estimate for the causal effect of SE on investment choices. Bernard et al. (2014) find that the treated farmers increased their investment, especially in education. This suggests that SE differences explain differences in economic behaviour across a relatively broad spectrum of contexts, at least across horticultural export crop producers in West-Africa and traditional subsistence farmers in East-Africa. There is also suggestive evidence from Germany (Grothmann & Reusswig, 2006) and the Netherlands (van Duinen et al., 2014) pointing towards SE being associated with innovation adoption, and opportunity recognition (Tumasjan & Braun, 2012; Krueger & Dickinson, 1993, 1994).

The concept has interesting implications for both economic theory and practice. It contributes to the emergent literature on individual endogenous preferences and constraints (Carter 2015; Hoff & Stiglitz, 2016; Wuepper et al., 2017). If we acknowledge SE to affect what individuals want and what they actually achieve, this implies that we need to ask how policy recommendations might change in this new light. Many studies using observational data conclude that credit constraints are a major constraint for the adoption of innovation. However, it seems that if the farmers really want, they are able to find investment capital (Karlan et al., 2012), but if they are not convinced about their ability to make a difference, they do not use credits effectively (Banerjee & Duflo 2011), or do not even want to take them at all (Banerjee et al., 2011, Karlan et al., 2012). The experiment of Bernard et al. (2014) shows that raising SE significantly raises credit taking, which means that indeed existing supply side constraints are not the full story of explaining the causes of credit constraints. It thus seems that in many studies, SE differences are an alternative explanation to the identified ones.

Raising SE is most effective in the long term, as much of it is developed (or not) during childhood. Uncertainty and negative shocks are significant barriers to the development of SE, which has potential for a poverty trap (Dercon & Krishnan, 2009; Dercon & Sánchez, 2013; Dercon & Singh 2013). On the other hand, Krishnan & Krutikova (2013) present experimental evidence from India that it is possible to significantly increase the SE of poor students with mentoring, challenging activities, active support, and special lectures. In general, all targeted measures help that provide mastery experience, vicarious mastery experience, verbal persuasion, and physiological arousal in doing successful things

SE clearly does not guarantee success. As Bandura (1997) extensively discusses, SE allows individuals to better exploit their opportunities, to make the most of what they have and extent their potential by learning. But humans are not in full control of the course of things and SE only influences one´s own behaviour. A farmer f.ex. is also dependent on infrastructure and bio-geographic circumstances. Suri (2011) e.g. shows that investment behaviour of Kenyan farmers is explained by binding infrastructure constraints, which simply render investments unprofitable.

There are, however, many instances where farmers face non-binding constraints, and SE differences have a large influence on whether they are overcome or appear as binding. Efficient policies should address external incentives and constraints (credit, insurance, infrastructure) as well as internal ones (SE, trust, self-control).

7. Theoretical Considerations on Self-Efficacy-Driven Modernization

Finnish researchers found a "Flynn-effect"-like increase of certain economically valuable personality traits which points towards the here claimed suitability of SE for development policies. In their 15-year study of 419,523 Finnish men, born between 1962 and 1976, representing 79% of their cohorte. Jokela, Pekkarinen, Sarvimäki, Terviö & Uusitalo (2017) researched development of personality traits that are correlated with economic success over a period of fifteen years: self-confidence, sociability, leadership motivation, activity energy, achievement striving, dutifulness, deliberation, and masculinity. While controlling for other factors like family background, they found a significant increase for all surveyed traits except masculinity Their findings of short term changes of traits, which are largely components or outcomes of SE, show that these can actually adapt quickly if environmental/circumstantial incentives foster it.

The relevance of SE for development and modernization gets questioned by the argument that it solely concerns intentional action and hence does not change immediate material conditions, like occur-rence of the tze-tze fly, lack of infrastructure, corrupt government or unfair terms of trade, all of which impede progress and demand dauntless action. This is true, but as long as some material base exists and efforts are not actively hampered, only in the short run. The ability of people to recognize and use opportunities, persevere in their efforts, comply with a change of methods and be resilient in case of setbacks is certainly decisive also for the success of traditional development aid or other policy measures. SE can be key to an upward cycle of development. It greatly influences the capability to make best use of what an environment offers, and aggregates over time in a kind of swinging movement. Employing material conditions in one state of SE produces results, which then act back on the actor´s SE to start another cycle of change on a higher level. We can assume a large multiplier effect as SE develops i.a. from vicarious experiences; herd behaviour and group conformity add to the effect. Growing economic success is a great incentive, vicarious experience with someone to identify with or relate to makes the attractive goal achievable!

High SE collectives develop more supportive institutions and invest productively instead of in dubious causes (cmp. the present surge in evangelical churches in Kenya and Ghana who skim off vast funds from the productive economy with promises of divine lifting from poverty after people lost hope in earthly relief). People with higher SE tend to produce and *demand* a more supportive, integrative, cooperative political and economic surrounding (on political efficacy i.a. Caprara, Vecchione; on econo-mic decision making McCloskey, Mokyr, Boyd, Richerson, Hendrich) while people with lower SE suffer from a lack of opportunity reckognition and utilization (Tumasjan & Braun, 2012; Krueger & Dickson, 1993, 1994). The former produces a virtuous cycle of rising SE with growing political participation and economic welfare while the latter produces an attraction of "strong-man" politics and further economic segregation as Kakkar & Sivanathan (2017) show in their study of 140k people in 69 countries. The fact that dictatorships can produce high economic growth rates for a while does not contradict this correlation.

The natural process of positive reinforcement can be interrupted by external shocks that can lock countries (or groups) in a state of stagnation or down-turn comparable to a post-traumatic stress disorder, and like this, require pro-active individual *and* group SE building. I believe, institutional and other SE proxies that allow for eluding the evolutionary pressures to develop individual SE, until average sinking SE in the population reaches a tipping point, endanger this process and could have a considerable share explaining downturns of formerly successful cultures.

Self-efficacy building is not the silver bullet of development as it needs material conditions to work with, but it is its seed and fertilizer: decisive for an empowerment that affects all other policy measures by enhancing peoples´ capacity for positive change.
Tetzlaff (2017, p.24ff) differentiates three theoretical schools of growth and modernization: those that count on economic growth to create i.a. a trickle-down effect; theories of political change to build capacities of adaptation and self-organization; and theories of mental and social change which include cultural and individual adaptations. Economic development-by-growth-theories (f.ex. Ragmar Nurske, Arthur W. Lewis, Paul Rosenstein-Rodan, Walt E. Rostow, and Gunnar Myrdal) (see Tetzlaff, 2017; Menzel, 2010) are less concerned with historic sequence and complexity, but rather focused on material factors like available capital that could be controlled, manipulated or produced by – possibly foreign – intervention with hopefully short-term results. In the aftermath of Keynes, scientists like Rostow concentrated on identifying specific target industries and respective policies – via market forces or state interventions like taxes or five-years-plans. Material action needs humans - individuals and groups - who are able and capable to make use of the newly available potential.

Social and political theories treat the development of integration, modernization, participation, welfare and allocation capacities (Gabriel Almond, Lucian W. Pye), and Karl W. Deutsch added thoughts on international adaptive and self-regulating capacity to analyze differences between political systems in their abilities to react constructively to challenges. Above mentioned scientists and others like Dankwart Rustow, James S. Coleman, Sidney Verba, Myra Winer, Stein Rokkan, and David Lerner identify three universal functions of a political system: legitimization through political socialization; incorporation of elites, articulating and grouping of interests and political communication; and finally, mobilizing and allocating resources like taxes, stability of political order and peaceful foreign relations (Tetzlaff, 2017; Menzel, 2010). Their insights help to analyze and categorize the expected modernization crises grouped

around problems of governmental penetration/state-building; integration of different societal groups; national identity and nation-building; legitimization of modern institutions and powers; political participation and politicization of institutions; and the allocation/re-allocation of national wealth, security and welfare to growing groups of entitled people. (based on Tetzlaff, 2017; Menzel, 2010). Political self-efficacies, as shown by Caprara et al. (2009) and Vecchione & Caprara (2009), have been found to be fundamental for active as well as electoral political participation in the democratic process. The correlation of SE with cooperation, trust and economic performance constitute an important positive factor in the political process providing for participation, democraticy and rule of law.
The third school of development and modernization theories treat the field of mental and social change, represented prominently by David Lerner, Karl W. Deutsch and Everett Hagen (see chpt. 3) who see the motor of change in the individual human being who has to ascend four (universal) stages of personal development on her way to modernity which is projected as a state of a mobile, educated, politically and economically fully integrated and participating individual with growing income. At this stage, she is expected to develop universal empathy (David Lerner, 1971). Tetzlaff (2017, p. 27) criticizes Lerner for underestimating cultural persistence, which would lead to cultural filtering of modern values, disorientation and hybrid forms of culture between traditional and modern personal demands. Political self-efficacy, the belief to be able to exert influence in and via the political process, and general self-efficacies step in to enable personal change and learning as shown explicitly earlier (chpt. 4 on learning, and 2.2. on identity): SE helps to master identity threatening and destabilizing effects of modernization for individuals and the collectives that make up a society´s structure.

Habermas locates his "project of modernity" (Tetzlaff, 2017, p. 20) in four parts: individualism as the unfolding of all individually particular peculiarities; the right to critique, meaning that nobody should be forced to accept anything they have not found legitimate; autonomy of acting; and finally, in the idealistic (constructivist) philosophy itself (ibid). If the concept of SE is analyzed under these – individualistic - premises, it is so as a factor that existed as an intrinsic human feature *before* formal education, state institutions, infrastructure and banks for capital supply were created, that grew *further* as development progressed, and which is now found to have had an important part in creating the material signs of progress. But it is, as Habermas claims, a factor that builds individual agency for an individual-driven modernization. This offers the chance to overcome earlier imperialistic imposition of alien elements through modernization policies that empower people to become agents of their own development, and break up progress-impeding collective structures. Strengthening individualism, though, may pose a special strain to some people, groups, societies, which makes the identification of different utilities of learning (chpt.4) vital for integration or cooptation policies.

My early chapters discussed the work of scientists aiming to identify factors promoting and hindering development and modernization to reduce poverty and human suffering, and add to peaceful international cooperation. Their hope was to find universal causes, universal chronological steps, universal processes or structures to possibly repeat, produce, and orchestrate economic and social development. Talcott Parsons defined this positive development as growing adaptive capacity of a social system to its environment, as well as modifying instead of enduring its conditions (cmp. Tetzlaff, 2017, pp.18ff; Menzel, 2010, pp. 73f). Parsons regards development as outcome of human abilities which were found to be directly correlated to the trait of (growing) SE (see chpt. 6 on SE developing naturally in reaction to environmental stimuli); he consequently differentiated traditional from modern societies by this capacity as reflected in specialization and differentiation of societal roles and their institutional analoga in education, law, banking, reli-gion etc. Proceeding to normative stages of a higher order, less survival stress and less human suffering, as described by Harrison (2000) and found by Lübbe (2005, pp.65ff) through growing SE, helps to dissolve the antagonism between the known and the unknown as well as between familiar traditions and alien modernity as SE empowers for developing a transcending identity.

Adaptive necessities frequently lead to destabilization (Huntington) as inner structures of people and communities get questioned, f. ex. their identity-defining hierarchies; status quo profiteers feel endangered, while status quo losers often lack the capacities to channel their wishes into constructive change. And worse, Western donor countries bring Western-style modernization along with their money, which has been received as neo-colonialism and cultural imperialism; it has become a project of "what" and "how-to" designed by the interests of those financing a major part of it, instead of increasing peoples′ agency to create their own pathways. Modernization within Western countries similarly left behind parts of their population and created growing integration barriers for migrants and their second and third generation offspring, because again, pre-prescribed ways to modernize are limiting peoples′ capabilities in controlled and controllable ways instead of setting free their potential.

The general question that has been raising doubts about applicability and desirability of transferring the European model not only in its results but also in its conduct was, if whatever enabled the production of economic and social welfare in unprecedented amounts, *can* be, and how much of it *must* be, transferred – assuming it would produce similar results under different limiting conditions. Accusations and animosities about cultural imperialism, neo-colonialism combined with real dangers of losing privilege, have helped to slow down modernization and discredit development aid to the point of defaming the term "development" altogether as Tetzlaff rightly states (Tetzlaff, 2017, p.19; Dirmoser et al., 1991, p.11; Moyo, 2010). Menzel (2010) went further in his critique by declaring the modernization ideal dead, and the potential good of development policy to be limited to economic, medical, military and political emergency aid.

Scientists identify numerous aspects of "First World" economic development and "Third World" economic slagging, and how to overcome it. Tetzlaff (2017, p. 23) counts about two dozens theories, theorems, paradigms, and models of development in the past sixty years. When important factors or strategies are identified like capital (de Soto, 2000; Yunus, 1999), neo-colonial, exploitive trade and business structures (Ziai,

2014; W. Sachs, 2002) institutions (Acemoglu & Robinson, 2012; Alesina & Guiliano, 2013; North, 1990), governance and democratization (Jacobeit et al, 2014; Schubert & Tetzlaff, 1998; Nohlen, 2005) or culture (Weber 2010; Etounga-Manguelle, 2000; Kabou, 1993; Elwert, 1997), we are left with doubts if our analysis of the situation of poverty and its causes were comprehensive in the first place: starting with Ghandi, Karl Polanyi, Ivan Illich, Michel Foucault, Edward Said, Stuart Hall, and Gustavo Estevan suggested that the misery of the non-Western world was partly a constructed myth based on the wish to continue exploitation after the end of colonialism and the ignorance, arrogance and disrespect for non-Western traditions. One example is the disregard for subsistence and other traditional institutions of production in an informal sector, which was rightly criticized by "Bielefelder Verflechtungsansatz" (a theory of coexistence and partial integration of the formal and informal sector by a team from University of Bielefeld). This critique of Hans-Dieter Evers (1987) and others opened a more grass-root view onto an ignored reality of reproduction (Hennings, 2009), and the female role in it. Similarly, we cannot be sure to have correctly and completely identified all factors that caused the European rise, as historic singularisms might have occurred to produce unrepeatable synergetics and prohibit drawing parallels.

The apparent attraction of at least the material results the Western model (Tetzlaff, 2017; Lübbe, 2005) however, answers transformation processes that have been taking place since the 17th century (Tetzlaff, 2017, p.19; similar: North, 1990; Diamond, 1997, 2005) to produce the present level of wealth and welfare. They took place in a certain chronological order, possibly implying a certain causal relation; reversing the chronological order cannot be expected to reverse the causal relationship as well. In Europe f.ex, economic growth of a kind produced the spreading of schools and universities. Without this initial "more" of economic substance, however, growing levels of education lead to growing frustration and unemployment with all its secondary destabilizing social effects (as in the North Africa). Squicciarini &Voigtlaender (2015) find f.ex. that "*although studies of contemporary economies find robust associations between human capital and growth, past research has found no link between worker skills and the onset of industrialization*" (p.1; their findings are supported by Mokyr, 2002, and Mokyr & Voth, 2009); rather they find that this early phase was driven by a small knowledge elite.

If at all Europe´s rise holds helpful information for future modernization and development processes, it is worth a look at what was there before there were supportive institutions, political/business alliances as in Venice, infrastructure, industrialization, universities, enough venture capital, and only *people* who brought all of this about in their producing economic and social welfare. David Brooks wrote the New York Times column:
"Roughly speaking, there are four steps to every decision. First, you perceive a situation. Then you think of possible courses of action. Then you calculate which course is in your best interest. Then you take the action. Over the past few centuries, public policy analysts have assumed that step three is the most important. Economic models and entire social science disciplines are premised on the assumption that people are mostly engaged in rationally calculating and maximizing their self-interest. But during this financial crisis, that way of thinking has failed spectacularly. As Alan Greenspan noted in his Congressional testimony last week, he was "shocked" that markets did not work as anticipated. "I made a mistake in presuming that the self-interests of organizations, specifically banks and others, were such as that they were best capable of protecting their own shareholders and their equity in the firms."So perhaps this will be the moment when we alter our view of decision-making. Perhaps this will be the moment when we shift our focus from step three, rational calculation, to step one, ***perception****." (NYT, Oct 27, 2008)*
And indeed, Hendrich et al. (2010) find that the people of the Northern hemisphere differ significantly in their perception of themselves and the world (cmp. Chpt. 8 below) from other people on this planet: they are generally "WEIRD", from Western, Educated, Industrialized, Rich, and Democratic societies and differ greatly in: "*visual perception, fairness, cooperation, spatial reasoning, categorization and inferential induction,*

moral reasoning, reasoning styles, self-concepts and related motivations, and the heritability of IQ.“ (p.61).

In a worldwide study on “Global Evidence on Economic Preferences“ of 80,000 people in 76 countries, representatively chosen to cover 90% of the world population, Falk et al. (2015) measured time preference, risk preference, positive and negative reciprocity, altruism, and trust. They found *“that preferences differ substantially across countries, but heterogeneity within countries is even more pronounced. The preferences vary with plausibly exogenous individual characteristics – gender, cognitive ability, and age – but relationships are in some cases culturally specific. Preferences also vary with cultural differences as captured by language structure, and with country-level characteristics like geography. Individual level economic outcomes, including savings decisions, labor market choices, and prosocial behaviours, are correlated with the preferences, and these relationships are similar across countries. Important aggregate outcomes, ranging from economic development to the frequency of armed conflicts, also vary with country-level averages of preferences.*

The measured indicators correlate with constituent factors of SE: time preference, risk preference, and trust which correlate with reciprocity and altruism and may be deduced from the general belief in one´s abilities to make it (well), making trust and cooperation less costly or risky. Interestingly, in an earlier research on “The Relationship between Economic Preferences and Psychological Personality Measures“ a team around Armin Falk (Becker et al., 2012) researched the Big Five (openness to experience, conscientiousness, extraversion, agreeableness, neuroticism, and locus of control) and found only low correlation with economic preferences. They did find though, complementary results when looking at economic life outcomes: labour market success, health status, and life satisfaction. Falk et al. (2015) empirically find what scientists from Max Weber to David Landes, George Akerloff, Joseph Henrich, Dambisa Moyo, Moletski Mbeki and Daniel Etounga-Manguelle have propagated: that cultural factors as in human perceptions are decisive for the outcome of intentional human actions. This includes not only economic decision making but all of the political process and its outcomes like institutions; they result from human decisions based on circumstance/environment, historical pathway, preferences and opportunity, which Acemoglu & Robinson (2012) identify as single most important factor for successful development. I assume that many scientists find SE-at-work, but without consensus on terminology identify its better known aspects or effects.

Development models that build on democratization, class, gender, governance and regimes, build on enhancing human agency. In concert with Bielefeld Integration Theory they reveal a realistic view of the reproduction and political reality of large parts of the world´s population. This draws attention to women as the prototype of profiteering from learning and modernizing: a majority of women conduct their social and economic life in the informal sector. Women were identified as a large untapped source for modernization by the microcredit movement. Despite feminist criticism of functionalizing poor women, the insight that women tend to use capital more responsibly and reliably for their family´s is good for them and political decision makers. The destabilizing effects of modernizing processes have often hit women and girls especially hard and twice: by devaluing their work and status in the informal sector (cmp. Boserup, 1970/2007), and as a pressure release or reconstruction target for thus disconcerted men. Women and girls profit most and immediately from SE building, and twice again: from their own by freeing their historically restricted potential, and from males with higher SE. Various studies on European men find self-efficacious men to be more cooperative, more supportive, less over-masculine, more sociable, more dutiful and more agreeable; I interpret that potentially less aggressive and less suppressive.

The overall economic, political and social effect of empowering women and men via self-efficacy has an enormous multiplier effect on society at all levels and offers great potential far beyond the integration of migrants and the economically less competitive. Based on knowledge about decision making under uncertainty, expanded by prospect theory and taking endowment and risk biases into account, expanded further yet by the bias of SE, it is possible to spell out building blocks of an economic and social theory of human behaviour that offers the chance of a more successful development policy that

- is not culturally intruding, as it does not tell people what to do and how, but helps to give them the agency for change of their own making;
- integrates elites who have much to loose by leveating some threads of change, in promoting trust in their ability to still make it well after change; without or against them change is costly or impossible, or will be under continuous reconstruction pressures for the old structures;
- alliviates some threads of change for those who fear losing their self-identification, social role or privilege as man, cleric, or shaman by fostering trust in their ability to redefine their role and do well;
- empowers all those who lack capacities and faith in themselves to take the risk of change.

The existential human struggle for survival is the core of every culture, developed from common experience and knowledge about survival of a group of people in their habitat. Culture reflects this historic knowledge and develops specific self-efficacies in her such bequested associates. Culture and SE become a vital part of self-identification as they include survival knowledge, not folklore or outdated tradition: it is the notion that my culture encompasses knowledge that helps me survive. That is why culture is as persistent as it is. But it can be updated, enlarged, expanded or changed if and only if new information fulfills three criteria:

- it must offer me the belief that I am personally able to use it
- that I will be better off than before
- it leaves my self-construct intact from shame or fear of identity loss.

Building SE in people holds not only the potential to foster modernization in less developed countries or make them less painful in developed ones for all ranks of society, self-efficacy can play an important role in integrating migrants and following generations who suffer from disparate reference frames and outdated self-efficacies. It is important to pay attention to the fact that parts of the present elite with the power to influence modernization processes may have low self-efficacies for learning and change as well: everybody who profits from a status quo and got there possibly not fully by merit may fear change unless he has enough SE to trust in his abilities to stay put or profit from change.

The following schema offers a simplyfied overview of individual SE, how it naturally evolves or is intentionally fostered and which perception fields and economic, political and social behaviour qualities it influences:

Sources of Individual Self-Efficacy
mastery/success experience
vicarious experience
social persuasion
physical or emotional arousal during activity
Intentional policy measures to produce any of the above

Individual Preferences Influenced by SE	**Behaviour Outcomes Influenced by higher SE**
time discounting	persistent, longer planning horizon, deliberate
risk taking	more risk taking, less defensive against novelty
social interaction	cooperative, trusting, leadership, motivated, dutiful,
activity level	active, initiative, schievement striving,
curiosity	interested, open, seeking

8. Outlock on Further Research

We tend to underestimate the strength of the persisting forces in a society and overestimate those for modernizing, the reason for which lie in the personal costs and risks of change and have been amply discussed herein. Consistent with this are the underestimated forces of reconstruction pressing for a rollback of modernizing changes that were initiated through historic events as exemplified i.a. by the rapid changes in the Western World after WWII and the ongoing reconstructive political and social pressures since the 1980s (growing in the 1970s) or reconstructive currents after WWI.

The need for research on how to foster originary and sustainable modernization by people of all ranks of society learning is vast and diverse.

Questions for further research concern methodology as well as context in the application of the concept of SE in different social sciences. It is disputed how to identify SE in the data on human action in social, political and economic processes, and how to delimit it from competing concepts. Information could be hidden in data on risk taking, time discounting, inclination for cooperation, openness to-wards novelty, participation, empowerment, and others. Findings on aspirations, hope, growth mindset, grit and other self-concepts likely contain information on SE. It can be distinguished by strictly delimiting the data to the actual *process* that leads to a set of outcomes. As the above example of political efficacy shows, efficacy for the process of winning public support (which is similar to win-ning any leading or popular position) is quite different from efficacy to head a successful government and manage a complex administration. These are two different processes (winning or managing) with two different efficacies (for popular success or management), but one and the same outcome: winning an office! Research is needed to standardize the criteria and methods of identifying and delimiting SE, make data retrieved from error-prone self-evaluation superfluous.

Caprara et al., (2009) developed and tested scales for measuring political efficacy, Schwarzer & Jerusalem (1995), and Luszczynska, Scholz, & Schwarzer (2005)[103] developed scales for measuring general efficacies in different cultural context, both employed in quantitative-descriptive manners.

Bandura rejects all attempts to use scales, which leaves the question of standardazed testing and identification methods for SE unresolved and an important future task. Bandura´s theory on SE has suffered from a lack of wider acceptance in psychology as well as in interdisciplinary employment. According to his comments, this seems to be at least partially due to some misunderstanding and misinterpretations. This powerful concept deserves all the translation into economics, political science and sociology scientists can render, as it may hold the key to widespread individual empowerment and benefits thereof. Social, cultural, and economic measures to promote SE should be developed and their application scientifically surveyed to learn what works best in which setting.

Little is known about SE differences amongst and within populations, and its macroeconomic effects. There is research (f.ex. by Vecchione et al., 2016) on personality, value change, and openess to change, but not with regard to the different levels and domains of SE.

Research is needed on SE effects on leadership and elites, especially of crowding-out and proxy effects: the question if leadership efficacy or efficacy to obtain leadership have a crowding-out effect on other efficacies of leaders, and possibly other players as well, could have important institutional consequences. In light of growing attraction of political populism and oligarchic "markets", it may be vital for democratic countries to understand how SE proxies like reputation, money, and institutional power interact with the development of SE beliefs in their elites, leaders, electorate and workforce.

There is no empirical research on the relation between rational decision-making and SE. This would be important information for political deci-

---

[103] Bandura (2015, p.1028) comments critically on the "one-size-fits-all" aspect of these and other self-efficacy scales.

sion makers to increase their inclination for SE building measures for example in public schools or as part of professional training. Interesting in this context is the interaction between SE and cooperation:
How does higher SE influence ability and inclination to cooperate? Does higher SE of group members influence the type of leader or representation preferred? How do SE beliefs of leaders and leading elites influence the political and institutional system? Do self-efficacious leaders affect cooperation and efficacy within groups and by individuals, and through which mechanism?

Modernization and sudden environmental or circumstantial changes like climate change and migration can lead to people having maladapted SE beliefs about themselves in the changed habitat, concerning the necessary or desired behaviours and skills, and their wishes and desires (entitlement). More research is needed about these asymmetries that can cause destabilization in modernizing societies, including those not discussed herein of chronology and societal sphere, f.ex. unsynchronized developments in individual SE and political, societal and institutional reactions. Knowing more about these processes helps governments to promote a more orderly process for change to act more positively than unsettling, and help integrating people into their new and changing lifes. The latter is especially true for migrants and f.ex. people whose life is directly negatively affected from technological or other changes in their workplace or privately, from overwhelming complexity or financial pressures.

A very important question concerns institutions being able to offset a lack of individual SE, thereby falsely reducing the evolutionary pressure to develop it. As this could eventually lead to growing parts of populations of countries with well-working institutions to develop less SE until a tipping point is reached when the functioning of that society is endangered, research could help to explain long economic cycles and possibly add to our understanding of downturns of high cultures. Also, acknowledge the existence of such tipping points could be an important political incentive to launch counteractive policies.

A challenging task is to develop a formal model of self-efficacy including a standardized terminology, and thereby foster interdisciplinary social, political and economic analysis and policies. The complexity of societal progress in the face of rising environmental dangers and worldwide reawakening of undemocratic currents calls for a concerted approach that all human sciences could employ; SE could play an important role.

9. A Culture of Learning Instead of Knowing Needs Self-Efficacy

This work started with refering to the work of Acemoglu & Robinson stating inclusive institutions and teh rule of law as decisive for the success of society and economy. I totally agree, except that institutions are the result and symptom of another, prior and ongoing process on which their functioning and survival hinges, as we can observe daily in the news: institutions are the outcome of culture and political processes of the group of people they are to protect; institutions can protect people only as much as the people protect them and their functioning. As we can presently observe almost 90 years after the Germany fell into the hands of Nazis by means of democratic institutions, institutions can get undermined and employed to undermine democracy and inclusion as they can be hijacked from within the system.

Institutions mirror their creators and the culture they exist in; hierarchic culture cannot develop inclusive institutions and inclusive institutions cannot survive in a hierarchic culture. A culture that is to entertain political processes that develop non-extrative institutions is the culture of self-efficacious people who do not need to exploit nor allow to be exploited.

Continuous modernization and development is a necessity for developed and less developed countries, and it takes SE to do so. For modernization not to lead to destabilizing a society, all ranks of a population need high and robust SE, including leaders and leading elites to allow for change of the status quo. Origin, cultural transmission, effects and importance of SE for ongoing economic, societal and political modernization are traced here, and SE is identified as the tool for adaptation to environmental and circumstantial changes including climate change and migration as well as promotor of a virtuous circle of stable and sustainable modernization.

Henrich et al. (2010) find that much of empirical research in behavioural science was conducted on volunteering U.S. American university undergraduates, who had made it through the American educational system to a

good university, and on other Western sample populations. They identified the origin of most of the researched people as WEIRD – Western, Educated, Industrialized, Rich, Democratic. In global context, these people are indeed weird; they are outliers, not representative for the life realities of the vast majority of all other inhabitants of this planet. In comparing data from across populations, they found results from the WEIRD people as particularly unusual: *"The domains reviewed include visual perception, fairness, cooperation, spatial reasoning, categorization and inferential induction, moral reasoning, reasoning styles, self-concepts and related motivations, and the heritability of IQ. The findings suggest that members of WEIRD societies, including young children, are among the least representative populations one could find for generalizing about humans. Many of these findings involve domains that are associated with fundamental aspects of psychology, motivation, and behaviour". (p.61)* WEIRD people inhabit rich democratic countries and their outlying features resonate with the concept of self-efficacy:
Henrich et al. find a so far underrated aspect of development: populations whose efforts in a sufficiently calculable surrounding were generally rewarded for generations, and thereby developed higher and wider spread SE, creating a self-fulfilling prophecy of achievement and success.

The origins of these fundamental aspects of human traits were traced back to life conditions of European populations in the early Middle Ages. Outlining the different pathways Muslim and European countries have taken since, Tetzlaff (2016) finds the same differences in culture and institutions which Greif (1994) find in comparing early Maghrebini and North Italian traders, and Alesina & Guiliano (2013) as well as Alesina, Guiliano & Nunn (2013) find on the role of women and in persistence and interaction of culture and institutions to have prevailed since as early as 1200. They all find that the specific conditions of life in Europe with its specific climate and geography enabled a series of little steps, starting off with the kind of cultivated crop and domesticated animals (Tetzlaff, 2016, p.26f.) to developing financial systems based on institutions that provided for anonymous trade (instead of Maghreb family-based trust relations, Greif, 1994); today´s role of women developed from agricultural practices and female participation in them (Alesina & Guiliano); today´s culture, institutions, political participation, and wealth result from at least thousand years of history developing in a particular environment, and its population adapting to it. In this process, European populations deveoped self-efficacies that make them demand and provide for more political and economic participation, and respective political leadership and institutions. Their SE enabled more inclusion of more and different people with more individual freedom to unfold their potential, bringing about entrepreneurs as much as technological progress and creativity in exactly the liberal democratic diversity that Beinhocker (2007) showed to be conducive for innovation. This process is one of self-enforcing, non-linear, uncontrollable emergence through people with enough SE to co-operate, innovate, learn and cope with change and diversity. But without doubt, and proven in disastrous wars and rollbacks, this process is not irreversible, it rather has to be adapted and reproduced in every generation and demographic change, and supported by modernizing, change-adapting institutions. Existing theories explain important aspects of the evolution of poverty and wealth, and different pathways countries have taken but suffer from lack of an operational tool that causally links the parameters of human society together. I suggest this tool to be self-efficacy. WEIRD populations whom Henrich et al. identify as living in environments that foster SE, developed institutions that compensate for individual lack thereof to stabilize their achievements.

Moyo (2010) accuses the present form of development aid for not only feeding corruption of (low-SE) elites, but to keep whole nations in low-SE dependency and thereby undeveloped.[104] But there are also great dangers ahead for Western-style democracies and capitalism as Shiller & Akerloff (2016) point out. Capitalism and democracy both give great individual freedom to develop one´s potential, but need fair play and respect for democratic institutions to work. Fair play needs potent institu-

[104] Cmp. experiences with too much training in Ghana above.

tions and self-efficacious players as all others will tend to corrupt the game; by definition those who do not believe to be able to get what they want the regular way will aim to get it by force or manipulation. Shiller & Akerloff bemourn the latter having produced mafia-style capitalism. Their demand for stricter regulation and stronger institutions is as much correct as a dilemma: the SE compensating effect of institutions described above has dampened the evolution of individual SE. At the same time, marketing and advertising at worldwide annual spending expected to surpass U.S.$1 trillion[105] in 2017 and annual growth rates of presently 4% p.a. helped to create ever increasing desires and perceived entitlement. Such undesired asymmetries between SE and entitlement endanger the system that created them, seemingly leading to a classic case of pathological learning: develop will to learn only after damage occurred.

Empirical data from Ghana show cultural transmission of SE to imply that SE which deveoped naturally without targeted measures, is based on information from the past and therefore regularly maladapted to changing conditions. If the environment fostered low SE in the past, the level of people´s SE is probably not high enough to recognize and make the best of new opportunities when they finally arise f.ex. through aid projects or migration! This underlines that people need support to update their SE quicker than they would by themselves in reaction to environmental stimuli. I elaborate on the negative effects of low, and the potential of high SE, and plead for it as a major policy tool with several multiplier effects as it enhances the outcome of most other policy measures.

Low SE in leaders and elites is especially dangerous as it makes people less inclined to pursue their interests with norms obeying methods, and more inclined to cling to the status quo and stifle development of SE in others. Democracy and more levelled distribution of wealth, income and opportunities require and produce higher levels of SE in more individuals

---

[105] Not even included are expenditure on direct marketing, promotions, retail trade spending and discounting according to strategy analytics, rapid research and world federation of advertisers, prnews.com and online research.

and more diverse social ranks, as much as more authoritarian regimes produce and are produced by lower SE in more individuals and amongst elites. With the exception of modernization dictatorships, modernization as the great change bringer clearly happens more regularly under high SE conditions, but with the constant danger of producing a double hazard to the process: institutional crowding-out effects, and creating the odd twist of uniting low SE individuals from the top with those from lower social ranks; both fear to lose through change while their SE is too low to belief in their abilities to keeping or regaining their status. The alliance of the billionaire Trump with his unsettled electorate serves as an unfortunate, but telling example.

Self-efficacious populations and leadership have the best potential to develop and modernize without alienating parts of a population, and stabilize what would otherwise be a constant threat to the newly built economic potential. Developed countries could profit in their continuous challenges by employing SE-building measures for the integration of all parts of society: future generations, immigrants, less educated, less cooperative, those low in SE but high in entitlement to consumption, power and prestige, and those low in SE but high in enduring, and possibly most importantly, bring about leaders and leading elites who are high enough in SE to be able to cooperate and share power in democratic manner. The present tendency for dictatorial powers aspiring politicians is also a sign of people and leaders having developed less SE then would be needed for them to feel secure and able for the present and growing complexity of environmental and other challenges, and consumption lures.

One of the most effective policy areas can be found in the empowerment of women whose vital role in the development process has been amply shown. Women are the one worldwide group who profit most from SE building policies. Power of people over people is often power of those who have too little SE and too much perceived entitlement to get what they want through rules-obeying trading, convincing, cooperation and compromise. Power compensates for this inability or excess desires by using violence, threatening to use violence or manipulating which is a form of violence through lying (I omit the odd case of power through merit-earned reputation[106].) Women who have often been taught to endure suffering and suppresion rather than changing it, can be expected to profit twofold from higher SE: by their own virtue in the above described ways of goal setting and achieving action, and through higher male SE leading to more cooperative, conciliatory treatment of women and children. An efficacious person does not need to suppress others as their efficacy is a sign of high, robust and general belief in their abilities to act successfully. A multiplier effect of push-and-pull economic, societal and political steps can be achieved for any country, at any point in their development, be more supportive to include more people on their necessary pathway of continuous adaptation, and peacefully move from a hierarchic culture of knowing to a democratic culture of learning.

---

[106] leaning on Max Weber´s schema of power here.

Acknowledgements

Throughout the long course of this work, I enjoyed generous support and inspiration from many people to whom i want to extent my deeply felt gratitude. Especially, I want to thank my untiring, critical and thorough co-author of several papers, Dr. David Wüpper, ETH Zürich.

I am deeply thankful to Prof. Rainer Tetzlaff, Prof. Matthias Basedau, German Institute for Global and Area Studies, Hamburg, and Prof. Andreas von Staden, University of Hamburg, who enabled me to conduct and finish this work successfully, and who went out of their way to do so. Prof. Maarten Jongsmaa, Wageningen generously discussed specific questions on genetics and Prof. Pavel Pelikan, Karl´s University Prague, kindly provided literature and encouraged me to attent to the controversial issue of cultural and genetic coevolution.

Innumerous discussions and inspirations over the years helped me detect new aspects or rethink ideas for which I owe many thanks to Prof. Hans Joachim Giessmann, Hamburg, Prof. Hans Halm, Tübingen, Prof. Sophia Al-Sharkawy, Cairo/Ryadh, Prof. Jens Weidner, Lüneburg, Baha Gungör, Cologne, Dr. Michael Kröher and Udo Latsch, Hamburg. I also owe a special thank you to Prof. Dennis J. Snower, and Dr. Steffen Ahrens, then IfW Kiel.

My dear friends David Horgan and Janusz Gawronski read, discussed, questioned, inspired and improved different parts and versions of the manuscript. Sarah Blackwell, Charles Hanson, and Christine Hunter stood by for questions, and Maureen Herzfeld for an inspiring discussion on learning.

On a personal account, many thanks to Dr. Atul Agarwala, Brigitte Agarwala, Michael Schalla and Kirsten Eckmann. Thank you also to Marie Düppe for your help and a huge mille grazie to the team of Federico in the Guesthouse Hotel in Lugano, who provided every effort to get my bag including labtop and hard disk with the only copies of this work back to me.

I want to take the opportunity to thank two institutions, which supported much of my academic self-efficacy development: The Studienstiftung des Deutschen Volkes and the Canadian United World College, the Lester B. Pearson College of the Pacific, and last but not least the University of Hamburg as my academic home.
Finally, thank you to Lea and Ruben for everything: Lea especially for her extraorinary artwork on the front cover and solving every computer problem, and Ruben for his culinary and practical support: I couldn´t have done it without yo

References

Abramson, Lyn Y., Seligmann, Martin E., and John D. Teasdale (1978), Learned helplessness in humans: Critique and reformulation, in: Journal of Abnormal Psychology, Vol. 87(1), 49-74.

Acemoglu, Daron (2009), Introduction to modern economic growth, Princeton.

Acemoglu, Daron, Simon Johnson, and James A. Robinson (2001), The colonial origins of comparative development: An empirical investigation, in: American Economic Review, Vol. 91, 1369-1401.

Acemoglu, Daron, Simon Johnson, and James A. Robonson (2001b), Reversal of Fortune: Geography and Institutions in the Making of the Modern World Income Distribution, NBER Working Paper No. 8460.

Acemoglu, Daron, and James A. Robinson (2012), Why Nations Fail. The Origins of Power, Prosperity, and Poverty, New York.

Adler, Alfred (1920/1974), Praxis und Theorie der Individualpsychologie. Vorträge zur Einführung in die Psychotherapie für Ärzte, Psychologen und Lehrer, Frankfurt a. M., (Erstausgabe: J. F. Bergmann, München / Wiesbaden 1920)

Akerloff , George A., and Robert J. Shiller (2009), Animal Spirits. How Human Psychology Drives the Economy, and Why It Matters for Global Capitalism, Princeton.

Akerlof, George A., and Rachel E. Kranton (2010), Identity Economics. How Our Identities Shape Our Work, Wages, And Well-Being, Princeton.

Akman, Wardatul (2002), Women's Education and Fertility Rates in Developing Countries, With Special Reference to Bangladesh, in: Eubios Journal of Asian and International Bioethics, Vol. 12, 138-143.

Alatas, Syed Hussein (1977), The Myth of the Lazy Native. A Study of the Image of the Malays, Filipinos and Javanese from the 16th to the 20th Century and its Functions in the Ideology of Colonial Capitalism, Milton Park, digital print 2006, https://books.google.de

Alesina, Alberti, and Roberto Perotti (1996), Income distribution, political instability, and investment, in: European Economic Review, Vol. 40 (6), 1203ff.

Alesina, Alberto, and Paola Giuliano (2013), Culture and Institutions, NBER Working Paper No. 19750.

Alesina, Alberto F., Paolo Giuliano, and Nathan Nunn (2013), On the Origins of Gender Roles: Women and the Plough, in: The Quarterly Journal of Economics, Vol. 128 (2), 469ff

Alon, Uri (2013), How To Go Into The Unknown, TEDxLausanne, 02/06/2013.

Altonji, Joseph G., Todd E. Elder and Christopher. R. Taber (2005), Selection on Observed and Unobserved Variables: Assessing the Effectiveness of Catholic Schools, in: Journal of Political Economy Vol. 113(1).

Al-Rawi, Rosina-Fawzia (2002), Tante Fatima kauft einen Teppich. Mein Leben im Morgenland der Frauen. Basel.

Amin, Samir (1974), Zur Theorie von Akkumulation und Entwicklung in der gegenwärtigen Weltgesellschaft, in: Senghaas, Dieter (ed.), Peripherer Kapitalismus. Analysen über Abhängigkeit und Entwicklung, Frankfurt/M., 71ff.

Amin, Samir (1979), `Self-reliance` und die Neue Internationale Wirtschaftsordnung, in: Senghaas, Dieter (ed.), Kapitalistische Weltökonomie. Kontroversen über ihren Ursprung und ihre Entwicklungsdynamik, Frankfurt/M., 317ff.

Aplin, Lucy M., Damien R. Farine, Julie Morand-Ferron, Andrew Cockburn, Alex Thornton, and Ben C. Sheldon (2014), Experimentally induced innovations lead to persistent culture via conformity in wild birds, in: nature, online.

Arthur, Brian W., Yuri M. Ermoliev, and Yuri Kaniovski, 1987, Path-dependent processes and the emergence of macro-structure, in: European Journal of Operational Research, Vol. 30 (3), Modeling Complex Systems II, 294-303.

Arthur, Brian W. (2014), All Systems Will Be Gamed: Exploitive Behaviour in Economics and Social Systems, Santa Fe Institute Working Paper #14-06-016.

Athanasopoulos, Panos (2015), How the language you speak changes your view of the world, online: theconversation.com/how-the-…, April 27, 2015.

Aulinger, Andreas (2008), Verfahren kollektiver Intelligenz zur Evaluation von Verbundnetzwerken, in: Aulinger, Andreas (Ed.), Netzwerk-Evaluation: Herausforderungen und Praktiken für Verbundnetzwerke, 171-190.

Austin, Gareth (2005), Land, Labor and Capital in Ghana: from slave to free labor in Asante, 1807-1956, Rochester NY.

Bandura, Albert (1963), Social learning and personality development, N.Y.

Bandura, Albert (1965), Influence of models reinforcement contingencies on the acquisition of imitative response, in: Journal of Personality and Social Psychology, Vol. 1, 589-595.

Bandura, Albert (1977), Social Learning Theory. Oxford.

Bandura, Albert, (1977b), Self-efficacy: toward a unifying theory of behavioural change, in: Psychological Review, Vol. 84 (2), 191-215.

Bandura, Albert (1986), Social foundations of thought and action: A social cognitive theory, Englewood Cliffs.

Bandura, Albert (1989), Human agency in social cognitive theory, in: American Psychologist, Vol. 44, 1175–1184.

Bandura, Albert (1990), Perceived self-efficacy in the exercise of control over AIDS infection, in: Evaluation and program planning, Vol. 13(1), 9-17.

Bandura, Albert (1993), Perceived self-efficacy in cognitive development and functioning, in: Educational psychologist, Vol. 28 (2), 117-148.

Bandura, Albert (1994), Self-efficacy, in: V.S. Ramachaudran (ed.), Encyclopedia of Human Behaviour, Vol. 4, 71-81, New York.

Bandura, Albert (1997), Self-efficacy: The exercise of control, New York.

Bandura, Albert (2000), Exercise of Human Agency Through Collective Efficacy, in: Current Directions in Psychological Science, Vol. 9 (2), 75-78.

Bandura, Albert (2005), Guide for Constructing Self-Efficacy Scales, in: Pajares, Frank and Tim Urdan, Self-Efficacy Beliefs of Adolescents, Greenwich, 307ff.

Bandura, Albert (ed.)(2008/1995), Self-Efficacy in Changing Societies, Cambridge.

Bandura, Albert (2012), On the Functional Properties of Perceived Self-Efficaccy Revisited, in: Journal of Management, Vol. 38 (1), 9-44.

Bandura, Albert (2015), On Deconstructing Commentaries Regarding Alternative Theories of Self-Regulation, in: Journal of Management, Vol. 41 (4), 1025ff.

Bandura, Albert, Claudio Barbaranelli, Gian V. Caprara, and Concetta Pastorelli, (1996), Multifaceted impact of self-efficacy beliefs on academic functioning, in: Child development, Vol. 67(3), 1206-1222.

Bandura, Albert, Claudio Barbaranelli, Gian V. Caprara, and Concetta Pastorelli, (2001), Self-efficacy beliefs as shapers of children´s aspirations and career trajectories, in: Child development, Vol. 72 (1), 187-206.

Banerjee, Abhijit V. (1992), A Simple Model of Herd Behaviour, in: Quarterly Journal of Economics, Vol. CVII (8), 797-817.

Banerjee, Abhijit, and Esther Duflo (2011), Poor Economics. A Radical Rethinking of the Way to Fight Global Poverty, New York.

Banerjee, Abhijit, Esther Duflo, Raghabendra Chattopadhyay, and Jeremy Shapiro (2011), Targeting the Hard-Core Poor: An Impact Assessment, Institute for Financial Management and Research - Centre for Micro Finance WP.

Banfield, Edward C. (reprint 1967/1958), The moral basis of a backward society, N.Y.

Barrett, Christopher B., Maren E. Bachke, Marc F. Bellemare, Hope C. Michelson, Sudha Narayanan and Thomas F. Walker (2012), Smallholder participation in contract farming: comparative evidence from five countries, in: World Development, Vol. 40 (4),715-730.

Beck, Ulrich, Anthony Giddens, and Scott Lash, 1996, Reflexive Modernisierung. Eine Kontroverse, Frankfurt.a.M.

Becker, Anke, Thomas Deckers, Thomas Dohmen, Armin Falk, and Fabian Kosse (April 2012), The Relation Between Economic Preferences and Psychological Personality Measures, IZA Discussion Paper No. 6470, in: Annual Review of Economics, Vol. 4, 453-478.

Becker, Gary S., and Kevin M. Murphy (2000), Social Economics: Market Behaviour in a Social Context, Cambridge, MA.

Beinhocker, Eric (2007), The Origin of Wealth, Evolution, Complexity, and the Radical Remaking of Economics, London.

Belsky, Jay, and Michael Pluess, (2009), The Nature (and Nurture?) of Plasticity in Early Human Development, in: Perspectives On Psychological Science, Vol. 4 (4), 345-52.

Bénabou, Roland, and Jean Tirole (2002), Self-confidence and personal motivation, in: Quarterly journal of economics, 871-915.

Bénabou, Roland (2009), Groupthink: Collective Delusions in Organizations and Markets, NBER Working Paper No. 14764.

Bénabou, Roland, Davide Ticchi, and Andrea Vindigni (2015), Forbidden Fruits: The Political Economy of Science, Religion, and Growth, NBER WP No. 21105.

Bénabou, Roland (2015), Religion and Innovation, NBER WP No. 21052.

Benin, Samuel, Alejandro Nin Pratt, Stanley Wood, and Zhe Guo (2011), Trends and spatial patterns in agricultural productivity in Africa, 1961–2010, ReSAKSS-Africa Wide Annual Trends and Outlook Report 2011. International Food Policy Research Institute.

Benjamin, Jonathan, Lin Li, Chavis Patterson, Benjamin D. Greenberg, Dennis L. Murphy, and Dean H. Hamer (1996), Population and familial association between the D4 dopamine receptor gene and measures of novelty seeking, in: Nature Genetics, Vol. 12 (1), 81-84.

Berger, Thomas (2001), Agent-based spatial models applied to agriculture: a simulation tool for technology diffusion, resource use changes and policy analysis, in: Agricultural Economics Vol. 25 (2-3), 245-260.

Bernard, Tanguy, Stefan Dercon, Kate Orkin, and Alemayehu Seyoum Taffesse, (22nd April 2014), The Future in Mind: Aspirations and Forward-Looking Behaviour in Rural Ethiopia, CSAE Working Paper WPS/2014-16, Oxford.

Bisin, A. and T. Verdier (2001), The economics of cultural transmission and the dynamics of preferences, in: Journal of Economic Theory, Vol. 97 (2), 298-319.

Bisin, Alberto and Thierry Verdier (2010), The economics of cultural transmission and socialization, NBER WP No. 16512.

Boeke, Julius (1953), Economics and Economic Policy of Dual Societies, N.Y.

Boyd, Robert, and Peter J. Richerson (1985), Culture and the Evolutionary Process, Chicago.

Boyd, Robert, and Peter J. Richerson (1995), Why does culture increase human adaptability? In: Ethology and Sociobiology, Vol. 16 (2), 125 -143.

Boyd, Robert, Peter J. Richerson, and Joseph Henrich (2011), The cultural niche: Why social learning is essential for human adaptation, in: Proceedings of the National Academy of Sciences, 108 (Supplement 2), 10918-10925.

Boserup, Ester (1970/2007), Woman´s Role in Economic Development, London.

Braudel, Fernand, Georges Duby, and Maurice Aymard (1987), Die Welt des Mittelmeeres: zur Geschichte und Geographie kultureller Lebensformen, Frankfurt a. M.

Brooks, David (2008), "The Behavioural Revolution", in: New York Times, oped of Oct 27, 2008.

Brooks-Gunn, Jeanne, Pamela K. Klebanov, and Greg J. Duncan (1996), Ethnic Differences in Children's Intelligence Test Scores: Role of Economic Deprivation, Home Environment, and Maternal Characteristics, in: Child Development, Vol. 67 (2), 396–408.

Burke, Marshall, Solomon Hsiang, and Edward Miguel (2015), Global nonlinear effect of temperature on economic production, online in: nature 15725.

Camerer, Colin, and Dan Lovallo (1999), Overconfidence and Excess Entry: An Experimental Approach, in: American Economic Review, Vol. 89 (1), 306-318.

Camerer, Colin F., George Loewenstein, and Drazen Prelec (2005), Neuroeconomics: How Neuroscience can Inform Economics, in: Journal of Economic Literature, Vol. XLIII, 9-64.

Camerer, Colin. F., George Loewenstein, and Matthew Rabin (Eds) (2011), Advances in behavioural economics, Princeton.

Cantoni, Daniele (2014), The Economic Effects of the Protestant Reformation: Testing the Weber Hypothesis in the German Lands, in: Journal of the European Economic Association, Vol. 13 (4), 561-598.

Caprara, Gian.V (2008), Will Democracy Win? in: Lanning, Kevin (Ed.), ibid, 639-661

Caprara, Gian V., Michele Vecchione, Cristina Capanna, and Minou Mebane, (2009), Perceived Political Self-Efficacy, in: European Journal of Social Psychology, Vol. 39 (6), 1002-1020.

Carter, M. R. (2015), What Farmers Want: The "Gustibus Multiplier" and other Behavioural Economic Insights on Agricultural Technology Adoption and Investment, WP UC Davies.

Centola, Damon, Uri Wilensky and Eamon Mckenzie (2000), A hands-on modeling approach to evolution: Learning about the evolution of cooperation and altruism through multi-agent modeling-The EACH Project, in: B. Fishman & S. O'Connor-Divelbiss (Eds.), Fourth International Conference of the Learning Sciences, Mahwah, NJ, 166-73.

Chabris, Chistopher. F. et al. (2012), Most Reported Genetic Associations with General Intelligence Are Probably False Positives, in: Psychological Science, Vol. 23 (11), 1314–23.

Chakraborty, Shanka, Jon C. Thompson, and Etienne B. Yehoue (2015), Culture in Development. The World Bank Economic Review, lhv018.

Chamorro-Premuzic, Tomas (2013), Why Do So Many Incompetent Men Become Leaders?, in: Harvard Business Review, Aug. 22, 2013.

Chanda, Areendam, C. Justin Cook, and Louis Putterman (2014), Persistence of Fortune: Accounting for Population Movements, There Was No Post-Columbian Reversal, in: American Economic Journal: Macroeconomics, Vol. 6 (3), 1-28.

Chaney, Eric (2008), Tolerance, Religious Competition and Fall of Muslim Society, unpublished manuscript, http://citeseerx.ist.psu.edu/viewdoc/download?doi=10.1.1.153.3085&rep=rep1&t

Chen, ChuanSheng, Michael Burton, Ellen Greenberger, and Julia Dmitrieva (1999), Population migration and the variation of dopamine D4 receptor (DRD4) allele frequencies around the globe, in: Evolution and Human Behaviour, Vol. 20 (5), 309–324.

Chesnay, Margaret A., Torsten B. Neilands, Donald B. Chambers, Jonelle M. Taylor, and Susan Folkman (2010), A validity and reliability study oft he coping self-efficacy skale, in: Behavioural Medicine, Vol. 36 (1), 12-23.

Chiapa, Carlos, José Luis Garrido, and Silvia Prina (2012), The effects of social programs and exposure to professionals on the educational aspirations of the poor, in: Economics of Education Review, Vol. 31 (5), 778-98.

Clark, Gordon L. (2010), Human Nature, The Environment, and Behaviour: Explaining the Scope and Geographical Scale of Financial Decision-Making, in: Geografiska Annaler: Series B, Human Geography, Vol. 92 (2), 159-173.

Collier, Paul (2007), The Bottom Billion: Why the Poorest Countries are Failing and What Can Be Done About It, Oxford.

Collier, Paul, and Stefan Dercon (2014), African Agriculture in 50 Years: Smallholders in a Rapidly Changing World?, in: World Development, Vol. 63, 92-101.

Cooter, Robert D., and Hans-Bernd Schäfer (2012), Solomon´s Knot. How Law Can End the Poverty of Nations, Princeton.

Conley, Timothy G., and Christopher R. Udry (2010), Learning about a new technology: Pineapple in Ghana, in: The American Economic Review, Vol. 100 (1), 35-69.

Dalton, Patricio S., Sayantan Ghosal, and Anandi Mani (2016), Poverty and Aspirations Failure, in: The Economic Journal, Vol. 126 (590), 165-188.

Demele, Isolde, Wolfgang Schoeller und Roald Steiner (1989), Modernisierung oder Marginalisierung. Investierbarer Überschuss und kulturelle Transformation als Grundlagen der Entwicklung, Frankfurt/M.

Dercon, Stefan, and Pramila Krishnan (2009), Poverty and the psychosocial competencies of children: evidence from the young lives sample in four developing countries, in: Children, Youth and Environments, Vol. 19 (2), 138ff.

Dercon, Stefan, and Alan Sánchez (2013), Height in mid-childhood and psychosocial competencies in late childhood: Evidence from four developing countries, in: Economics & Human Biology, Vol. 11 (4), 426-432.

Dercon, Stefan and Abhijeet Singh (2013), From nutrition to aspirations and self-efficacy: gender bias over time among children in four countries, in: World Development, Vol. 45, 31-50.

Diamond, Jared (1997), Guns, Germs, and Steel. A Short History of Everybody for The Last 13,000 Years, New York.

Diamond, Jared (2005), Kollaps. Warum Gesellschaften überleben oder untergehen. Frankfurt/M.

Dietz, Thomas, and Tom R. Burns (1992), Human Agency and the Evolutionary Dynamics of Culture, in: Acta Sociologica, Vol. 35, 187-200.

Delgado, Mercedes, and Christian Ketels (2014), Does the past still dictate our prosperity, on: World Economic Forum, Sep. 22, 2014; Delgado, Mercedes, Christian Ketels, Michael E. Porter, and Scott Stern, The Determinants of National Competitiveness, NBER Working Paper No. 18249.

Dirmoser, Dietmar, Marianna and Reimer Gronemeyer, and Georgia Rakelmann (Hrsg.)(1991), Mythos Entwicklungshilfe. Entwicklungsruinen: Analysen und Dossiers zu einem Irrweg, Giessen.

Donath, Orna (2015), Regretting Motherhood. A Sociopolitical Analysis, in: Signs, Vol. 40 (2), University of Chicago Press, 343-367.

Donath, Orna (2016), JAZ interview: "Reue ist nichts Schlimmes" (*regret is nothing bad*, transl. bd), Jüdische Allgemeine, No. 6/16 of Feb. 11, 2016, 18

Doepke, Matthias, and Fabrizio Zilibotti (2014), Culture, Entrepreneurship, and Growth, in: Handbook of Economic Growth, Edition 1, Chapter 1, Vol. 2, 1-48.

Drosten, Barbara (2016), Self-Efficacy and Modernization. On the Origin of Change, Hamburg.

Duesenberry, James S. (1949), Income, Saving, and the Theory of Consumer Behaviour, Cambridge, MA, (ref. via Hodgson, 2003, ibid, 172).

Duflo, Esther, Michael Kremer, and Jonathan Robinson (2011), Nudging Farmers to Use Fertilizer: Theory and Experimental Evidence from Kenya, in: The American Economic Review, Vol. 101(6), 2350-2390.

Easterly, William (2006), The White Man´s Burden: Why the West´s Efforts to Aid the Rest Have Done So Much Ill and So Little Good, Oxford.

Eberle, Ute (2013), Die Insel des Vergessens (Island of Forgetting), in: Geo Kompakt: Die Geburt der Zivilisation, No. 37, 12/2013.

Ebstein, Richard P., Olga Novick, Roberto Umansky, Beatrice Priel, Yamima Osher, Darren Blaine, Estelle R. Bennett, Lubov Nemanov, Miri Katz, & R H. Belmaker (1996), Dopamine D4 receptor (D4DR) exon III polymorphism associated with the human personality trait of novelty seeking, in: Nature Genetics, 12(1), 78-80.

Eibl-Eibelsfeld, Irenäus (1997), Die Biologie des menschlichen Verhaltens. Grundriss der Humanethologie, Weyarn.

Elsenhans, Hartmut, (1982), Die Überwindung von Unterentwicklung durch Massenproduktion für den Massenbedarf – Weiterentwicklung eines Ansatzes, in: Nohlen & Nuscheler, 1982, ibid, 152-193.

Elwert, Georg (1997), Schmückendes Gerede und reale Entwicklungsbedingungen – Über soziokulturelle Bedingungen der Entwicklung, in: Manfred Schulz (Hrsg.), Entwicklung. Die Perspektive der Entwicklungssoziologie, 261-290.

Eng, Kynan, Matti Mintz, Tobi Delbrück, Rodney J. Douglas, Adrian M.Whatley, Jonatas Manzolli, and Paul F.M.J. Verschure (2006/updated 2014), An Investigation of Collective Human Behaviour in Large-Scale Mixed Open Spaces, in: Presence, Vol. 15 (4), 403-418.

Engermann, Stanley L., and Kenneth L. Sokoloff (1997), Factor Endowments, Institutions, and Differential Paths of Growth Among New World Economies: A View from Economic Historians of the United States, in: Harber, Stephen (Ed), How Latin America Fell Behind, Stanford.

Engermann, Stanley L., and Kenneth L. Sokolof (2002), Factor Endowments, Inequality, and Paths of Development Among New World Economies, NBER Working Paper 9259.

Engermann, Stanley L., and Kenneth L. Sokolof (2006), The Persistence of Poverty in the Americas. The Role of Institutions, in: Bowles, Samuel, Steven N. Durlauf, and Karla Hoff (eds.), Poverty Traps, Princeton.

Epstein, Joshua M., & Robert Axtell (1996), Growing Artificial Societies, Washington, D.C.

Erikson, Erik H. (1954), Identity and Totality: Psychoanalytic Observations on the Problem of Youth, in: Human Development Bulletin, 5th Annual Symposium, cited from Strauss, ibid, 78.

Etounga-Manguelle, Daniel (2000) Does Africa Need a Cultural Adjustment Program? in: Harrison & Huntington, 65ff.

Evers, Hans-Dieter (1987), Subsistenzproduktion, Markt und Staat. Der sogenannte Bielefelder Verflechtungsansatz, in: Geographische Rundschau, Jg. 39, Heft 3, 136-140.

Falk, Armin (2012), The Relationship between Economic Preferences and Psychological Personality Measures, in: Annual Review of Economics (4), 453ff

Falk, Armin, Anke Becker, Thomas Dohmen, Benjamin Enke, David B. Huffman, and Uwe Sunde (2015), The Nature and Predictive Power of Preferences: Global Evidence, IZA Discussion Paper No. 9504.

Faraone, Stephen, Alysa Doyle, Eric Mick, & J. Biederman (2001), Meta-analysis of the association between the 7-repeat allele of the dopamine D4 receptor gene and attention deficit hyperactivity disorder, in: American Journal of Psychiatry, Vol. 158 (7), 1052-1057.

Farmer, J. Doyne and Duncan Foley (2009),The economy needs agent-based modelling, in: Nature, Vol. 460(7256), 685-686.

Feder, Gershon, Richard E. Just, and David Zilberman (1985), Adoption of agricultural innovations in developing countries: A survey, in: Economic Development and Cultural Change, Vol. 33 (2), 255-298.

Fenske, James (2010), A causal history of Africa: A response to Hopkins, MPRA Paper No. 24458, http://mpra.ub.uni-muenchen.de/24458

Festinger, Leon (1962), Cognitive dissonance, in: Scientific American, Vol. 207 (4), 93 –107.

Feola, Guiseppe, and Claudia Binder (2010), Why Don´t Pesticide Applicators Protect Themselves? Exploring the Use of Personal Protecting Equipment among Columbian Smallholders, in: International Journal of Occupation and Environmental Health, 11-23.

Feola, Guiseppe, and Claudia Binder (2010b), Towards an improved understanding of farmers' behaviour: The integrative agent-centred (IAC) framework, in: Ecological Economics, Vol. 69 (12), 2323–2333.

Fernandez, Antonia, Marina Della Giusta, and Uma S. Kambhampati (2015), The Intrinsic Value of Agency: The Case of Indonesia, in: World Development, Vol. 70 (C), 92-107.

Finkelstein, Israel (2015), Das vergessene Königreich – Israel und die verborgenen Anfänge der Bibel, München.

Foster, Andrew D., and Mark R. Rosenzweig (2010), Microeconomics of technology adoption, in: Annual Review of Economics, Vol. 2(1), 395-424.

Freund, Caroline (2016), Rich People Poor Countries: The Rise of Emerging-Markets Tycoons and their Mega Firms, books.google.com.

Fuglesang, Andreas (1982), About Understanding: Ideas and Observations on Cross-Cultural Communication, Uppsala, Dag-Hammerskjöld Foundation.

Fullerton-Batten, Julia, 2015, Feral Children, Photo-Project, London, online at juliafullerton-batten.com.

Gallup, John Luke, Jeffrey Sachs, and Andrew D. Mellinger (1999), Geography and Economic Development, in: International Regional Science Review, Vol. 22 (2), 179-232.

Galor, Oded, and Stelios Michalopoulos (2012), Evolution and the growth process: Natural selection of entrepreneurial traits, in: Journal of Economic Theory, Vol. 147 (2), 759-780.

Galor, Oded, and Ömer Özak (2014), The Agricultural Origins of Time Preference. NBER WP No. 20438 (CEPR Discussion Paper DP10122).

Galtung, Johan, Peter O´Brian, and Roy Preiswerk (1980), Self-Reliance: a strategy for development, online at http://agris.fao.org/agrissearch/search.do?recordID=XF2015013348

Gantzel, Klaus Jürgen (1992), Krieg – Lernen aus den Folgen oder was folgt für das Lernen, in: Politische Vierteljahresschrift, Vol. 33 (4), 673-676.

Gatune, Julius, Mitchris Chapman-Kodam, Kwesi Korboe, Francis Mulangu, and Manitra Raktoarisoa (2013), Analysis of Trade Impacts on the Fresh Pineapple Sector in Ghana. FAO Commodity and Trade Policy Research WP No.41, Rome.

Gebhardt, Christian, Friedrich Leisch, Petra Schüssler, Klaus Fuchs, Thomas Stompe, Werner Sieghart, Kurt Hornik, Siegfried Kasper und Harald N. Aschauer (2000), Non-association of dopamine D4 and D2 receptor genes with personality in healthy individuals, in: Psychiatric Genetics, Vol. 10 (3), 131-137.

Gebrehiwot, Tagel, and Anne van der Veen (2015), Farmers prone to drought risk: why some farmers undertake farm-level risk-reduction measures while others not?, in: Environmental Management, Vol. 55(3), 588-602.

Geiger, Klaus (2015), Warum Ärzte und Ingenieure in den Dschihad ziehen (why doctors and engineers go to jihad, bd), in: Die Welt v. 19.11.2015.

Gennaioli, Nicola, and Ilia Rainer (2007), The modern impact of precolonial centralization in Africa, in: Journal of Economic Growth, Vol. 12 (3), 185-234.

Gigerenzer, Gerd, and Wolfgang Gaissmaier (2011), Heuristic decision making, in: Annual review of psychology, Vol. 62, 451-482.

Gilboa, Itzhak, Andrew Postlewaite, and David Schmeidler (2012), Rationality of Belief, in: Synthese, Vol. 187(1), 11-31.

Goetze, Dieter (2000), Modernisierung, in: Nohlen, Dieter (Hg) (2000), Lexikon der Politik, Bd 4, Die östlichen und die südlichen Länder, Berlin, 380-384.

Golub, Benjamin and Matthew O. Jackson (2010), Naive Learning in Social Networks and the Wisdom of Crowds, in: American Economic Journal: Microeconomics, Vol. 2 (1), 112-149.

Gottfredson, Linda S. (1981), Circumscription and compromise: A developmental theory of occupational aspirations, in: Journal of Counseling Psychology, Vol. 28 (6), 545-579.

Government of Ghana (2010). Medium-term national development policy framework: Ghana shared growth and development agenda, 2010 – 2013, Vol. 1.

Greif, Avner (1994), Cultural Beliefs and the Organization of Society: A Historical and Theoretical Reflection on Collective and Individual Societies, in: The Journal of Political Economy, Vol. 102 (5), 912-950.

Gross, Jessica (2013), How languages can affect the way we think, on: ideas.ted.com of 2/19/2013.

Grothmann, T., and F. Reusswig (2006), People at Risk of Flooding: Why Some Residents Take Precautionary Action While Others Do Not, in: Natural Hazards, Vol. 38 (1), 101-120.

Grundmann, Siegfried (2004), Einsteins Akte. Wissenschaft und Politik – Einsteins Berliner Zeit. Berlin.

Guiso, Luigi, Paola Sapienza, and Luigi Zingales (2008), Trusting the stock market, in: The Journal of Finance, Vol. 63 (6), 2557-2600.

Guiso, Luigi, Paola Sapienza, and Luigi Zingales (2010), Civic capital as the missing link, NBER Working Paper No. 15845.

Guiso, Luigi, Paola Sapienza, and Luigi Zingales, 2008/2013/2014/2015, Long-Term Persistence (Was Putnam Right?), Northwestern Kellogg University, Faculty Publication; the citation is from their June 2014 online version.

Hagen, Everett C. (1961), Psychology´s Role in Economic Development. Is there an identifiable personality trait that promotes or retards economic progress in societies? In: Science, Vol. 134 (3490), 1608-1609.

Harari, Yuval Noah (2014), Sapiens. A Brief History of Humankind, London.

Harrison, Lawrence E. (2000), Why Culture Matters, in: Harrison & Huntington, 2000, ibid.

Harrison, Lawrence. E., (2000), Promoting Progressive Change, in: Harrison & Huntington, 2000, ibid.

Harrison, Lawrence E., and Samuel P. Huntington (2000), Culture Matters: How Values Shape Human Progress, New York.

Heath, Chip, and Amos Tversky (1991), Preference and Belief: Ambiguity and Competence in Choice under Uncertainty, in: Journal of Risk and Uncertainty, Vol. 4 (1), 5-28.

Heisey, Paul W., and Wilfred Mwangi (1996), Fertilizer Use and Maize Production in Sub-Saharan Africa, CIMMYT Economics Working Paper 96-01, Mexico, D.F.

Hennings, Werner (2009). Entwicklungsforschung. Eine Bestandsaufnahme am Beispiel Samoa. Frankfurt/New York.

Henrich, Joseph (2014), Rice, Psychology, and Innovation, in: Science, Vol. 344 (6184), 593-594.

Henrich, J. (2015), The secret of our success: how culture is driving human evolution, domesticating our species, and making us smarter, Princeton.

Henrich, Joseph, Steven J. Heine, and Ara Norenzayan (2010), The Weirdest People in the World?, in: Behavioural and Brain Science, Vol. 33 (2-3), 61-83.

Henrich, Joseph, Robert Boyd, Samuel Bowles, Colin Camerer, Ernst Ferch, and Herbert Gintis (eds.)(2004), Foundations of Human Sociality – Economic Experiments and Ethnographic Evidence from Fifteen Small-Scale Societies, Oxford.

Hermanns, William (author), and Adolph Caso (ed)(1983)(ebook 2011), Einstein and the Poet: In Search for the Cosmic Man.

Hesse, Helmut und Hermann Sautter (1977), Entwicklungstheorie und –politik, Bd.1, Entwicklungstheorie, Tübingen.

Hessel, Stéphane (2011), Tanz mit dem Jahrhundert. Erinnerungen, Berlin.

Hodgson, Geoffrey M. (2003), The hidden persuaders: institutions and individuals in economic theory, in: Cambridge Journal of Economics, Vol. 27, 150-175.

Hodgson, Geoffrey Martin, and Thorbjørn Knudsen (2006), Why we need a generalized Darwinism, and why generalized Darwinism is not enough, in: Journal of Economic Behaviour and Organization, Vol. 61, 1-19.

Hodgson, Geoffrey M. (2012), Agreeing on generalized Darwinism: a response to Pavel Pelikan, in: Journal of Evolutionary Economics, Vol. 22 (1), 9-18.

Hoff, Karla, and Joseph Stieglitz (2016), Striving for balance in economics: Towards a theory of the social determination of behaviour, in: Journal of Economic Behaviour and Organization, Vol. 126, 25-57.

Hondrich, Karl Otto, 1992, Lehrmeister Krieg, Reinbek bei Hamburg.

Hopkins, A.G. (2009), A New Economic History of Africa, in: The Journal of African History, Vol. 59 (2), 155-177.

Humphreys, Colin J. (2003), The Miracles of Exodus: a Scientist Reveals the Extraordinary Natural Causes Underlying the Biblical Miracles, New York.

Hulleman, Chris S., Sheree M. Schrager, Shawn M. Bodmann, and Judith M. Harackiewicz (2010), A meta-analytic review of achievement goal measures: Different labels for the same constructs or different constructs with similar labels? In: Psychological Bulletin, Vol. 136 (3), 422-449,

Huntington, Samuel P. (1968), Political Order in Changing Societies, New York.

Huntington, Samuel P. (1997), Kampf der Kulturen. Die Neugestaltung der Weltpolitik im 21. Jahrhundert, München.

Huntinton, Samuel P. (2000), Culture Counts, in: Harrison & Huntington (2000), ibid.

Hyden, Göran (1983), No Shortcuts to Progress. African Development Management in Perspective, Berkeley.

Ibrahim, Solava, and Sabina Alkire (2007), Agency & Empowerment: A proposal for internationally comparable indicators, in: OPHI WP Series, online.

Inglehart, Ronald, and Christian Welzel (2009), How Development Leads to Democracy, in: Foreign Affairs, Vol. 88 (2), 33-48.

Jakobeit, Cord et al. (2014). Einleitung: Entwicklungstheorien, in: Franziska Müller et al. (Hrsg.), Entwicklungstheorien, 5-40.

Jarcho, Johanna M., Elliot T. Berkman, and Matthew D. Lieberman (2010), The neural basis of rationalization: cognitive dissonance reduction during decision-making, in: Social Cognitive Affective Neuroscience, Vol. 6, 460–467.

Janssen, Marco A. (2005), Agent-based modelling, in: Modelling in Ecological Economics, 155-172.

Johnson, Dominic P., and James H. Fowler (2011), The evolution of overconfidence, in: Nature, Vol. 477 (10384), 317-320.

Jokela, Markus, Tuomas Pekkarinen, Matti Sarvimäki, Marko Terviö & Roope Uusitalo (2017), Seculiar rise in economically valuable personality traits, in: PNAS, June 20, 2017, Vol. 114 (25) 6527-6532.

Kabalak, Alihan, Elena Smirnova, and Juergen Jost (2014), Game Theory in Biology and Anthropology, Santa Fe Institute Working Paper #14-06-019 of June 23, 2014.

Kabou, Axelle (1993), Weder arm noch ohnmächtig. Eine Streitschrift gegen schwarze Elite und weiße Helfer. Aus dem Französischen 1991, Basel.

Kahneman, Daniel (2012), Schnelles Denken, Langsames Denken, München.

Kahneman, Daniel, and Amos Tversky (1979), Prospect Theory. An Analysis of Decision Under Risk, in: Econometrica, Vol. 47 (2), 263-291.

Kahneman, Daniel, Jack L. Knetsch, and Richard H. Thaler (1991), Anomalies: The Endowment Effect, Loss Aversion, and Status Quo Bias, in: The Journal of Economic Perspectives, Vol. 5 (1), 193-206.

Kakkar, Hemant, and Niro Sivanathan (2017), When the appeal of a dominant leader is greater than a prestige leader, in: PNAS, Vol. 114 (26), 6734-6739.

Kandel, Eric R. (2007), In search of memory: The emergence of a new science of mind, NY

Kant, Immanuel (1974), Die Kritik der Reinen Vernunft, Werkausgabe, Bd. III, Wilhelm Weischedel (Ed.), Berlin.

Kappel, Robert (2015), Hürden für die Industrialisierung in Afrika, GIGA Focus Afrika 07/2015, Hamburg.

Kappel, Robert (2015a), Auf dem "Nullpunkt". Deutschland braucht eine neue Afrikapolitik. Fünf Vorschläge für eine koordinierte Strategie, in: IPG Internationale Politik und Gesellschaft.

Kappel, Robert, and Esther Ishengoma (2011), Business Environment and Growth Potential of Micro and Small Manufacturing Enterprises in Uganda, in: African Development Review, Vol. 23 (3), 352-365.

Karlan, Dean, Robert D. Osei, Isaac Osei-Akoto, and Christopher Udry (2012), Agricultural decisions after relaxing credit and risk constraints, NBER Working Paper No. 18463.

Kauffman, Stuart A. (1993), Origins of Order: Self-Organization and Selection in Evolution, Oxford.

Kenning, Peter, and Hilke Plassmann (2005), Neuroeconomics: An Overview from an Economic Perspective, in: Brain Research Bulletin, Vol. 67, 343-354.

kff.org/other/state-indicators (2013), state-indicators on infant mortality rate by race/ethnicity for 2013, retrieved online 6/27/2015.

Kleemann, Linda, and Awudu Abdulai (2013), Organic certification, agro-ecological practices and return on investment: Evidence from pineapple producers in Ghana, in: Ecological Economics, Vol. 93, 330-341.

von Kleist, Heinrich (1801), letter to Wilhelmine von Zenge, Berlin, March 22, 1801, online at *gutenberg.spiegel.de/buch/briefe-7043/3.*

Krishnan, Pramila, and Sofya Krutikova (2013), Non-cognitive skill formation in poor neighbourhoods of urban India, in: Labour Economics, Vol. 24, 68-85.

Krueger Jr., Norris, and Peter R. Dickson (1993), Self-efficacy and perception of opportunities and threads, in: Psychological Reports, Vol. 72(3), 1235-1240.

Krueger Jr., Norris, and Peter R. Dickson (1994), How Believing in Ourselves Increases Risk Taking: Perceived Self-Efficacy and Opportunity Recognition, in: Decision Science, Vol. 25(3), 385-400.

Kuhn, Thomas (1962), The Structure of Scientific Revolutions, Chicago.

Kumar, Krishna, (2014), Modernization, britannica.com/topic/modernization, retrieved on 1/5/2016.

Landes, David S. (1999), The Wealth and Poverty of Nations: Why Some Are So Rich and Some So Poor, New York.

Landes, David S. (2000), Culture almost makes all the difference, in: Harrison & Huntington (2000), ibid, 2-13.

Lanning, Keith (2008), Democracy, Voting and Disenfranchisement in the United States: A Social Psychological Perspective, in: Lanning, Keith (Ed)(2008), Democracy and Disenfranchisement, Journal of Social Issues, Vol. 64 (3), 431ff.

Lehmann, Jana (2012), Die Bedrohung des Selbst als Ursache von Stress – eine experimentelle Operationalisierung des SOS-Konzeptes, Bern.

Lerner, Daniel (1971), Die Modernisierung des Lebensstils: eine Theorie, in: Wolfgang Zapf (Hrsg.), Theorien des sozialen Wandels, Köln, 362-381

Lim, Lin Lean (2002), Female Labour-Force Participation, online at un.org/esa/population/publications/completingfertility/RevisedLlMpaper.

Lipset, Seymour Martin (1960), Political Man. The Social Basis of Modern Politics, New York.

Lipsey, Richard. G., Gordon R. Sparks, and Peter O. Steiner (1973/1976, 2nd ed.), Economics, New York.

Locke, Edwin A., and Gary P. Latham (1990), A theory of goal setting and task performance. Englewood Cliffs.

Loewenstein, George, Scott Rick, and Jonathan Cohen (2008), Neuroeconomics, in: Annual Review of Psychology, Vol. 59, 647-672.

van der Loo, Hans und Willem van Reijen (1997), Modernisierung. Projekt und Paradox. München.

Lübbe, Hermann (2005), Die Zivilisationsökumene. Globalisierung kulturell, technisch und politisch, München.

Luszczynska, Aleksandra, Urte Scholz, and Ralf Schwarzer (2005), The General Self-Efficacy Scale: Multicultural Validation Studies, in: The Journal of Psychology: Interdisciplinary and Applied , Vol. 139 (5), 439-457.

Luszczynska, Aleksandra, Benicio Gutiérrez-Doña, and Ralf Schwarzer (2005), General self-efficacy in various domains of human functioning: Evidence from five countries, in: International Journal of Psychology, Vol.40 (2), 80-89.

Lybbert, Travis J., and Bruce Wydick (2016), Poverty, Aspirations, and the Economics of Hope: A Framework for Study with Preliminary Results from the Oaxaca Hope Project.

Kumar, Krishna (2014), Modernization, online at: www.britannica.com/topic/modernization retrieved on 1/5/2016.

MacLeod, Jay (1987), Ain´t No Makin´It, Boulder.

Macours, Karen, and Renos Vakis (2009), Changing Households´ Investments and Aspirations through Social Interactions. Evidence from a Randomized Transfer Program. The World Bank, Latin America and the Caribbean, Poverty Sector Unit, Policy Research Working Paper 5137.

Maddux, James E. (1995), Self-Efficacy Theory, in: ---- (ed), Self-Efficacy, Adaptation, and Adjustment. Theory, Research and Application, The Springer Series in Social Clinical Psychology, N.Y., 3-33.

Maher, Shiraz (2015), The Roots of Radicalization. It´s Identity, Stupid, in: The Guardian, June 17.

Malthus, Thomas Robert (1798), An Essay on the Principle of Population, as it Affects Future Improvements of Society, 2012, Kindle Edition.

Martens, René (2016), Als Aktiver kaltgestellt. Sportgeschichte, in: Jüdische Allgemeine, March 10.

Mayshar, Joram, Omer Moav, Zvinka Neeman, and Luigi Pascali (2015), Cereals, Appropriability and Hierarchy, at //http.economics.mit.edu/files/10771, (also CEPR Discussion Paper, 10742).

Mbeki, Moeletsi (2009), Architects of Poverty: Why African Capitalism needs Changing, Johannesburg.

Mbeki, Moeletsi (Ed.)(2011), Advocates for Change: How to Overcome Africa´s Challenges, Johannesburg.

McCarroll, Michele L., Shannon Armbruster, Heidi E. Frasure, M. David Gothard, Karen Gil, Mary Beth Kavanagh, Steven Waggoner, and Vivian E. von

Gruenigen (2014), Self-efficacy, quality of life, and weight loss in overweight/obese endometrial cancer survivors (SUCCEED): A randomized controlled trial, in: Gynecologic Oncology, Vol. 132 (2), 397-402.

McClellant, David C. (1961), The Achieving Society, Princeton.

McCloskey, Deirdre Nansen (2015), It was ideas and ideologies, not institutions, which changed in North Western Europe, 1600-1848, in: Journal of Evolutionary Economics, Vol. 25 (1), 57-68.

McElreath, Richard (rapporteur), Robert Boyd, Gerd Gigerenzer, Andreas Glöckner, Peter Hammerstein, Robert Kurzban, Stefan Magen, Peter J. Richerson, Arthur Robson, and Jeffrey R. Stevens (2008), Individual Decision Making and the Evolutionary Roots of Institutions, in: Engel, Christoph, and Wolf Singer (Eds.), Better Than Conscious? Decision Making, The Human Mind, and Implications for Institutions, Cambridge, MA, 325-342.

McFadden, Daniel (2000), Economic Choices, Prize lecture, at: www.Nobelprize.org/nobelprizes/economic-sciences/laureates/2000/mcfadden-lecture.

McFadden, Daniel (2001), Keynote Address, University of California, Berkeley´s 133th Charter day Celebration (March 23): Economic Choices. Economic Decisions of Individuals, online: homepage McFadden.

Meadows, Dennis (1972), Die Grenzen des Wachstums. Bericht des Club of Rome zur Lage der Menschheit, Stuttgart.

Mednick, Sarnoff A., William F. Gabrielli, Jn., and Barry Hutchings (1984), Genetic influences in criminal convictions: evidence from an adoption cohort; in: Science, 224 (4651), p.891-894

Menzel, Ulrich (2010), Teil 1: Entwicklungstheorie, in: Reinhard Stockmann, Ulrich Menzel und Franz Nuscheler, Entwicklungspolitik. Theorien – Probleme – Strategien, München, 11-159.

Meredith, Martin (2005/2011), The State of Africa. A History of the Continent Since Independence, London.

Michalopoulos, Stelios, Louis Putterman and David N. Weil (2016), The Influence of Ancestral Lifeways on Individual Economic Outcomes in Sub-Saharan Africa, NBER Working Paper 21907.

Moyo, Dambisa (2010), Dead Aid, Why Aid is Not Working and How There is Another Way for Africa, London.

Mokyr, Joel (1990), The Lever of Riches. Technological Creativity and Economic Progress, New York.

Mokyr, Joel (2002), The Gifts of Athena: Historical Origins of the Knowledge Economy, Princeton.

Mokyr, Joel (2007), The European Enlightenment, the Industrial Revolution, and Modern Economic Growth, Max Weber Lecture Series, 2007/06.

Mokyr, Joel (2008), The Institutional Origins of the Industrial Revolution, in: Elhanan Helpman (ed.),Institutions and Economic Performance, Cambridge, 64ff

Mokyr, Joel, and Hans Joachim Voth (2009), Understanding Growth in Europe, 1700-1870: Theory and Evidence: Volume 1, 1700-1870, in: S. Broadberry, & K. H. O'Rourke (Eds.), The Cambridge Economic History of Modern Europe: Vol. 1, 1700-1870 Cambridge.

Mousavi, Shabnam, and Gerd Gigerenzer (2014), Risk, uncertainty, and heuristics, in: Journal of Business Research, Vol. 67 (8), 1671-1678.

Montier, James (2006), Behaving Badly, in: ssrn 890563, Feb 2.

Müller, Ruth, Stephan Sievert und Reiner Klingholz (2016), Krisenregion Mena. Wie demographische Veränderungen die Entwicklung im Nahen Osten und Nordafrika beeinflussen und was das für Europa bedeutet, Studie, Berlin-Institut für Bevölkerung und Entwicklung.

Mullainathan, Sendhil (2005). Development economics through the lens of psychology. Paper presented at the Annual World Bank Conference in Development Economics: Lessons of Experience.

Munafò Marcus R., Binnaz Yalcin, Saffron A. Willis-Owen & Jonathan Flint (2008), Association of the dopamine D4 receptor (DRD4) gene and approach-related personality traits: meta-analysis and new data, in: Biological Psychiatry, Vol. 63 (2), 197–206.

Mundlos, Christina (2015), Wenn Mutter sein nicht glücklich macht. Das Phänomen Regretting Motherhood, München.

Munk, Nina (2013), The Idealist. Jeffrey Sachs and the Quest To End Poverty, New York.

Myint, Hla (2014), Economic development, britanni-
ca.com/topic/modernization,
retrieved on 1-5-2016.

Neisser, Ulric, Gwyneth Boodoo, Thomas J. Bouchard, Jr., A. Wade Boykin, Nathan Brody, Stephen J. Ceci, Diane F. Halpern, John C. Loehlin et al. (1996), Intelligence: Knowns and Unknowns, in: American Psychologist, 51 (2), 77ff.

Neufeld, Gordon, and Gabor Maté (2013), Hold on to Your Kids. Why Parents need to Matter More than Peers, Toronto.

Nisbett, Richard E., and Dov Cohen (1996), Culture of honor: the psychology of violence in the south, Boulder.

Nohlen, Dieter und Franz Nuscheler (1982), Was heißt Dritte Welt?, in: idem (Hrsg.), Handbuch der Dritten Welt, Bd. 1, Unterentwicklung und Entwicklung: Theorien – Strategien – Indikatoren, Hamburg, 11-47.

Nohlen, Dieter und Franz, Nuscheler(1982), Was heißt Unterentwicklung? In: idem, ibid, 25-47.

Nohlen, Dieter (2005), Entwicklungstheorie und Transitionsforschung. Ein ressourcenorientierter Theorievergleich, in: Engel, Ulf, Cord Jakobeit, Andreas Mehler und Gunter Schubert (Hrsg.), Navigieren in der Weltgesellschaft. Festschrift für Rainer Tetzlaff, Münster, 313-336.

North, Douglas C. (1990), Institutions, Institutional Change and Economic Performance, Cambridge.

Nunn, Nathan (2007), The Long-Term Effects of Africa´s Slave Trades, NBER Working Paper No. 13367.

Nunn, Nathan (2008), Slavery, Inequality, and Economic Development in the Americas: An Examination of the Engermann-Sokoloff-Hypothesis, in: Helpman, Elhanan (Ed), Institutions and Economic Performance, Cambridge, MA, 148-179.

Nunn, Nathan, and Leonard Wantchekon (2009), The Slave Trade and the Origins of Mistrust in Africa, NBER Working Paper No. 14783.

Nunn, Nathan (2012), Culture and the Historical Process, in: Economic History of Developing Regions, Vol. 27 (sup1), 108-126. NBER Working Paper 17869.

Nunn, Nathan (2014), Historical Development, in: Philippe , A., and N. D. Steven (Eds.), Handbook of Economic Growth, Chapt. 7, Elsevier, Vol. 2, 347ff.

Nyerere, Julius (1967), Education for Self-Reliance, in: The Ecumenical review, Vol. 19 (4), 382-403.

Oishi, Shigehiro, and Thomas Talhelm (2012), Residential Mobility. What Psychological Research Reveals, in: Current Directions in Psychological Science, Vol. 21 (6), 425-430.

Paalova, Jouni, and W.Neil Adger, 2005, Institutional Ecological Economics, in: Ecological Economics, Vol. 53, 353-368.

Pajares, Frank (1997), Current directions in self-efficacy research. Advances in motivation and achievement, Vol. 10 (149), 1-49.

Pajares, Frank, and Héfer Bembenutty (2007), The Last Word: An Interview With Frank Pajares: God, the Devil, William James, the Little Prince, and Self-Efficacy, online http://www.uky.edu/~eushe2/PajaresInterview2007.pdf

Pajares, Frank (2002), Overview of social cognitive theory and self-efficacy, online at: http://www.emory.edu/EDUCATION/mfp/eff.html.

Pareto, Vilfredo (1906/2014), Manual of Political Economy, Oxford. http://books.google.de/books?hl= de & id=M3ZYAwAAQBAJ &q=psychology# v=snippet&q=psychology&f=false.

Parsons, Talcott (1964), Evolutionary Universals in Society, in: American Sociological Review, Vol. 29, 339-357.

Pelikan, Pavel (2003), Bringing Institutions into Evolutionary Economics: Another View With Links to Changes In Physical and Social Technologies, in: Journal of Evolutionary Economics, Vol. 13 (3), 237-258.

Pelikan, Pavel (2013), A conceptual instruction-centered model of evolutionary and developmental processes as a source of insights into the issues of group selection, multi-level selection, and the origins of order. http://kie.vse.cz/english/new-pavel-pelikans-working-paper/

Philips, Wendell, and Theodore C. Pease (1891), Speeches, Lectures and Letters of Wendell Phillips: Volume 1, online at http://www.perseus.tufts.edu/hopper/text?doc=Perseus%3Atext%3A2001.05.0188%3Achapter%3D17%3Apage%3D333.

Putnam, Robert D., Robert Leonardi, and Raffaella Y. Nanetti (1993), Making Democracy Work: Civic Traditions in Modern Italy, Princeton.

Putterman, Louis (2008), Agriculture, Diffusion, and Development: Ripple Effects of the Neolithic Revolution, in: Economica, Vol. 75 (300), 729-748.

Prebisch, Raul (1976), A critique of peripheral capitalism, in: CEPAL Review, 9-76.

Purzycki, Benjamin.G., Coren Apicella, Quentin D. Atkinson, Emma Cohen, Rita Anne McNamara, Aiyana K. Willard, Dimitris Xygalatas, Ara Norenzayan, and Joseph Henrich (2016), Moralistic gods, supernatural punishment and the expansion of human sociality, in: Nature, doi:10.1038/nature16980.

Rabin, Matthew (1998), Psychology and Economics, in: Journal of Economic Literature, Vol. XXXVI (11).

Ramirez, Ricardo, and Wendy Quarry (2009), Communication for Another Development: Listening Before Telling, London.

Rees, Debbie, Andrew Westby, Keith Tomlins, Quirien Van Oirschot, Muhammad U. Cheema, Eric Cornelius and Mohammad Amjad (2012), Tropical root crops, in: Rees, Debbie, Graham Farrell, and John Orchard (Eds.), Crop Post-harvest: Science and Technology, Perishables, Chichester/UK.

Richerson, Peter J., and Robert Boyd (2008), Not by genes alone: How culture transformed human evolution, Chicago.

Richerson, Peter J., Robert Boyd, and Joseph Henrich (2010), Gene-culture coevolution in the age of genomics, in: Proceedings of the National Academy of Sciences, Vol. 107 (Supplement 2), 8985-8992.

rif.org/pdf/literacy-facts.

Sachs, Jeffrey (2000), Notes on a New Sociology of Economic Development, in: Harrison & Huntington (2000), ibid.

Sachs, Jeffrey (2006), The End of Poverty, New York.

Sachs, Jeffrey (2011), The Price of Civilization: Reawakening American Virtue and Prosperity, New York.

Sachs, Wolfgang (2002), Nach uns die Zukunft. Der globale Konflikt um Gerechtigkeit und Ökologie, Frankfurt am Main.

Sautter, Hermann (1985), Underdevelopment through isolationism? Dependency theory in retrospect, in: Intereconomics, Vol. 20 (4), 180-187.

Schnaidberg, Allen (1970), Measuring Modernism: Theoretical and Empirical Explorations, in: *American Journal of Sociology*, Vol. 76 (3), 399-425, http://www.jstor.org/stable/2775730 .

Schnaidberg, Allen (1994), The Political Economy of Environmental Problems and Policies: Consciousness, Conflict, and Control Capacity, in: Freese, Lee (Ed.), Advances in Human Ecology, Vol. III, Greenwich.

Schubert, Gunter und Rainer Tetzlaff (Hrsg.) (1998), Blockierte Demokratie in der Dritten Welt, Opladen.

Schultz, Theodore W. (1972), The Increasing Value of Human Time, in: American Journal Of Agricultural Economics, Vol. 54 (5), 843-850.

Schultz, Theodore W. (1975), The Value of the Ability to Deal with Disequilibria, in: Journal of Economic Literature, Vol. 13 (3), 827-846.

Schultz, Theodore W. (1980), Nobel Lecture: The Economics of Being Poor, in: Journal of Political Economy, Vol. 88 (4), 639-651.

Schumpeter, Josef A. (1934/1983). The theory of economic development: An inquiry into profits, capital, credit, interest, and the business cycle, N. Brunswik.

Schwarzer, Ralf, and Matthias Jerusalem (1995), Generalized Self-Efficacy Scale, in: Weinman, J., S. Wright, & M. Johnston, Measures in health psychology: A user's portfolio. Causal and control beliefs, Windsor, 35-37.

Schwarzer, Ralf (2000), Stress, Angst und Handlungsregulation, Stuttgart.

Schwarzer, Ralf (Ed.)(1992/2014), Self-efficacy: Thought control of action. Milton Park.

Sen, Amartya (1988), Freedom of Choice. Concept and Content, in: European Economic Review, Vol. 32 (2-3), 269–294.

Sen, Amartya (1999), Development as Freedom, Oxford/New York.

Sen, Amartya (2000), Culture and Development, Presentation Script for the World Bank Tokyo Meeting of Dec 13, 2000, online at google scholar.com or http://ricardovillasmil.com/site/wp-content/uploads/2014/11/culture-sen.pdf

Sen, Amartya (2004), How does culture matter? In: Rao, Vijayendra, and M. Walton (Eds.), Culture and Public Action: Rationality, Equality of Agency, and Development, 37-58, Stanford.

Sen, Amartya (2007), Die Identitätsfalle. Warum es keinen Krieg der Kulturen gibt. München.

Sen, Amartya (2012), Development as Capability Expansion, in: Defillippis, J. and S. Saegert (Eds.), The Community Development Reader, N,Y., 319-327.

Senghaas, Dieter (Hg.) (1974), Peripherer Kapitalismus. Analysen über Abhängigkeit und Entwicklung. Frankfurt/M.

Senghass, Dieter (Hg) (1979), Kapitalistische Weltökonomie. Kontroversen über ihren Ursprung und ihre Entwicklungsdynamik, Frankfurt/M.

Senghaas, Dieter (1992), Wider den gelehrten Bellizismus, in: Leviathan, Vol. 20 (1), 141ff

Sherif, Musafa and Carolyn W. Sherif (1964), Reference groups: exploration into conformity and deviation of adolescents, New York.

Shibutani, Tamotsu (1962/2007), Reference Groups and Social Control, in: Rose, A. M. (Ed.), Human Behaviour and Social Processes: An Interactional Approach, Milton Park, 128-147.

Shiller, Robert J., and George A. Akerloff (2016), Phishing for Fools, Princeton.

Simon, Herbert A. (1955), A Behavioural Model of Rational Choice, in: Quarterly Journal of Economics, Vol. 69 (1).

Smith, Adam (1776/2000), The Wealth of Nations (intro. by Robert Reich), N.Y.

Sokoloff, Kenneth L., and Stanley L. Engermann (2000), History Lessons: Institutions, Factor Endowments, and Paths of Development in the New World, in: Journal of Economic Perspectives, Vol. 14, 217-232.

Solhaug, Trond (2006), Knowledge and Self-efficacy as Predictors of Political Participation and Civic Attitudes: With Relevance for Educational Practice, in: Policy Futures in Education, Vol. 4 (3), 265-279.

Soto, Hernando de (2000), The Mystery of Capital. Why capitalism Triumphs in the West and Fails Everywhere Else, New York.

Squicciarini, Mara P., and Nico Voigtländer (2015), Human Capital and Industrialization. Evidence from the Age of Enlightenment, in: Quarterly Journal of Economics, Vol. 130 (4), 1825-1883.

Der Spiegel, Nr. 52, 20.12.2014: Die Geburt Gottes. Archäologen entdecken den Ursprung der Bibel.

Stajkovic, Alexander D., and Fred Luthans (1998), Self-efficacy and work-related performance: A meta-analysis, in: Psychological Bulletin, 124 (2), 240ff.

Steele, Claude M., and Joshua Aronson (1995), Stereotype threat and the intellectual test performance of African Americans, in: Journal of Personality and Social Psychology, Vol. 69 (5), 797-811.

Stockett, Kathryn (2009), The Help, New York.

Strauss, Anselm (1959), Transformation of Identity, in: Rose, A. (Ed.) (1967/2007), Human Behaviour and Social Processes. An Interactionist Approach, The International Library of Sociology. The Sociology of Behaviour and Psychology, Vol. VI, Milton Park, 63-85.

Suri, Tavneet (2011), Selection and comparative advantage in technology adoption, in: Econometrica, Vol. 79 (1), 159-209.

Tabellini, Guido (2010), Culture and institutions: economic development in the regions of Europe, in: Journal of the European Economic Association, Vol. 8 (4)

al-Tahawy, Miral (2016), Der Frauenkörper ist das Ziel eines Klassenkampfs, in: www.spiegel.de/kultur/gesellschaft/frauenrechte-und-islam, retrieved 2/ 5, 2016.

Talhelm, T., Zhang, X., Oishi, S., Shimin, C., Duan, D., Lan, X., & Kitayama, S. (2014), Large-scale psychological differences within China explained by rice versus wheat agriculture, in: Science, Vol. 344 (6184), 603-608.

terra mater (3/2018), Schule heisst Chance, p16.

Tetzlaff, Rainer (1975), Die Ursachen von Unterentwicklung in der Dritten Welt und das Problem ihrer Überwindung. Eine Einführung, in: Friedensanalysen, Vol. 1, 150-181

Tetzlaff (1982), Perspektiven und Grenzen der Neuen Weltwirtschaftordnung, in: Nohlen & Nuscheler, 1982, ibid, 273-291.

Tetzlaff, Rainer (2005), Europa´s islamisches Erbe. Orient und Okzident zwischen Kooperation und Konkurrenz, Hamburger Beiträge zur Friedensforschung und Sicherheitspolitik, Heft 138.

Tetzlaff, Rainer (2016), Der Islam, die Rolle Europas und die Flüchtlingsfrage. Islamische Gesellschaften und der Aufstieg Europas in Geschichte und Gegenwart, Opladen.

Tetzlaff, Rainer and Cord Jakobeit (forthcoming-2017), Afrika in Vergangenheit und Gegenwart, Hagen.

Thaler, Richard (1988), Anomalies. The Winner´s Curse, in: Journal of Economic Perspectives, Vol. 2 (1), 191-202.

Thomas, X Zhang, S. Oishi, C. Shimin, D. Duan, X. Lan, and S. Kitayama (2014), Large-Scale Psychological Differences Within China Explained by Rice Versus Wheat Agriculture, in: Science, Vol. 344 (6184).

Tierney, Pamela and Steven M. Farmer (2011), Creative self-efficacy development and creative performance over time, in: Journal of Applied Psychology, Vol. 96 (2), 277-293.

Traulsen, Arne, Dirk Semmann, Ralf D. Sommerfeld, Hans-Jürgen Krambeck, and Manfred Milinski (2010), Human strategy updating in evolutionary games, in: PNAS, Vol. 107 (7), 2962–2966.

Tumasjan, Andranik, and Reiner Braun (2011), In the eye of the beholder: How regulatory focus and self-efficacy interact in influencing opportunity recognition, in: Journal of Business Venturing, Vol. 27, 622-636.

Tversky, Amos, and Daniel Kahneman (1986), Rational Choice and the Framing of Decisions, in: Journal of Business, Vol. 59 (4), pt.2, 251-278.

Tversky, Amos, and Daniel Kahneman (1992), Advances in prospect theory: Cumulative representation of uncertainty, in: Journal of Risk and Uncertainty, Vol. 5 (4), 297-323.

Udry, Christoper (2011), Land Tenure, in: The Oxford Companion to the Economics of Africa.

Udry, Christopher, and Santosh Anagol (2006), The Return to Capital in Ghana, in: The American Economic Review, Vol. 96 (2), 388-393.

van Duinen, Rianne, Tatiana Filatova, Peter Geurts, and Anne van der Veen (2014), Coping with drought risk: empirical analysis of farmers' drought adaptation in the south-west Netherlands, in: Regional Environmental Change, Vol. 15 (6), 1081-1093.

Vecchione, Michele, and Gian V. Caprara (2009), Personality determinants of political participation: The contribution of traits and self-efficacy beliefs, in: Personality and Individual Differences, Vol. 46 (4), 487-492.

Vecchione, Michele, Shalom Schwartz, Guido Alessandri, Anna K. Döring, Valeria Castallani (2016), Stability and change of basic personal values in early adulthood: An 8-year longitudinal study, in: Journal of Reseach in Personality, Vol. 63, 111-122.

Venkatachalam, Suri (2001), Guns, Germs and Steel, in: Resonance (Jan), 84-86.

Voigtlaender, Nico and Hans-Joachim Voth (2012), Persecution Perpetuated: The Medieval Origins of Anti-Semitic Violence in Nazi Germany, in: Quarterly Journal of Economics, Vol. 127 (3), 1339-1392.

Waaktaal, Trine and Svenn Torgersen (2013), Self-efficacy is mainly genetic, not learned: a multiple-rater twin study on the causal structure of general self-efficacy in young people, in: Twin Research and Human Genetics, Vol.16 (03).

Warren, Elisabeth (2016), cited after: time, Vol. 187 (12), 6.

Wallerstein, Immanuel (1974), The Rise and Future Demise of the World Capitalist System: Concepts for Comparative Analysis, in: Comparative Studies in Society and History, Vol. 16 (4), 387-415.

Weber, Elke, Ann-Renée Blais, and Nancy E. Betz (2002), A Domain-Specific Risk-attitude Scale: Measuring Risk Perceptions and Risk Behaviour, in: Journal of Behavioural Decision Making, Vol. 15, 263-290.

Weber, Max (1973), Soziologie. Universalgeschichtliche Analysen. Politik, Stuttgart.

Weber, Max (2010), Die protestantische Ethik und der Geist des Kapitalismus, München.

Webster´s Seventh New College Dictionary (1965), London/Springfield.

Wehler, Hans-Ulrich (1975), Modernisierungstheorie und Geschichte, Göttingen.

Welzel, Chrstian (2013), Freedom rising, Cambridge University Press.

Welzel, Christian, and Ronald Inglehart (2014), Evolution, Empowerment and Emancipation: How Societies Ascend the Utility Ladder of Freedoms, in: World Development, Vol. 64, 33-51.

Wessling, Ewald (1991), Individuum und Information: die Erfassung von Information und Wissen in ökonomischen Handlungstheorien, Tübingen.

Whitbeck, L.B., R.L. Simons, R.D. Conger, K. Wickrama, K.A. Ackley, & G.H. Elder Jr. (1997), The effects of parents' working conditions and family economic hardship on parenting behaviours and children's self-efficacy, in: Social Psychology Quarterly, 291ff.

Wilde, Oscar, 1895/2011, An Ideal Husband, kindle edition.

Williams, David M. (2010), Outcome Expectancy and Self-Efficacy. Theoretical Implications of an Unresolved Contradiction, in: Personality and Social Psychology Review, Vol. 14 (4), 417-425.

Williams, Sarah C.P. (2014), Genes Don´t Just Influence Your IQ – They Even Determine How Well You Do In School, online on: science, 2014 (10), news.

Woodruff, S.L., and J.F. Cashman (1993), Task, Domain, and General Efficacy: A Re-examination of the Self-Efficacy Scale, in: Psychological Reports, Vol. 72 (2), 423-432.

World Bank (2011), Horticultural Exports from Ghana: A Strategic Study. Agriculture and Rural Development, Working Paper by Peter Jaeger.

Worland, Justin (2016), The Anthropocene should bring awe – and act as a warning, in: time magazine , Sept 12-19, p.8.

Wu Jing, Haifan Xiao, Hongjuan Sun, Li Zou and Ling-Qiang Zhu (2012), The role of dopamine receptors in ADHD: a systematic meta-analysis, in: Molecular Neurobiology, Vol. 45 (3), 605–620.

Wuepper, David, and Barbara Drosten (2015), Economic Implications of Historically Evolved Self-Efficacy: Agent-based Modeling and Empirical Evidence from Rural Ghana, MPRA Paper No. 65413.

Wuepper, David, and Barbara Drosten (2016), Historic Returns on Investment and Current Economic Outcomes: The Cultural Evolution of Investment Self-Efficacy, WP August 2016, at: researchgate.net/publication/307560803

Wuepper, David, and Johannes Sauer (2016), Explaining the performance of contract farming in Ghana: The role of self-efficacy and social capital, in: Food Policy, Vol. 62, 11ff.

Wuepper, David, Tanguy Bernard, and Alemayehu Seyoum Taffesse (forthcoming), Self-Efficacy and Economic Behaviour, in: Annual Review of Resource Economics, Vol. 9 (2017).

Wuepper, David, David Zilberman, and Johannes Sauer (2016). Self-Efficacy or Farming Skills: What matters more for the Adaptive Capacity of Ghana's Pineapple Farmers? WP.

Wuepper, David, Hannes Lang, and Emmanuel Benjamin, forthcoming, The Accumulation of Human Capital amongst Descendants of African Nomads.

Young, Oran R. (1999), Institutional dimensions of global environmental change, in: Public Administration and Policy, Vol. II.

Yunus, Muhammad (1999), Banker to the Poor. The Story of the Grameen Bank, London.

Ziai, Aram (2014), Post-Development-Ansätze: Konsequenzen für die Entwicklungstheorie, in: Franziska Müller et al. (Hrsg.). Entwicklungstheorien, 405-434.

* * *

Christian Ungruhe
Lasten tragen, Moderne befördern
Wanderarbeit, Jugend, Erwachsenwerden und ihre geschlechtsspezifischen Differenzierungen in Ghana
Wanderarbeit ist fester Bestandteil eines Lebensverlaufs vieler junger Männer und Frauen aus Nordghana. Die Begleitung von Lastenträger*innen (weibliche kayayei und männliche truck pusher) auf Märkten und Busstationen im südlichen Ghana und in ihre Heimat verdeutlicht diese Praxis als diffizile soziale Aushandlung um Lebensphasen einer modernen Jugend und des Erwachsenendaseins. Teilhabe an diesen äußert sich als kollektives (kayayei) oder zunächst verborgenes (truck pusher) Bestreben, deren Bedeutung sich erst mit der Rückkehr in den Norden erschließt. Die Begleitung der Wanderarbeiter*innen zeichnet diesen Prozess nach und zeigt so die Bedeutung geschlechtsspezifischer und multilokaler Perspektiven auf Jugend, Wanderarbeit und soziale Mobilität jenseits populärer Exklusionszuschreibungen von Jugend in Afrika auf.
Beiträge zur Afrikaforschung, Bd. 89, 2018, 456 S., 54,90 €, br., ISBN 978-3-643-14011-1

Justice Anquandah Arthur
The Politics of Religious Sound
Conflict and the Negotiation of Religious Diversity in Ghana
"Justice Arthur presents a wealth of intriguing material, an impressive thick description of the conflict and a thorough analysis of the many, very complex factors that contribute to the conflict. His work on the multiple dimensions of the conflict is knowledgeable, comprehensive and plausible and it clearly shows that the so-called religious conflicts are never about 'religion' only." – Prof. Dr. Eva Spies (University of Bayreuth, Germany).
"Justice A. Arthur has laid out a multidisciplinary, multi-perspective and long-term analysis of the clashes on the noise ban in Accra. The chapters are convincingly set up in order to manage the complexity of approaches, covering religious studies, theology, mission studies as well as anthropology, legal and political studies." – Prof. Andreas Heuser (University of Basel, Switzerland).
Beiträge zur Afrikaforschung, vol. 86, 2018, 358 pp., 39,90 €, pb., ISBN 978-3-643-90982-4

Johannes Flosbach
Financial Performance of Microfinance Institutions in Ghana and Uganda
Development and Application of the Achievement Stages Model
Beiträge zur Afrikaforschung, vol. 59, 2015, 372 pp., 39,90 €, pb., ISBN 978-3-643-90600-7

Christiane Voßemer
"I want to be somewhere!"
Young Malawian Nurses' Perspectives on Migration
Perspectives on Development, vol. 2, 2019, 232 pp., 29,90 €, pb., ISBN 978-3-643-90872-8

Matteo Landricina
Nkrumah and the West
"The Ghana Experiment" in British, American, German Archives and Ghanaian Archives
Studien zur Afrikanischen Geschichte, vol. 34, 2018, 440 pp., 34,90 €, br., ISBN 978-3-643-90972-5

Gerald Leppert
Social Risk Management Strategies and Health Risk Exposure
Insights and Evidence from Ghana and Malawi
Social Protection in Health, vol. 2, 2016, 324 pp., 34,90 €, pb., ISBN 978-3-643-90642-7

Pascal Schmid
Medicine, Faith and Politics in Agogo
A history of health care delivery in rural Ghana, ca. 1925 to 1980
Schweizerische Afrikastudien, vol. 13, 2018, 366 pp., 54,90 €, pb., ISBN 978-3-643-80261-3

Hans Scheutz
Die vergessene Kultur
Terrakotten aus Nordghana
Forschungen zu Sprachen und Kulturen Afrikas, Bd. 15, 2016, 248 S., 39,90 €, gb., ISBN 978-3-643-50780-8